Beyond Vision

training for work with visually impaired people

Beyond Vision

training for work with visually impaired people

Karen Maychell and David Smart

NFER-NELSON

Published by The NFER-NELSON Publishing Company Ltd.,
Darville House, 2 Oxford Road East,
Windsor, Berkshire SL4 1DF, England.

First published 1990
© 1990, The National Foundation for Educational Research

British Library Cataloguing in Publication Data
Maychell, Karen
Beyond vision : training for work with visually impaired people.
1. Great Britain. Welfare workers. Professional education.
Curriculum subjects. Welfare work with visually handicapped persons
I. Title   II. Smart, David
362.4'1'071141
ISBN 0-7005-1245-4

Typeset by David John Services Ltd, Slough
Printed by *Billing & Sons Ltd, Worcester*

Note: this book has been recorded by the RNIB's fast reading service. A taped version can be obtained by writing with your name and address to the NFER Library, NFER, The Mere, Upton Park, Slough, Berkshire SL1 2DQ.

ISBN 0 7005 1245 4 (Hardback)
Code 8336 02 4

ISBN 0 7005 1246 2 (Paperback)
Code 8337 02 4

Contents

List of Tables and Figures

The National Foundation for Educational Research

The National Foundation for Educational Research in England and Wales was founded in 1946 and is Britain's leading educational research institution. It is an independent body undertaking research and development projects on issues of current interest in all sectors of the public educational system. Its membership includes all the local education authorities in England and Wales, the main teachers' associations and a large number of other major organizations with educational interests.

Its approach is scientific, apolitical and non-partisan. By means of research projects and extensive field surveys it has provided objective evidence on important educational issues for the use of teachers, administrators, parents and the research community. The expert and experienced staff that has been built up over the years enables the Foundation to make use of a wide range of modern research techniques and, in addition to its own work, it undertakes a large number of specially sponsored projects at the request of government departments and other agencies.

The major part of the research programme relates to the maintained educational sector – primary, secondary and further education. A further significant element has to do specifically with local education authorities and training institutions. The current programme includes work on the education of pupils with special needs, monitoring of pupil performance, staff development, national evaluation and major curriculum programmes, test development and information technology in schools. The Foundation is also the national agency for a number of international research and information exchange networks.

The NFER-NELSON Publishing Company are the main publishers of the Foundation's research reports. These reports are now available in the NFER *Research Library*, a collection which provides the educational community with up-to-date research into a wide variety of subject areas. In addition, the Foundation and NFER-NELSON work closely together to provide a wide range of open and closed educational tests and a test advisory service. NFER-NELSON also publish *Educational Research*, the termly journal of the Foundation.

Acknowledgements

The project team would like to express their gratitude to all those people whose assistance has enabled this study to be undertaken. In particular, our thanks are due to the Department of Health and Social Security, who funded the research; the management and course tutors at the National Mobility Centre, the North Regional Association for the Blind and the South Regional Association for the Blind, for their willingness to be interviewed on several occasions and their co-operation in responding to our requests for information; and the students on each of the courses for agreeing to be interviewed.

The mobility officers and technical officers to whom we owe our thanks are too numerous to mention, but we are grateful to all those who returned a questionnaire and to those whom we subsequently interviewed at some length. Special thanks are due to the workers who were the focus of a case study for allowing us to accompany them during the course of their work and for arranging interviews with colleagues, gaining access for client visits and preparing accounts of their daily routines.

Within the NFER we wish to thank Dr Seamus Hegarty, the project director, for contributing a great deal of time and work in shaping the nature of the project and its outcome, Dougal Hutchison, for help in the statistical analyses, Dr Judy Bradley, for reading and commenting constructively on the draft of this report, and our secretary Deborah Billings, for ensuring the smooth running of the project and her competence and patience in typing the report. Thanks are also due to Roda Morrison, Jane Picton and Hilary Hosier for their assistance in the final stages of producing this report.

Preface

The research described in this report was commissioned by the Department of Health and Social Security (DHSS). Its aim was to conduct a comprehensive study of the training provided for mobility officers (MOs) and technical officers (TOs) and the work carried out by them. This entailed examining how the training related to the requirements of the work, within the twin contexts of social services provision and the needs of visually impaired people. The project concentrated on three main areas of inquiry:

1. training courses;
2. student characteristics and recruitment; and
3. the work and working environment of practising MOs and TOs.

The study was conducted by research officers of the National Foundation for Educational Research (NFER); it started in October 1985 and was due to finish by October 1987. However, the introduction of a 'joint' training course at each of the three centres led the sponsor to request an extension in order to enable a brief examination of the new course and its relationship with existing courses. This necessitated extending the finishing date to April 1988.

Please note that this report has been recorded by the RNIB's fast reading service. A taped version can be obtained by writing with your name and address to: The NFER Library, The Mere, Upton Park, Slough, Berkshire SL1 2DQ.

1 Introduction

I am aware of the long-standing and growing need which exists to find a suitable way of integrating visual handicap training into normal patterns of social service training. I am also aware of the enormous thought and effort which has been put into attempts to meet this need, over a number of years. Tony Newton, Minister of State [Social Security and the Disabled], 1984).

For many years the qualifications associated with working with visually impaired people have been the Technical Officer (TO) Certificate and the Mobility Officer (MO) Certificate. The TO training is mainly concerned with skills associated with communication and daily living and the MO training is mainly concerned with skills related to mobility. The majority of TOs and MOs are employed by local authorities; some work for voluntary societies. Most are based in social services departments and operate as peripatetic workers providing a domiciliary service to clients (mainly adults) in a given area or, sometimes, the whole authority. There is no fixed ratio of workers to clients and local authority provision in this respect varies a good deal. Also, within the personal social services departments, there is no obvious location for these workers, with the result that there is great diversity in the teams to which they are attached.

Background

For many years there has been debate about the training of those working with the visually impaired. Doubts have been raised about its effectiveness in preparing these workers for the tasks they are expected to undertake. Questions have also arisen regarding the scope of the training in equipping TOs and MOs to function as fully integrated officers of social services departments, or to tap the resources of these departments, the National Health Service (NHS) and other agencies as effectively as they might.

The training for MOs and TOs is provided within the voluntary sector: the National Mobility Centre (NMC) in Birmingham, the North Regional Association for the Blind (NRAB) in Leeds and the South Regional Association for the Blind (SRAB) in London. The courses are assessed and accredited by the centres themselves. Attempts to integrate the training into mainstream social services training have so far been unsuccessful.

Traditionally, the NMC trained only MOs and the two regional associations for the blind trained only TOs. The NMC course on orientation and mobility was a six-month course which centred on training in outdoor mobility, mainly through the use of the long cane. This training started indoors before moving on to outdoor mobility, with the ultimate aim of independent travel. The two regional associations ran seven-month courses in technical work for blind and partially sighted people. These mainly involved training in daily living skills (cooking, home and personal care and indoor mobility) and communication skills (braille, moon and typing), with the aim of safety and independence for visually impaired people inside their homes.

In recent years the training agencies have introduced changes to existing courses and have begun new ones. This started with the NRAB which, in addition to its TO course, ran its first MO course in 1983. Three years later, the SRAB began a three-month MO 'top-up' course for qualified TOs. Then, in September 1985, the NRAB began a rehabilitation officer (RO) course which was a nine-month course (one academic year). Most recently, the three agencies have launched what they describe as a joint rehabilitation worker (RW) course, which started at the SRAB in September 1987 and at the NMC in January 1988. (The NRAB has continued, with modifications, to run its existing RO course.) It is claimed by the NMC and the SRAB that once the demand for top-up training from workers who hold a single MO or TO qualification has ceased, the RW course will replace the existing, separate, TO and MO training. The NRAB has so far continued to offer MO or TO training to people who have neither of these qualifications. Chapter 2 describes the historical context of the current training for workers with the visually impaired, outlines the training centres' relations with the Central Council for Education and Training in Social Work (CCETSW) and considers the search for independent external validation and accreditation

Research structure and report outline

MO and TO courses and students

The first stage of the research involved several visits to each of the training centres to obtain detailed information on students and courses. Individual interviews were held with students on each of the training courses to obtain information on their gender, age, education and training, as well as their views on the selection procedures and the training provided. The total group comprised 32 students: 6 NMC (MO); 14 NRAB (7 TO, 1 MO, 6 RO); and 12 SRAB (8 TO and 4 MO). Information on MO and TO student characteristics and recruitment is given in Chapter 3.

Chapter 4 describes the structure, content and assessment procedures of each of the TO and MO courses. (The development of the new RO/RW course, together with its content, structure, assessment and students, is described in Chapter 9.) The information was obtained from a series of interviews with the General Secretary and Training Officer at each of the regional associations, the Principal of the NMC and separate interviews with each of the tutors at each centre, as well as some observation of the teaching. Course documentation was also examined. However, in many cases documentation was very limited, and what was said in interviews contrasted with the written material, so that further inquiries were necessary to clarify what actually occurred. In order to ensure that our descriptions of the various courses were accurate, the training centres were provided with drafts of the relevant sections of Chapter 4 and a meeting was held with each to discuss their views. Following these meetings, certain changes were made where we felt these to be justified.

Visual impairment workers

The second stage of the inquiry focused on the work of MOs and TOs and their working environment. The findings of this phase are incorporated in Chapters 5 to 7. The data was obtained from a workers' questionnaire, follow-up interviews with a sample of these workers and case studies in six locations. The questionnaire sought information on workers' age and qualifications, supervision, team situation, the proportion of time spent on various activities and the number of hours per week in contact with clients.

Questionnaire sample

It was intended that the questionnaire be sent to the total population of qualified MOs and TOs. The NMC indicated that it had trained 344 MOs from the British Isles; the NRAB had trained 232 TOs; and the SRAB 138 TOs. Thus the total number of workers trained was 714. However, information from the NMC indicated that approximately one-quarter of those trained had left the profession and a further 23 MOs worked in Scotland or Northern Ireland and were therefore outside the remit of this research. Although the regional associations were unable to supply comparable information, it seems reasonable to assume that a similar situation pertained. The effective sample size (i.e. those for whom addresses were available) was 408; questionnaires were sent out to these workers in May 1986. Some 371 questionnaires were returned, giving a response rate of 91 per cent. However, 51 respondents had left the field for some reason (for example, other employment, retirement) and were therefore taken out of the study. A further 13 were employed by the Guide Dogs for the Blind Association, whose role was outside the scope of this inquiry and who were consequently not included in the report data. Therefore, the questionnaire data cited in this report refers to information supplied by 307 workers: 154 MOs; 125 TOs; and 28 who had both qualifications.

Interviews with workers

On the basis of information obtained from the questionnaire, a sample of workers was selected for interview. These workers were chosen to reflect variations in working environments, amount of specialist work done and recency of training. A total of 20 TOs, 17 MOs and ten dual qualified workers were interviewed during summer–autumn 1986. These provided more detailed information on working environment, supervision and duties, and also covered new areas such as links with other social services and NHS employees, the nature of the work with clients, views on training, reasons for working with the visually impaired, work background and career plans.

Case studies

From the interviews a sub-sample of six locations was selected for intensive case study. These allowed a closer examination of the different kinds of working environment which were found to exist and their implications for workers. Locations were selected to provide a variety of worker qualifications, work practices, geographical locations and organizational structures, including one voluntary society. These case studies involved extended visits to each of the six locations. Further interviews were conducted with the visual impairment workers themselves and individual interviews were held with team colleagues and other workers with whom there was professional contact. Interviews also took place with the workers' supervisors and managers. In each location we were able to observe a variety of dealings with clients, including teaching sessions. At the end of the visits, workers were asked to provide the team with a self-completion diary outlining their working patterns over a fortnightly period.

Workers' and students' views

Chapter 8 shifts the attention again to training. While the MO and TO courses are the subject of Chapter 4, in this chapter the workers and students, through interviews, comment on their experience of the various courses. For the workers, this is directly related to their subsequent experiences in the field.

New rehabilitation officer/worker training

The extension to the project allowed a brief examination of the new RW course and the changes in the NRAB RO course. In addition to examining what course documentation was available, the project team visited each of the training agencies and again held individual interviews with teaching staff, some of whom had been recruited since the original visits. All discussion of the new course has been incorporated in Chapter 9. The format is similar to Chapter 4 (which describes the MO and TO training), with each module of the course considered in turn. There is an outline of the origins of the course, which includes the RO course introduced at the NRAB in 1985. Students from the first NRAB RO course were interviewed and their comments reported. Details are also provided of students on the first joint RO/RW courses.

Analysis and recommendations

In Chapter 10 the conclusions drawn from the research are presented. This mainly involves a detailed analysis of each of the courses at each centre. There follows a brief discussion of the new rehabilitation officer/worker training courses. Finally, recommendations for future training are made.

2 History and Context of Training Provision

Background to current service provision

The nature of welfare provision changed in post-war Britain with the National Health Service Act 1946, the National Assistance Act 1948 and the Children Act 1948. In response to this legislation, local authority service provision became the responsibility of two – sometimes three – separate departments: children, health and welfare; or children and health/welfare. At that time, the visually impaired came under the welfare department.

The next set of structural changes came 20 years later, in the wake of the Seebohm Report. In 1965 a committee was appointed under Frederick Seebohm, with a remit as follows:

> to review the organization and responsibilities of the local authority personal social services in England and Wales, and to consider what changes are desirable to secure an effective family service.

The subsequent Seebohm Report (1968) indicated that the existence of separate departments was widely felt to be problematic: wasteful of resources and confusing for clients and their families who could be visited by workers from some or all of the three departments. The Report went on to make a series of recommendations regarding the provision of welfare services by local authorities. Principally, these concerned the establishment in each local authority of a unified department dealing with all aspects of welfare provision:

> The new department will have responsibilities going beyond those of existing local authority departments, but they will include the present services provided by children's departments, the welfare services provided under the National Assistance Act 1948, educational welfare and

child guidance services, other social work services provided by health departments, day nurseries, and certain social welfare work currently undertaken by some housing departments.

The Report said that the needs of clients and their families should normally be attended to by one social worker. This echoed the earlier Younghusband Report (1959), which had contained the recommendation that there should no longer be specialist workers for each specific client group. The main thrust of the Seebohm Report was enshrined in the Local Authority Social Services Act 1970.

Aside from the legislative changes, a particular interpretation was made of Seebohm which was to be the focus of some future debate. The Barclay Report (1982) said:

[social services] departments interpreted the Seebohm Committee's view that, as far as possible, an individual or family in need should be served by a single social worker as requiring early abandonment of former specialisms. The notion of a generalist social worker was seized upon and put into practice, rather than a notion of a generalist team.

The disappearance of welfare departments and the new demand for generic social workers meant that those who had specialized in work with a specific client group were now expected to deal with a range of clients. There were particular consequences for those who had worked only with the visually impaired: there was generally little recognition of their training and, as a consequence, in most areas they were placed in 'unqualified' positions such as social work assistants. In contrast, workers who had been concerned with children, whose qualifications were recognized, were placed in 'qualified' and therefore more senior positions.

Training for workers with the visually impaired

Training for workers with the visually impaired stemmed from, and to a large extent has continued under the auspices of, voluntary or charitable organizations. The first formal qualification for workers with the visually impaired was the Home Teacher Certificate, introduced in the early 1920s. It had quickly become a requirement for people working with the visually impaired to have this certificate. The (then) Northern Counties Association for the Blind – later the North Regional Association for the Blind – developed a training course leading

Association for the Blind _ developed a training course leading to the qualification of home teacher. Later the Southern and Western Regional Association for the Blind also offered a Home Teacher Certificate. However, students did not necessarily attend a training centre full-time to obtain the qualification. Often workers covered topics on a similar basis to a correspondence course before taking a final examination alongside other potential home teachers in a central location.

The training was primarily concerned with craft instruction and communication skills, but also covered any benefit entitlements which were available. In later years, as the concept of rehabilitation was developed, the training came under criticism for placing too much emphasis on craft activities and on regular contact with the visually impaired in a 'caring' capacity.

Much later the two regional associations for the blind (described later in this chapter) introduced a new course which led to the Social Welfare Officer for the Blind Certificate (SWOB) and replaced the Home Teacher's Certificate. This course lasted for one academic year and involved instruction at the training centres and a series of placements. At the end, there was a residential week during which students took examinations. Between them, the regional associations for the blind were eventually training approximately 50 social welfare officers for the blind each year (more than the average number of TOs trained per year).

However, a role for specialist workers was virtually defined out of existence in the early 1970s with the interpretation of the Seebohm Report's recommendations. The implementation of these meant that the demand for specialists dwindled as more social services departments reorganized and required workers to take on generic caseloads. The last group of social welfare officers for the blind took their qualifying examinations in 1973. It was a difficult period in which to present working with the visually impaired as an attractive or even clearly identifiable career, at least in local authorities, since there was uncertainty about whether any separate, specialist training should be maintained. One of the training agencies was reported as stating that:

> the indecision about training for work with blind people has had a marked effect on the number coming forward for interview, and only two from the region have been accepted for the last two courses (New Beacon, 1973, p.8).

While changes were made in the structure of social services, the responsibilities of local authorities to their visually impaired residents remained. The Chronically Sick and Disabled Persons Act 1970 reaffirmed the statutory rights of the handicapped, disabled or impaired, though the exact effect of this legislation has been the subject of some debate (Oliver, 1983, pp.102–6). The Local Government Act 1972 required authorities to provide services geared to the *rehabilitation* of the handicapped, disabled or impaired. The main thrust was towards enabling people to live independently in the community.

To replace the training previously provided for those working with the visually impaired, and following discussions with DHSS over a number of years, the regional associations for the blind started a new course in 1973: the course for technical work with blind and partially sighted people. This was designed as a temporary measure to fill the vacuum created by the ending of previous training. The course was intended to run only until such time as specialist training was 'incorporated within the overall framework of training devised by the Central Council for Education and Training in Social Work (CCETSW)' (Southern and Western Regional Association for the Blind, 1978, p.9). The regional associations for the blind recognized the low status of workers with the visually impaired and intended that this new qualification would improve the status of these workers. In planning the new course, great emphasis was placed on skills teaching, notably on communication and 'daily living' skills.

However, though the TO course had been developed with the knowledge and assistance of DHSS and CCETSW, there was no formal accreditation by CCETSW. Instead, the regional associations' for the blind own inter-regional committee issued certificates to those students who completed the course to the satisfaction of the agencies.

North Regional Association for the Blind (NRAB)

The NRAB was founded in 1906 as an organization for the various counties and voluntary associations in the north of England. Although registered as a charity, it is supported by central and local government: 50 per cent of its funding is from the DHSS, and 50 per cent from its local authorities. Affiliation of local authorities is voluntary, but almost all the NRAB's respective authorities are currently members. Authorities which choose to opt out are exempt from the affiliation fee which is a per capita sum based on the number of registered blind in the authority. However, these authorities are not eligible for the substantial concessions on the cost of the training. The member authorities have majority representation on the NRAB's executive committee and take the chair and vice-chair.

The NRAB's first involvement in training started with a course for home teachers in 1923–4. The emphasis of the training offered has changed since the early days:

> Whereas previously the specialist officer had to care for all aspects of blind people, today the specialist officers are responsible for their rehabilitation. This has been brought about by the difference in society's attitude to handicapped people and more acceptance by society that handicapped people could, with training, be independent (NRAB, *Eighty-first Annual Report*, p.7).

Initially, training was conducted in schools in Manchester and Liverpool before the NRAB moved to its own premises in Manchester and later to the present location in Leeds. As well as the full-time training, the NRAB offers one- or two-day, in-service training courses. In addition to its training function, it also acts as a centre for advice on matters relating to the visually impaired and the deaf-blind.

South Regional Association for the Blind (SRAB)

The NRAB was instrumental in setting up a similar organization in the south, which became the Southern and Western Regional Association for the Blind (SWRAB), and later the South Regional Association for the Blind. The SRAB is funded in the same way as the NRAB. According to the SRAB, some two-thirds (68 per cent) of the country's visually impaired population are in its area (SRAB, *Annual Report*, 1984–5). At the present time, four authorities in the SRAB region have opted out of affiliation. The voluntary societies have a much greater role on the SRAB committee than at the NRAB – i.e. there is equal membership of the local authorities and the voluntary societies on the executive committee, and the chair and vice-chair are taken by representatives from the voluntary sector.

The SRAB, like the NRAB, has organized home teacher training, social welfare officer for the blind training and TO training, and it too offers short, in-service training courses. The

SRAB also has a role, again similar to the NRAB, as a regional centre for information and advice on matters relating to the visually impaired.

The National Mobility Centre (NMC)

A system of training visually impaired people to become independently mobile is a comparatively new development in the UK, having been introduced from the USA in the 1960s. Mobility training, based on a new type of cane and a structured programme of learning, began there during the Second World War, with war-blinded people as the specific client group involved (for a further discussion of this, see Bledsoe, 1980). In 1966 the Midlands Mobility Centre was set up as a two-year research project (later to be granted a year's extension because of its perceived success), funded by the Nuffield Foundation, to: 'investigate the feasibility of non-residential mobility training for blind people based on the use of the long cane, and to produce a few mobility specialists – peripatologists' (Thornton, 1968, p.13).

In the initial stages, the centre was involved in training visually impaired people and sighted instructors. After the project ended in 1969, a permanent training centre was established with funding from the Royal National Institute for the Blind (RNIB), St Dunstan's and Birmingham Royal Institution for the Blind. The National Mobility Centre, as it was renamed, aimed:

> to make personal mobility training based on the long cane system available to as many blind people as need it... Great emphasis is placed on training the students under blindfold in the skills they will be expected to teach when they qualify. (Biggs, 1982, p.226)

Since its inception, the NMC has offered a training course to two types of workers: a six-month course in orientation and mobility (MO course) 'for people to work with *adults* in local authorities or voluntary organizations' (advertisement, *New Beacon*; July 1986, p. 223; emphasis added); and a three-month course – i.e. the same course but without a fieldwork placement, for 'school teachers of the visually handicapped who wish to have a specialised knowledge of mobility training and its use in schools for the visually handicapped' (*ibid.*). Since 1985 this one-term option has also been available to the Guide Dogs for the Blind Association's instructors. As with the regional associations for the blind, there is no external validation of the training courses at the NMC. The Centre awards its own certificates.

Course fees

The course fees for TO training at the two regional associations were very similar:

	Affiliated authorities	Non-affiliated authorities
NRAB	£550	£2,750
SRAB	£500	£2,550

However, there was a much greater discrepancy in the charges made for MO training:

NMC		£2,550
NRAB	Affiliated authorities	£550
	Non-affiliated authorities	£2,750
SRAB		£1,000

(NRAB documentation; interview with General Secretary and Training Officer, SRAB; and interview with Principal, NMC.)

The SRAB said it charged less than the NMC for its MO training because it was a much shorter course. Clearly, however, the difference in the funding arrangements between the NMC and regional associations for the blind was the main reason for the discrepancy in fees. The NRAB said it had a policy of charging its affiliated authorities the minimum; hence its MO training cost around 20 per cent of that at the NMC. The NMC claimed that the cost of its course reflected more accurately the true cost of MO training which was necessarily high in terms of staffing because of the amount of one-to-one teaching which took place.

The independent special option

For some years the training of specialist workers continued in much the same vein, although many modifications were said to have been made by each of the training agencies. However, in 1978 at an SWRAB conference which included representatives from social services, CCETSW, DHSS, the NMC and voluntary societies for the blind, calls were made for a joint training course combining TO and MO skills. This was not a new idea; over the years there was increasing pressure to offer training which would equip one worker with all the rehabilitation skills needed by the visually impaired. Subsequent negotiations between the three training centres led to a decision that a new course should be developed.

The postscript to the report on the 1978 Conference said:

> plans should be prepared for a joint training course for a rehabilitation officer as an independent special option within the Certificate in Social Service. This planning has the approval and the active support of the Central Council for Education and Training in Social Work. (SWRAB, *Regional Review*, 1979, p.60)

The proposed training was based on a series of modules. While each centre would offer some common modules, those sections related to the MO course were to be offered by the NMC, and those related to the TO training by the NRAB or the SRAB. The modular system was adopted, at least in part, to allow visually impaired students to take the course; they would take options other than the mobility module, which was restricted to those who were 'sighted'.

The proposal was approved by CCETSW in May 1981. However, the course was never run. One reason given by the centres was that they had trouble attracting the number of students specified by CCETSW as a prerequisite (for further discussion on the failure of the Independent Special Option to get off the ground in all specialist areas, see CCETSW, 1983). Despite the failure of the Independent Special Option, both of the regional associations for the blind have given some training to students taking a Certificate in Social Service (CSS).

Continuing negotiations with CCETSW

In June 1984 a joint statement was issued by the three agencies, the RNIB and CCETSW which said that training for workers with the visually impaired should be located within the broad spectrum of social work training, and that the training agencies should work 'towards the promotion of a national training resource' (joint statement on training for work with visually handicapped people, June 1984). The three training agencies acknowledge that their main objective in trying to establish the training for work with the visually impaired in the social work field is to secure independent validation by a recognized body (i.e. CCETSW); the latter, for its part, reported:

> CCETSW should continue to work towards the provision of specialist training for workers with visually handicapped people within its policies for qualifying training, while acknowledging that the specialist training provided by the regional associations and the National Mobility Centre will need to continue temporarily. Assuming continued collaboration between these bodies and the move towards a more 'rounded' rehabilitation officer, combining the skills of existing TOs and MOs, CCETSW might have a useful interim contribution to make with regard to training for the counselling aspect of the work. (Ash, 1985, p.16)

The thrust of CCETSW's interest was to integrate, in some way, specialist training within its plans for the Qualifying Diploma in Social Work (QDSW), proposed for the 1990s. One option which was suggested by CCETSW at a meeting in February 1987 (involving representatives of CCETSW, DHSS, RNIB, NRAB, NMC, SRAB and NFER) was for the training agencies to link with local further education establishments and offer training in conjunction with them. This would bring the agencies more into mainstream training and open up the potential for a new field of student recruitment for the training centres. At that meeting, CCETSW emphasized that a high level of commitment from each of the training centres was necessary in order to make arrangements in time for the 1990 proposals, and that this may be the last chance for the training centres to come under the auspices of CCETSW. However, it seemed that no progress in this direction had been made by January 1988. Instead, the training agencies had begun negotiations with the National Council for Vocational Qualifications (NCVQ) for accreditation. The outcome of these talks was still uncertain in January 1988, but the training agencies expressed confidence that accreditation would be given.

Associations for visual impairment workers

There are three organizations which specifically represent workers with the visually impaired: the National Association of Orientation and Mobility Instructors (NAOMI); the National Association of Technical Officers for the Blind (NATOB); and the Association for the Education and Welfare of the Visually Handicapped (AEWVH). Some visual impairment workers are members of the main white-collar local government trade union, the National Association of Local Government Officers (NALGO), instead of, or in some cases in addition to, these bodies.

NAOMI was established in 1976. In 1985 it claimed a membership of 25 per cent of qualified MOs and described itself as 'the only professional body whose sole concerns are the interests of Mobility Instructors, their employers and their clients' (NAOMI, 1985). It has formal representation on a number of committees, including the advisory committee of the NMC. Because of the historical development of mobility training, until very recently NAOMI members were all (with the exception of one worker trained in the USA) trained at the NMC. Indeed the NAOMI constitution stipulated that members must possess a certificate issued by the Midlands Mobility Centre or the NMC. The recent introduction of mobility training at both the NRAB and the SRAB has complicated the situation. NAOMI has expressed reservations about these courses, particularly that at the SRAB, because of what it sees as a reduction in the time allocated to the teaching and practice of long-cane mobility and the use of the blindfold in training. It seems that MOs trained at the regional associations may apply for membership, but NAOMI does not guarantee acceptance: '[NAOMI]...is committed to the maintenance of professional standards, and to this end it seeks assurance from applicants that they can satisfy its executive committee of their competence to teach long cane travel' (Dodds, 1987, p.72).

NATOB was formed by a group of students on the 1978 TO course at the SRAB. The main reasons for its inception were described by the originators as concern about the implications for single-trained workers of the proposed introduction of joint training in the form of a rehabilitation course and dissatisfaction with the current training for TOs. It has a similarly low membership to that of NAOMI.

AEWVH also has members who are workers with the visually impaired, though primarily these are in the educational field rather than in social services. However, in the light of the new rehabilitation officer/worker course, recent merger negotiations between NAOMI and NATOB, the belief that common goals exist and, perhaps most significantly, the failure to recruit members in social services, AEWVH has proposed a merger of all three bodies.

3 Student Characteristics and Recruitment

This chapter outlines the arrangements for the recruitment and selection of students, both in employing agencies and the training centres, and looks at the backgrounds and characteristics of the students in training in 1986. It is based on interviews with one full intake from each of the courses at each training centre. Twenty-six students were interviewed in all (excluding RO students, who are discussed in Chapter 9). Table 3.1 gives a breakdown by training centre and type of course.

Table 3.1: *MO and TO students interviewed at each training centre*

	NMC	NRAB	SRAB	TOTAL
	N	N	N	N
MO students	6	1*	4	11
TO students	–	7	8	15
Total	6	8	12	26

* There were two MO students at NRAB, but one was not available during the interviewing period.

Job advertising and recruitment

According to the training centres, most of their applicants had been offered secondment by a local authority/voluntary agency, or hoped to secure such secondment if accepted for training. A few applicants who did not manage to obtain secondment funded themselves with a view to seeking future employment with the visually impaired. Sometimes, applicants who were already employed by a local authority funded themselves. This because they did not intend to stay for two years in the same post – the usual condition upon which secondment was offered.

In most cases, local authorities or voluntary agencies which advertised the post of specialist worker would have preferred to appoint a qualified person. However, such applicants were relatively few, which is why many were prepared to offer training secondment to successful candidates who were unqualified. Most students who were seconded to training courses (and by far the majority of them were) had secured funding in this way.

A few employers offered training secondment to someone already working for them, either because they were currently deployed with the visually impaired (possibly without any visual impairment qualification) or because they appeared suitable for a vacant post.

Each local authority conducted its own interviews and made the offer of secondment conditional upon the candidate being accepted by one of the training centres. Such a situation naturally allowed for rivalry between the three centres; secondees who were refused a place by one training centre had, on occasion, applied to another and been successful. The discrepancy in the fees charged by each of the centres was another important aspect in secondment (see Chapter 2).

Occasionally, where a local authority was interviewing a number of applicants for MO training with a view to an NMC place, the Principal from the NMC[1] was invited to sit in and advise on their suitability. If he felt that several candidates were acceptable, he advised those who were not selected by that particular authority to apply for secondment elsewhere, and to contact him when they had been successful.

The NRAB's General Secretary and Training Officer were also involved in this type of local authority interviewing. Also they sometimes held local authority interviews at the NRAB. Recently the SRAB had been involved in similar interviewing situations, though not on their own premises.

The main condition local authorities and voluntary agencies usually made of their secondees was that they would work for them for a further two years after qualifying. Some students had been asked to sign contracts to this effect, while others

---

1   During the period of the research the Principal at the NMC left and was succeeded by a member of the teaching staff. For the purpose of clarification in the report, 'the Principal' refers to the former who was in post when the first stage of the research (relating to the training courses) was being carried out. His successor is referred to as 'the new Principal'.

described it as an understanding between themselves and their employers which had not been formalized in writing, but which they felt would still be binding. The project team heard of two students who did not subsequently complete the two-year period with the sponsoring authority and had to repay some of the cost of training.

In recruiting visual impairment specialists local authorities sometimes indicated certain criteria which are of note. First, it was not uncommon to see advertisements for TOs which stipulated that they must have a driving licence. Secondly, local authorities sometimes indicated a preference for a qualification from one training centre over another; for example, an advertisement for a rehabilitation officer said, 'Preference will be given to holders of either the Rehabilitation Officer Certificate (NRAB) or Mobility Officer and Technical Officer Certificate (NRAB/NMC)'.

Fifteen of the 26 students interviewed were seconded by local authorities. Five of the students were receiving Manpower Services Commission (MSC) funding through its Training Opportunities Programmes scheme. They were eligible to apply for an MSC grant because they were themselves visually impaired. Three students were self-funding. Two of them were already TO-trained and worked with visually impaired people. The third self-funding student had no specialist visual impairment qualification, although she had been working as a self-care skills supervisor in a rehabilitation centre for the visually impaired. Of the remaining three students, one received funding from the health authority in which she was employed as a staff nurse on a ward for mentally handicapped patients. Another received funding from his local education authority, and the other was funded by her local voluntary association for the blind, although she was to be employed by the local authority, once qualified (Table 3.1).

Course entry requirements

MO course

Academic

The NMC required five GCE O-levels or equivalent as a minimum standard of entry. However, this might be waived if a candidate showed 'a distinct aptitude for this specialized work' (NMC course booklet). The NRAB requirements were virtually the same, but with one important difference. The NRAB course booklet stated that 'normally five GCE subjects at Ordinary level or equivalent are required as a minimum standard of education for entry, but this requirement might be waived for mature candidates who show an aptitude for this work'. The NRAB added that 'candidates will be given a written test of their ability to study to 'O' level standard'. By this, it meant that applicants who appeared suitable and who performed to an acceptable level in the written work which was set as part of the entry procedure, but who did not possess the necessary academic qualifications, would be accepted. There was no indication in the entry requirements that the NRAB MO course was only available as a 'top-up' course for those who already had a visual impairment qualification. However, all the students who had taken the course up to 1986/7 had either a TO qualification or a Home Teacher Certificate. Furthermore, the course content and structure was geared towards students who already had a visual impairment qualification (see Chapter 4). The entry requirements stipulated by the SRAB for its MO course mirrored the outcome criteria for the TO course, which meant that only those who had passed the TO course were acceptable. Moreover, the Training Officer said that some people who had done the TO course a long time ago would not have covered all the necessary elements and would have to do some pre-course training to be eligible. This was because the MO course at the SRAB was only three months long and designed as a 'top-up' to the TO course rather than a qualification in its own right.

Age

The NMC and SRAB said that students should be between 21 and 45 years, whereas the NRAB stated that candidates should normally be between 20 and 50 years of age at commencement of the course.

Physical

The NMC required candidates to be sighted and 'to undergo physical and audiometric examinations'. The NRAB demanded that candidates 'should have normal vision, i.e. any defects in visual acuity can be corrected by wearing spectacles where the field of vision is normal'. Also an audiogram, signed by an audiologist and showing that the candidate had a normal range of hearing, was required by the NRAB.

Table 3.2: *Entry requirements for MO course at each of the training centres*

	NMC	NRAB	SRAB
Age	21 – 45 years	20 – 50 years (normally)	21 – 45 years (normally)
Physical	Must be sighted; must pass physical and audiometric exams	Normal vision (i.e. correctable with glasses); must pass audiometric exam	Medically fit; should normally meet the necessary sensory requirements
Academic	5 O-levels; may be waived if showing particular aptitude	5 O-levels; may be waived for mature applicants*	Recent TO qualification

* Although NRAB did not stipulate that applicants were expected to have a TO qualification, the course objectives seemed to assume this.

The SRAB stressed the physical demands of the course, and stated that: 'A certificate will not be awarded to anyone who will be unable to properly fulfil his required role, due to lack of fitness'. Regarding sensory requirements, it wrote: 'Applicants should normally meet the necessary sensory requirements in order to complete training, and be able to carry out the subsequent work to the satisfaction of their employer.'

The Training Officer said that he felt the phrasing of the above was sufficiently vague to allow for the SRAB to decide on the individual merits of each case in which a visually impaired person applied to do the MO course. A TO, who was registered blind, had been accepted on the 1988 MO course. Also, two TO students who were registered partially sighted said they had been told that they may be able to take the SRAB MO course in the future.

Overseas candidates

A condition of overseas students being accepted by the NRAB was that they 'must have an adequate knowledge of English, written as well as spoken, and must be prepared to undertake a proficiency test if required'. The Training Officer at the SRAB said that few overseas students had been trained there. He expressed reservations about accepting them because he believed that much of the course would lack relevance for them. In contrast, the Principal of the NMC believed its MO training to be applicable to any environment and claimed that the NMC had a worldwide reputation in this field.

Other considerations

The NMC handbook mentioned that 'because of the travelling involved in teaching mobility skills, local authorities usually require applicants to have a driving licence'. Also an NMC leaflet, 'Details for Applicants 1986–7', claimed that 'experience in a local authority social service department or blindness agency is also desirable'.

However, the Principal said that local authority experience was not essential. He stressed that he was looking for new blood, and said that when visiting local authorities he described the sort of person he had in mind – someone young and flexible who, in his opinion, would be more likely to respond to the type of training offered by the NMC than established social service workers. (Table 3.2 summarizes the entry requirements for MO training at the three centres.)

TO course

The inter-regional course booklet stated that for admission to the TO course at either of the regional associations, candidates 'should normally be between 20 and 50 years of age at commencement of the course'. The Training Officer at the SRAB said that a promising applicant over 50 but with a job to go to after training would be acceptable. However, he described the ideal candidate as someone between 25 and 35 years of age, with a university degree and good interpersonal skills. He stressed that good academic qualifications were not enough on their own – they were looking for 'good, practical students – at the end of the day that's what it's all about'.

The inter-regional course booklet also stated that students must:
- 'be approved by a selection board and produce evidence of medical suitability';

- 'pass a written test of their ability to study to 'O' level standard in the examination for the General Certificate of Education'; and
- '[in the case of] candidates who cannot read inkprint be able to type and read Grade II braille fluently (i.e. 40 w.p.m.)'.

Course selection procedures

Course advertising

Each of the three centres advertised their training courses at appropriate times of the year in certain visual impairment journals. In addition, the two regional associations circulated details of all their courses to their own affiliated local authorities. This course of action was not open to the NMC, since it did not have affiliated authorities, but in any case the Principal said that additional advertising was unnecessary as the NMC was sufficiently well known for offering MO training. Also in recent years more MOs had been employed in local authorities which, he believed, was publicity in itself. The NRAB, which asked its applicants where they heard about courses, said that most had read about them in journals or learnt about them from social workers, colleagues or friends.

Information available to applicants

Each of the three training centres produced some information on courses, which was available to potential applicants. The NMC, which at the beginning of the research offered only an MO course, published the booklet, National Mobility Centre. However, much of the information it contained was many years out of date, and acknowledged to be so by NMC staff; nevertheless, it continued to distribute the booklet to those seeking information on the MO course. A similar situation obtained with the booklet on the TO course, Course for Technical Work with Blind and Partially Sighted People, which was published by the inter-regional committee of the two regional associations for the blind.

For the MO course more recently introduced at the SRAB, the information available consisted of four pages covering a list of entry requirements and an outline of the course structure and content. The NRAB, for its MO course provided the booklet, *Course for Instructors of Advanced Mobility and Orientation with Blind and Partially Sighted People*, giving information on the training centre, training personnel, aims of the course, its structure, curriculum, assessment procedures, how to apply and conditions of acceptance. The NRAB produced additional information for applicants: a pamphlet on the background and work of the NRAB, and a pamphlet on the aims, admission criteria, length, subjects and assessment procedures of each of its courses.

Interviewing

NMC

The interviewing system at the NMC comprised solely of an interview with the Principal. Staff were unhappy with this situation and drew attention to the potential unfairness of a system which depended entirely on the decision of one person. Some also indicated concern that it did not enable the breadth of experience and awareness that a panel of interviewers could bring, while others expressed surprise that there were not more appeals against rejection, especially before 1983 when the NMC was the only centre in the UK offering MO training.

The interview involved questioning, followed by a brief trial with a blindfold, in which the applicant was introduced to basic room familiarization techniques and a sighted guide walk outside. A number of students felt that this was to assess how they responded to wearing a blindfold rather than to test their aptitude in learning the skills.

NRAB

The NRAB had a policy of interviewing *all* applicants. The selection procedure covered two consecutive days, described by the tutors as 'informal' and 'formal'. This system had been in operation since 1985, prior to which there was a formal interview only.

On the first day of the selection process each tutor was assigned a number of applicants, for whom they were expected to complete an assessment form by the end of the day.[2] After an informal, individual meeting with the allocated tutor, all

---

2   A copy of the assessment form is available on request from the authors.

applicants and tutors had lunch together during which their behaviour and interactions were observed. Lunch was followed by a group discussion on topics suggested by the tutors. The final task of the first day was a written test in which applicants had to list and discuss the main points of an article. This article was not necessarily concerned with visual impairment; it was intended to test applicants' critical faculties and ability to present 'good, written English'. On the second day each applicant had an individual interview with a panel of interviewers, comprising the General Secretary, the Training Officer, the chairperson of the NRAB and the chairperson of the Training Committee. Sometimes a fifth person made up the panel – i.e. a local visual impairment specialist. In the event of a disagreement, the committee members would overrule the tutors, although this had happened only once.

The admissions criteria did not stipulate previous experience with the visually impaired, although the panel preferred candidates to have met visually impaired people or demonstrated some interest in the field. Also, the panel was looking for people with a mature outlook who demonstrated the right attitude to the visually impaired. The Training Officer described this as someone who would promote clients' independence rather than seek to take over their lives. Academic qualifications were not essential although they made academic ability easier to assess. Sometimes the panel suggested to applicants that they re-apply in a year's time because it felt that the person was not ready for the work commitment required.

SRAB

The selection process at the SRAB involved a preliminary, informal conversation between applicants and tutors, followed by written work and a formal panel interview. The written exercise was not intended to be a test of applicants' knowledge, but to ensure that they could produce an acceptable standard of writing.

Not everyone passed on to the formal interview stage. The Training Officer usually expected applicants to have had some contact with visually impaired people. Those who had not were advised that they should gain such experience before re-applying. Sometimes he recommended a voluntary agency with which they might get in touch. The formal interview panel comprised the General Secretary, the Training Officer and two SRAB Education Committee members, one from a voluntary association and one (who was himself visually impaired) from a local authority.

Not all students interviewed had gone through this interview procedure. Five of the eight students had only had the panel interview, which lasted about half an hour. These five also said they had not been given a written test. One of them said that she had come prepared for one, and 'felt quite cheated' when this did not happen. Two students commented on the fact that they felt the interviewing panel was only interested in whether or not they were going to get funding.

Recruitment for the first SRAB MO course involved only the Training Officer and the mobility tutor. The latter said that students were selected very carefully because it was a new course. They were looking for students who would be able to deal with a flexible teaching approach to orientation and mobility. Four students were selected from 15 applications, and each had recently done the TO course at the SRAB.

Visually impaired applicants

The NMC did not accept visually impaired students for MO training; in its booklet it stated that candidates must be sighted. At the SRAB, as far as visually impaired applicants were concerned, the Training Officer believed that many who wanted to work in the field were looking for a way to help them come to terms with their own problems, and that such people made bad teachers; however, some students who were visually impaired were accepted. At the NRAB, the General Secretary felt that it received too many applications from visually impaired people who were not necessarily cut out for the work of a TO. The NRAB's *Seventy-eighth Annual Report* discussed the failure of a number of visually impaired students: 'it was believed that a considerable number of visually handicapped people who attended the Rehabilitation Centre at Torquay were recommended to apply for the course, although it was felt by the association that they were not suitable material.'

Student characteristics

Just under two thirds of the students were female (17 out of 26) and most, though not all, were quite young – in their twenties or early thirties. Six students were over 40.

Work experience

MO students

Students' work experiences and motivation for doing the training were very diverse. Among the six NMC mobility students, two had had work experience with the visually impaired. One had trained as a TO and had worked for nine years before being seconded for MO training; she saw the latter as a logical extension of her TO work. The other student had been employed as an unqualified member of a visual impairment specialist team. The authority later created an extra post for an MO and agreed to pay for him to train at the NMC. The remaining four NMC students all had experience which may be considered relevant: two had worked with visually/physically handicapped children, a third had been involved in voluntary work for an organization working with visually impaired people and the fourth, who had a brother who was a qualified MO, had also done some voluntary work with physically handicapped children. These four students each said that they were looking for a change of direction in their careers when they applied for training.

Three of the four MO students at the SRAB had just qualified as TOs there and had moved straight on to MO training. One of these was a qualified social worker who had been employed with the visually impaired for five years. Another had been employed in a variety of social services jobs and had also been involved in voluntary work with a local society for the blind. The third student had had no previous contact with the visually impaired, and had decided to apply for TO (and later MO) training after being introduced to the idea while on a community project. The fourth student had qualified as a TO from the SRAB six years earlier and was employed by a school for the blind.

TO students

Three of the seven TO students training at the NRAB had been working with visually impaired people prior to the commencement of the course. One had been a residential self-care skills supervisor at a rehabilitation centre for visually impaired adults. The second had been employed in a social services disability team as a social worker for the blind, despite having no relevant social work or visual impairment qualification. Although he was satisfied with this position, his authority requested that he go on the TO course. The third student had been employed for 18 months as an unqualified TO in a social services department. Each of the remaining students had had some contact with visually impaired people, and two of the students were visually impaired.

Of the eight SRAB TO students, two were qualified MOs and had worked in this capacity for five and three years respectively. Another was a registered nurse for the mentally handicapped and worked on a ward which brought her into contact with people who were visually, as well as mentally, impaired. Another student, who was registered blind, had become interested in doing the course through contact with his own TO. He had accompanied him in the course of his work for two days per week for a year. Two other students, both registered partially sighted, had heard about TO work when doing the rehabilitation course at RNIB, Torquay. Prior to this, they had not considered working with visually impaired people. Another student had done voluntary work with visually impaired children; she met their TO, and this had initiated her interest in the work. The remaining student had had no experience of working with the visually impaired, but she became interested in visual impairment through a friend who was an ex-home teacher.

Education and other training

Six of the 11 MO students already possessed the TO qualification. Four of these were at SRAB, where this was a prerequisite for acceptance on the course. Two of the MO students were graduates, and two students had other vocational qualifications. Of the 15 TO students interviewed, one had a degree, one was over half-way through an Open University degree and one had completed a four-year course in home and community studies. Two were qualified MOs; and another was a state- registered nurse for the mentally handicapped.

4 Training Courses

The information in this chapter was obtained from a series of interviews with training centre leaders and individual interviews with course tutors. Information was also taken from course documentation, where this existed. The NRAB had a written syllabus for each of its courses; the SRAB and the NMC did not. The course booklets contained syllabus outlines from these two centres; however, both said that the booklets were now out of date. In the absence of up-to-date documentation, the interviews were the main source of information from the SRAB and the NMC, although some tutors at the NMC provided lists of topics covered in their subjects and the SRAB provided its 1986 timetables. As none of the centres had a written breakdown of the time allocated to each subject, (and tutors could not easily put a number of hours to their subject), the hours indicated in this chapter are approximate. They have been approved by each of the training centres.

Technical officer training

The two regional associations for the blind ran their own TO course, usually once a year. Both involved 24 weeks' attendance at the training centre. The SRAB students had six weeks' practical placement; the NRAB students had only five weeks, but spent one week with deaf-blind people in a holiday location.

Course aims

The NRAB documentation spelt out four aims of the course:
1. to help students develop the skills necessary to undertake the duties of a TO;
2. to enable students to understand how services for the visually handicapped fit into the pattern of services

supplied by both the local authority and voluntary sectors;

3. to stimulate students into regarding their rehabilitative task in a positive light requiring professional skills;
4. to give students the confidence to examine, assess and improve their own work and skills.

The General Secretary at the NRAB said that the course aimed to focus attention on the students' ability to assess clients, to know what motivates a client and to use that motivation, and to make a teaching plan. New topics had been introduced in recent years because of an increasing awareness of the demands of the work. These included teaching and learning, social studies and counselling.

The SRAB had no written material on the aims of its TO course. The Training Officer said there were two main emphases: low vision, and assessing the whole person. The importance of dealing with clients as individuals with practical difficulties in a sighted world was stressed. According to the Training Officer, the course had changed so much in recent years that there was a need to update the training of some workers in the new aspects, such as low vision and counselling, which the course now incorporated. Both the NRAB and the SRAB said that recent courses had placed greater emphasis on developing the students' ability to teach clients certain skills as opposed to simply learning the skills themselves.

Detailed course content

The working day at the NRAB involved five $1\frac{1}{4}$ hour sessions, a total of $31\frac{1}{4}$ hours per week. On average, 24 hours a week were taught sessions. At the SRAB there were two $\frac{1}{2}$ hour sessions, and two 1 hour sessions per day, a total of 25 hours per week. On average, 19 hours per week were taught sessions. The subject areas and an approximate breakdown of hours for each of these at the two training centres were as follows:

NRAB	Total hours (to nearest hour)
Communications	240
Daily living skills	150
Medical studies	8

NRAB *(contd)*	*Total hours*
	(to nearest hour)
Basic mobility and guiding skills	11
Learning and teaching	60
Counselling	5
Social and other studies	60
Total	534

SRAB	
Communications	138
Daily living skills	78
Low vision and assessment and ophthalmology	33
Medical aspects and audiology	18
Mobility	47
Learning and teaching	6
Counselling	3
Other studies	84
Total	407

Communications

Both NRAB and SRAB courses included the following topics: braille, moon, typing and deaf-blind communication. At the NRAB these were allocated a total of 240 hours, and at the SRAB, 138 hours.

At the end of the NRAB course, students were expected:

- to have a knowledge of a range of aids and resources for people with a visual disability to facilitate their communicating abilities;
- to read and write braille and moon to Grade II standard, using a variety of appropriate methods;
- to have knowledge of basic touch-typing and associated apparatus;
- to use a range of communication methods appropriate to deaf-blind people;
- to have knowledge of resources developed for deaf-blind people;
- to be able to ensure the maintenance of handwriting skills using appropriate aids.

(NRAB documentation)

Braille. The teaching of braille was very similar at both training centres. Each based their braille teaching on the RNIB primer. At the NRAB the module consisted of formal lectures and seminars on the theory of braille, and practical sessions involving individual practice and role play exercises[1] performed by students in pairs with either the sleepshade or low-vision simulation spectacles. These were followed by group discussions. Students were assessed on the basis of seven braille tests, a piece of written work of not more than 1,000 words on some aspect of embossed communication and one role-play teaching practice.

The SRAB students were advised to become familiar with the braille alphabet, Grade I, before the start of the course. Once on the course, practical sessions involved individual practice and role-play sessions in pairs, just as at the NRAB. Similarly, role-play sessions were followed by a group discussion. The section had been reduced overall by about one-third, which reflected the Training Officer's belief that there was not much demand for braille in the field. Students were assessed on seven braille tests and a written assignment of about 500 words, discussing aspects of the braille system from the point of view of the teacher.

Moon. There was little formal teaching of moon at either training centre. By the end of the course, the NRAB students were required to be able to read moon while sighted at 40 words per minute. At the SRAB students were assessed on their ability by reading aloud a moon text to the Training Officer.

Typing. Students at both training centres received formal teaching in touch typing. At the NRAB, the tasks for assessment comprised nine typing exercises, three pieces of written work related to learning touch typing and one role-play teaching practice. At the SRAB, students were assessed through their performance in a series of typing exercises. The Training Officer questioned the usefulness of teaching students typing on the course; he felt that it would be far more productive if students arrived already proficient in this area.

---

1   Each of the training courses incorporated a certain amount of role play in practical subjects. This took one of two forms – i.e. each student was blindfolded or wore low-vision simulation spectacles and performed an allocated task, or students worked in pairs, one taking the role of instructor (specialist worker) and the other the part of the client wearing blindfold or low-vision simulation spectacles.

Deaf-blind communication. The NRAB said that this section concentrated specifically on communication skills, aids and resources for the deaf-blind. Practical role-play exercises were again utilized, with both earplugs and sleepshades or low-vision simulation spectacles being worn by the 'client'. Students also visited a number of deaf-blind residential units and participated in a 'Deaf-blind Week'. This involved TO students taking a group of deaf-blind clients away on holiday. The NRAB saw this week as an integral part of the course; it was designed to give students experience of being with clients on a one-to-one basis from morning to night. The performance of the students and their ability to communicate with clients and organize the necessary activities were assessed. In addition to the experience of working with real clients, tutors at the NRAB strongly believed that the week contributed to the development of a group identity among the students which they felt was very important.

At the SRAB a total of two teaching sessions were spent on deaf-blind manual and spartan communications, which the Training Officer considered 'ample': once the basic alphabet was mastered, it was simply a matter of building up speed. For this reason, four unsupervised practice sessions were timetabled. In addition, a talk was given by the RNIB special adviser to the deaf-blind. On the 1986 course students also attended a residential weekend organized by the National Deaf-blind and Rubella Association (SENSE) for the parents or guardians of multi-handicapped children and young people. The Training Officer explained that this replaced the deaf-blind holiday for which, he said, there was no rationale.

Daily living skills

The NRAB usually timetabled $6\frac{1}{4}$ hours daily living skills each week. At the end of the module, students were expected to:
- have a knowledge of aids, resources and techniques to enable people with a visual disability to lead an independent life;
- have a knowledge of facilities and aids available for hobbies, crafts, games, sports and gardening.

(NRAB documentation)

The tutor for the module said that students were being taught to teach 'survival' techniques. Two points were emphasized:

first, students had to be flexible enough to be able to adapt their training to any client or working environment; and secondly, the needs of the client had to be the focal point of any rehabilitation programme. The importance of maximizing clients' existing skills was stressed to students, in particular, the use of remaining vision, and recently students had been given much more opportunity to work with low-vision simulation spectacles.

Teaching normally followed a set pattern: a lecture to the whole group, which dealt with the correct approach to the teaching of a particular skill and included a task analysis; a practical teaching session with a teacher–student ratio of 1:4; and student write-ups of both these sessions. There were also occasional seminars in which students presented papers. Assessment took three forms: a student workbook, a role-play teaching practice and a 'dinner essay'. The latter had been introduced on the NRAB RO course, and subsequently incorporated into the TO course. It involved the preparation of a three-course meal while wearing a sleepshade or low-vision simulation spectacles; the workbook contained all the students' written work.

At the SRAB, about half as much time was spent on daily living skills – an average of just under $3\frac{1}{4}$ hours per week. Staffing difficulties at the SRAB meant that there was no opportunity to interview either of the daily living skills tutors engaged during this period. From interviews with TO students, it emerged that virtually no formal teaching had taken place. Instead the tutor had encouraged 'learning by error' or 'discovery learning'. Students worked on their own in practical sessions, using either the blindfold or low-vision simulation spectacles and the tutor intervened only when a problem arose. In the final few weeks of the course this tutor left the SRAB and was replaced (on a part-time, temporary basis) by a practising specialist who was dual trained. This tutor incorporated much more formal teaching and role-play teaching practice.

Low-vision assessment and ophthalmology

These subjects appeared as a separate section on the SRAB course only, where they were timetabled for an average of just over one hour per week. At the NRAB they were included under a general heading of 'Medical studies' (see next section).

At the SRAB, the Training Officer, who taught this part of the course, stressed that while this formed an identifiably separate section it was also interwoven with other subjects, especially mobility. It covered all aspects of low vision, ranging from initial client assessment to the use of low-vision aids. Teaching consisted of formal lectures, practical sessions with low vision aids and problem-solving group exercises.

The module was relatively new on the course and was intended to focus primarily on client assessment. The new module sought to move away from the strictly medical aspects of visual loss towards a consideration of the implications for individuals' sight. While the existing input on ophthalmology was retained, assessing individual clients' needs was given far more coverage.

Formal lectures were given by the Training Officer on the anatomy and physiology of the eye. As well as the tutor's input, outside speakers lectured on lighting, low-vision aids and diabetes.

Medical studies

At the NRAB this module included lectures on the eye, the ear and use of residual vision; eight hours was allocated, almost entirely taken up with outside speakers. Students spent an additional half day observing work at an ophthalmologist's clinic. At the end of the course the students were expected:

- to have knowledge of a range of medical disorders which might accompany visual disablement;
- to understand the structure and functions of the human visual system, visual disorders and their consequences;
- to be able to operate strategies to make the best use of poor vision, using light, size, contrast and vision training;
- to have a knowledge of appropriate resources and how to obtain them;
- to be able to assess vision, both clinically and functionally;
- to understand the structure and functions of the human hearing system, hearing disorders and their consequences;
- to be able to operate strategies to make the best use of poor hearing;

- to have a knowledge of appropriate resources and how to obtain them.

(NRAB documentation)

The medical section at the SRAB was entitled 'medical aspects and audiology' and was timetabled for a total of 18 hours. In fact, since ophthalmology and low vision had become a separate module, audiology formed the bulk of this section: the structure and function of the ear and implications of specific auditory conditions.

Mobility

The NRAB called this section 'basic mobility and guiding skills'; at the end of the course, students were expected:

- to have a knowledge of basic orientation and mobility skills;
- to have an understanding of alternative methods of independent travel and mobility resources.

(NRAB documentation)

Approximately 11 hours were allocated (a total of nine practical sessions were timetabled). Students usually worked with tutors on a one-to-one basis, although some role-play teaching practice occurred. One of the mobility tutors said that for over two-thirds of the time students worked with a blindfold, although the use of low-vision simulation spectacles had recently increased and would continue to do so. Teaching also included some seminars and lectures. Long cane mobility was not taught, although one session gave a demonstration of the technique, an outline of the role of an MO and suggested some types of client who might suitably be referred for mobility training.

Assessment of this module included: students' write-ups of each practical session; a short typed piece on a relevant topic and a map suitable for a visually impaired person; and a test of practical skills at the end of course.

At the SRAB, 47 hours were allocated to mobility. The main aim was to give students an introduction to basic mobility, particularly sighted guide skills. Emphasis was also placed on mobility in the home, so that students could help clients feel safe and confident in their own environment. They were told about the role of an MO and had a limited amount of practical experience of the long cane. They learned the basic cane techniques, so that in areas where there was no MO they would be able to teach new routes to experienced long cane travellers. This section was not assessed.

Learning and teaching

Only the NRAB had a separate section on learning and teaching; the SRAB incorporated it into 'other studies'. The NRAB module expected the following of students:

- to be able to undertake a comprehensive assessment of the individual, develop an appropriate treatment plan, effectively carry out that plan and evaluate its effectiveness;
- to have an understanding of adult learning and the development of skills.

(NRAB documentation)

Students at the NRAB received a $2\frac{1}{2}$ hour teaching block per week (a total of 60 hours). The tutor, who had many years' experience of teacher training, said she was trying to cover some of the same ground that she would have covered in teacher training, but found this extremely difficult with such limited time. Because of this, written handouts were issued which saved students having to take notes.

Written assignments were required on a regular basis, which enabled the tutor to monitor each student's progress. Two additional assignments, each of 1,500 words, were required for the formal course assessment. One had to be based on the application of learning theories, the other on teaching and learning related to a specific skill taught on the course.

The SRAB, as part of its 'other studies' section, timetabled a total of six hours for learning and teaching; it involved lectures on models of learning, and adapting these to meet the needs of individual clients. There was no assessment of this work.

Counselling

At the NRAB, counselling formed part of the 'Social and other studies' section. By the end of the course, students were expected 'to have an ability to undertake interviewing and counselling'. Four sessions were allocated (five hours), taught by guest tutors, one of whom was a marriage guidance counsellor. The Training Officer said these sessions covered awareness of what is meant by counselling, the skills involved, the student/workers' limitations, and referring a client on for more specialist counselling.

The SRAB had introduced a new section to their syllabus on counselling, and the intention was to allocate 30 hours to it. Due to staffing problems on the 1986 course, students received only two or three hours involving one lecture and a video.

Social and other studies

Students at the NRAB at the end of this section were expected:
- to understand the psychological and sociological factors which might affect visually disabled people and their families;
- to understand normal and deviant human growth and decline;
- to have an understanding of group dynamics;
- to understand the role of others working with visually disabled people;
- to have a knowledge of current relevant legislation and an appreciation of the historical background to the specialist service;
- to have a knowledge of relevant central and local government services and voluntary agency resources and how to obtain them for the benefit of visually disabled people;
- to have an understanding of the self-management skills required to fulfil the professional role;
- to have an ability to undertake effective case-recording;
- to have an ability to undertake interviewing and counselling;
- to have knowledge and understanding of non-verbal communication.

(NRAB documentation)

The NRAB Training Officer said that social studies covered four areas: a factual component (for example, legislation); social and psychological factors affecting rehabilitation; specific problems relating to certain client groups and where to go for help with them; and 'tools of the trade' – i.e. interviewing, caseload management, record-keeping, public speaking and committee work. In addition to these key areas, there were single sessions on local government and social services.

Students had two sessions per week (total 60 hours) throughout the course, which usually involved seminars or group discussions. There appeared to be a considerable amount of information to be covered in this time. Outside speakers played a major role in this section. Assessment was based on four essays, each of 1,500 words.

At the SRAB the social ('Other') studies section involved a series of lectures by tutors on legislation, leisure and the social services. Outside speakers gave lectures on current educational practice, leisure, multi-handicap, cultural implications of blindness and adult literacy.

Placement

NRAB

At the NRAB, TO students had a five-week placement in a social services department, school or rehabilitation unit. Of the 60 students who took the TO course between January 1983 and January 1986, approximately two-thirds were placed in social services and one-third were based with voluntary societies or education authorities. The two main objectives of the placement were 'to meet the individual student's needs [and] to offer varied and relevant work experience' (NRAB documentation).

Before the placement, a programme was negotiated between the NRAB, the student and the fieldwork supervisor, and students sometimes visited the placement location. Students were expected to keep a written account of their work and experiences during the placement and also had to complete a project while on placement which included a case study of a client.

The fieldwork supervisors were invited to the Centre for a two-day 'supervisors' course'. A four-page placement guide was also prepared, which detailed the purpose of the placement, the roles of the participants and their duties.

The responsibility for assessing the students' performance on the placements rested with the fieldwork supervisors. They were told to base their assessment on: teaching ability; interpersonal skills (for example interviewing, assessment); and organizational ability (for example professional knowledge, recording).[2] The sheet on which they had to indicate this assessment required

---

2   The NRAB practical fieldwork assessment form is available from the authors on request.

only a 'Yes' or 'No' response to the question: 'Has the student reached a satisfactory standard in [these three categories]?'

After the placement, students returned to the NRAB for approximately one week. During this time a feedback session, involving all staff and students, was scheduled. This focused on placement experiences, but also covered other aspects of the course.

SRAB

Fieldwork placement on the course at the SRAB lasted for six weeks. Most placements were in social services departments: 24 of the 31 TO placements which took place between January 1983 and January 1986 were in social services. The SRAB said that it was sometimes difficult to find suitable placement supervisors. Generally, but not necessarily, supervisors were ex-TO students, and there was a regular group on whom the SRAB relied.

The Training Officer was aware of (and had attended) the two-day course for supervisors run by the NRAB but was sceptical of its value and felt no need to offer anything similar. Instead, potential supervisors were invited to visit the SRAB for a day when they talked with the tutors and then with the students. Subsequently, students visited the placement to gain some idea of what awaited them.

While on placement, the SRAB expected the students to:
- [gain] experience in teaching at least one relevant skill e.g. daily living skills, braille, moon or typewriting;
- [make] appropriate visits to statutory and voluntary facilities for the visually impaired in the placement area;
- [gain] experience of a registration visit and an opportunity to examine procedures in the placement agency;
- [make] supervised and independent visits to a range of visually impaired clients with an opportunity to write up reports;
- [gain] experience of day centre activity, either specialist or general; and to;
- [have] an opportunity to discover the structure of the placement agency, its administrative and hierarchical methods, the place of the specialist within the agency,

and the method of assessing and meeting the needs of the visually impaired.
(SRAB documentation)

The Training Officer said that in the first and, depending on the student, the second week, the supervisor and student visited clients jointly. After this, they worked together for perhaps two sessions each week. For the remainder of the time the student worked alone.

As with the NRAB, the placement supervisors were entirely responsible for assessing students on placement. The SRAB were only involved in the assessment of a student on placement if the supervisor encountered any problems. Before students returned to the SRAB, they were expected to discuss their performance with the placement supervisor. The SRAB said they must have satisfied the supervisor of their ability to teach clients certain skills. The supervisor sent a written 'Placement Report' back to the SRAB which covered the following areas: competence in teaching; ability to build relationships both with colleagues and clients; response to criticism; reliability and punctuality; initiative; ability to apply theory to practice; flexibility in dealing with new situations and changes in plan; and how the placement expectations had been fulfilled. In addition to the written report from the supervisor, the students themselves were expected to write an account of their experiences.

Discussion at the SRAB took place in the week between the completion of the placement and the end of the course. A number of feedback sessions, covering the whole course, were arranged for this period.

Project

Students at both training centres were required to complete a project. At the NRAB this had to be:

an essay of approximately 5,000 words, or a project supported by an abstract, on any topic relevant to the field of visual handicap and covered on the technical officer's course. The project should demonstrate the student's understanding of the topic and his ability to analyse and discuss the relevant material. (NRAB documentation)

NRAB students submitted three project titles, one of which was chosen by tutors following discussions with the students. The General Secretary said that the topic finally selected was the one which would stretch the student the most. Although it did not need to be related to the placement, the NRAB preferred that a case study was included, wherever possible. The project was submitted at the end of the course.

At the SRAB, students were free to choose their own topic – though the SRAB had responded to what was described as the need of some students for some direction and provided a list of possible titles. Students secured the agreement of their tutor before work on the project began. In 1986, for the first time, students had to submit this before, rather than after, the placement. The Training Officer explained that the SRAB felt that students 'should not be doing any other work on the placement'. Furthermore, he questioned the value of the project, which to be accomplished properly, he felt, required far more input than the students had time to give.

Course assessment

Both centres used a system of continuous assessment for practical and written work. At the NRAB a pass mark of 50 per cent had to be achieved for each piece of work. Only a certain number of assignments in each subject area could be re-submitted; the number of permitted re-submissions varied between subjects, according to the total number of assignments required. Students who consistently failed to meet the required standard were advised to leave the course. Between January 1983 and January 1986 six students withdrew out of a total of 60 who took the course in that period.

In 1985/6 the NRAB produced an assignment evaluation sheet which allowed for a grade on various aspects of each piece of work, an agreed overall mark and tutors' and students' comments. This evaluation sheet was also used for the other courses run at the NRAB. With the exception of the placement, all assessment was carried out by course tutors. A retired worker was invited as an outside assessor to monitor all assessed course work (i.e. not the placement). This system of continuous assessment was relatively new to the NRAB.

At the SRAB, the system of continuous assessment was introduced in 1984. The Training Officer believed this system to be harder for students than the previous reliance on final examinations. No more than two pieces of work in any one subject could be re-submitted. There were no longer any outside assessors for this course. Between January 1983 and

January 1986 two students withdrew, and two failed, out of a total of 34 who took the course in that period.

Mobility Officer training

Each of the three training agencies ran an MO course. The NMC course was usually 24 weeks (depending on variations due to Easter): 12 weeks at the training centre, and 12 weeks' fieldwork placement. The NRAB course was 30 weeks: 16 weeks at the training centre, and two periods of fieldwork placement, totalling 14 weeks. The first SRAB course began in 1986, and was intended for people already possessing a TO qualification. It was 12 weeks: eight weeks at the centre, and four weeks on placement.

Course aims

The training at the NMC was based on a firm commitment to the long cane system. Although there was passing reference to the use of other mobility aids, the course booklet was unequivocal about the central role of the long cane:

> The centre believes in the fundamental value of the long-cane system and of its usefulness to a wide cross-section of visually handicapped people.

Along with this commitment was the belief that the best way to encourage clients to use a long cane was to ensure that students themselves were proficient users:

> Any student must have respect for and confidence in his teacher. Before taking those first brave steps into society the blind person needs the reassurance of knowing that his sighted tutor can fully understand the difficulties, not simply imagine them. For this reason all trainee instructors undergo training while blindfolded. They experience travelling without sight and gain confidence in the techniques they will be asked to pass on.

The Principal maintained that this was the purpose of the training. However, following a meeting at the NMC in October 1987, staff prepared a detailed statement of aims, which stated:

> The aim of the mobility course is to teach students the principles of orientation and mobility training based on the long cane system of training and to encourage students to adapt that system to suit the individual mobility needs of all visually impaired people.

The long cane system of mobility and orientation presents skills and learning opportunities in a carefully planned hierarchy of difficulty. The centre believes that this system forms an excellent basis for all work in orientation and mobility, including the training of clients whose primary travel aid is remaining vision.

Whilst mobility theory and discussion sessions form part of the training, the centre believes that the occluded travel (i.e. blindfold and low vision simulating spectacles) undertaken by all students is a vital part of the training. Through occluded travel students gain a better insight into the difficulties experienced by visually impaired people and are actively involved in problem solving techniques. They are also able to examine the teacher/student relationship through their own experiences as both learner and teacher and by experiencing a degree of success in their own occluded travel gain a confidence and belief that the training is effective.

However, both workers and students felt that these aims had not been wholly achieved (see Chapter 8).

The NRAB course aimed to equip students with the skills to assess client needs and provide individualized mobility teaching. The General Secretary and Training Officer stressed that the aim was to provide students with a knowledge of other aids and techniques, in addition to the long cane system. They also aimed to make students good mobility *teachers*. The mobility tutors at the NRAB said that the aim was not necessarily to produce good long cane travellers, but to provide students with experience of a long cane in a variety of situations and to ensure an understanding of the problems of visually impaired people.

The SRAB course was designed to provide mobility training for those people who already possessed a TO qualification (see Chapter 3 for discussion of entry requirements). This requirement was felt by the SRAB to justify the brevity of the course, since students had already covered a range of topics in their TO training, which the MO course did not seek to repeat. The Training Officer and mobility tutor said that in designing the course, they had intended a major departure from what was described as 'traditional' mobility training. Primarily, their aim was to move away from the emphasis on students being proficient long cane users under blindfold and to equip them instead with a variety of approaches to teaching mobility. This aim stemmed from their conviction that demand for long cane training among the visually impaired population was limited. This was linked to a second aim, which was to develop an understanding of the needs of low-vision clients in relation to mobility training and to equip students with a range of skills to enable them to train such clients.

Course structure and daily schedule

At the NMC, with the exception of mobility teaching, subjects were taught consecutively in a series of discrete blocks. At the NRAB and the SRAB, the structure followed a similar pattern to that of their TO courses – i.e. they taught most subjects each week.

The working week at the NMC comprised a $31\frac{1}{4}$ hour week, of which, on average, $18\frac{3}{4}$ hours were taught sessions. The NRAB had the same working week, but with an average of 11 hours taught sessions. At the SRAB there was a 25-hour week, of which 15 hours were taught sessions.

Detailed course content

The subject areas and hours allocated to each of these at the three training centres were as follows:

NMC	Total hours (to nearest hour)
Orientation and mobility – practical	75
Orientation and mobility – theory	13
Mapping	19
Anatomy and physiology of the eye	15
Audiology	14
Learning and teaching	9
Adjustment to visual handicap	4
Social services	6
Daily living skills	3
Other mobility aids	8
Braille	13
Counselling	6
Total	185

	Total hours (to nearest hour)
NRAB	
Orientation and mobility – practical*	75
Orientation and mobility – theory*	40
Anatomy and physiology of the eye	14
Audiology	14
Social studies and administration (incl. psychology of blindness)	19
Total	162

* These two subjects included work on mapping

SRAB	
Orientation and mobility – practical	70
Other subjects	34
Total	104

The NMC allocated a total of 88 hours to mobility, which represented 48 per cent of the taught sessions (i.e. excluding study time); and the NRAB allocated 115 hours to mobility, which constituted 71 per cent of the taught sessions. The SRAB allocated 70 hours to mobility, that is, 67 per cent of the taught sessions.

Practical orientation and mobility

This was the major element of all three courses. At the NMC and the NRAB, 75 hours were spent on practical mobility; and at the SRAB, there were 70 hours.

The NMC students had one session per day ($7\frac{1}{2}$ hours per week) of individual tuition in practical long cane mobility. The Principal of the NMC said: 'the main emphasis is on working (on long cane mobility) under blindfold.' The syllabus was described in the course booklet:

Learning to travel by the long cane method whilst blindfolded.

Included are:

- pre-cane skills, protective methods and indoor travel;
- outdoor travel in residential area and road crossing;
- orientation and mental mapping;

- pedestrian and traffic light crossings;
- use of public transport;
- techniques in heavily congested shopping areas;
- use of escalators, lifts, revolving doors;
- town centre travel;
- travel in adverse weather conditions; and
- rural area travel and adaptation of techniques to suit country tracks and terrain.

In recent years, an element of practice with low-vision simulation spectacles had been introduced, but this was minimal. Tutors said that this was increasing on each successive course.

At the beginning of the course, students were assigned to a tutor for one-to-one practical mobility teaching. Most tutors believed that practical mobility teaching would be positively dangerous under any other circumstances, though one tutor said that practical teaching of a group was possible, provided that the students were sufficiently advanced. The training was divided into three separate sections: (1) indoor mobility, during which students wore a blindfold or, occasionally, low-vision simulation spectacles, and which included basic safety techniques such as orientation and the use of senses other than sight; (2) basic outdoor mobility, which took students up to, but did not include, the point where they attempted a solo city centre journey; and (3) city centre travel, during which time was spent reinforcing earlier work, as well as on new aspects (for example traffic skills). It was felt that solo travel would demonstrate to students that visually impaired people could do the same.

Students were intended to gain practice in teaching the long cane technique in role-play sessions, called 'teachbacks'. These were observed by a tutor, who assessed the performance of the student taking the role of the MO. There was no set number of teachbacks on the course; tutors fitted them in when time permitted.

Students were required to write up each practical mobility lesson. In these notes they were expected to cover aims and objectives, teaching techniques and personal reactions to the lesson. Tutors read through and commented on these notes – and the 'notebooks' formed part of the formal assessment (see orientation and mobility theory, p. 50).

At the NRAB, each student had four one-to-one practical mobility sessions (five hours) per week. The first two weeks of the course were spent on indoor mobility and the remainder on outdoor work. The mobility tutors (each of whom had trained at the NMC) likened the course to that at the NMC, but said there were two main differences: first, they placed more emphasis on giving students practice in teaching the skills; and secondly, they had included much more work with low vision simulation spectacles.

Included in the practical mobility sessions were sessions on role play (i.e. what the NMC described as 'teachbacks'). In these role-play sessions students worked in pairs, with one student taking the part of the worker and the other that of the client. There was an attempt to simulate different visual abilities, age groups and additional impairments in these sessions. Some of the practical sessions were videoed and discussed with the tutor. Students also observed the tutor teaching another student mobility at least once a week, and these sessions were discussed in the mobility theory sessions.

Students were required to keep a workbook throughout the course in which they recorded details about their practical work, much along the lines of the NMC. It was assessed at the end of the course.

At the SRAB, students on the MO course normally received two practical sessions per day (10 hours per week). Very little of this was one-to-one teaching. Most was conducted either with another student present as an observer or with the tutor demonstrating an aspect to the whole group (four students) which they then practised in pairs – not necessarily under the supervision of the tutor. Practical teaching was the responsibility of one NMC-trained tutor. She stressed that she did not place a great deal of importance on the students' performance as long cane travellers and therefore kept the teaching programmes flexible, so that students were taken on to the next stage, once they had grasped the techniques.

At first, a blindfold was used to alert students to the importance of auditory skills. However, the tutor said that low-vision simulation spectacles were soon introduced because these more adequately represented the visual condition of most clients. The SRAB estimated that only about 20 per cent of the practical mobility training was spent under blindfold, compared with 80 per cent spent wearing low-vision simulation spectacles.

The initial stage of training involved students working indoors under blindfold. The tutor was most concerned that students acquired teaching skills. They regularly observed her teaching other students and were expected to consider how to teach the skills they learned. At the end of the indoor section there was a short role-play teaching exercise in which the students worked in pairs: each surveyed a route and then taught it to their partner. The next stage involved students working individually on mental mapping. Starting with an indoor area, they had to draw a map of the route they had travelled under blindfold.

The rest of the practical training was devoted to outdoor work which students generally tackled in pairs. Again, the tutor taught the skill to one of the students while the other watched, and vice versa. They were expected to make written notes on the teaching points. They also had two role-play exercises per week, which involved surveying an outdoor route and teaching this to another student who was wearing low-vision simulation spectacles. The tutor observed this session and focused particularly on the teaching skills used rather than the skill of the student in using a long cane.

For their practical mobility training, as at the other two centres, students had to keep a notebook. In addition, when a new route was covered, students had to make out a route map or sketch of the area they thought was covered in the lesson. These notes were checked by the tutor regularly and were returned to students with written comments.

(Note: The remaining subjects at the NMC and the NRAB came under similar headings and are described together in the following sections. However, the SRAB course was markedly different in coverage because of its design and aims and is therefore described later in a separate section.)

Orientation and mobility: theory

At the NMC this was allocated 13 hours. It involved a weekly group session, led by the Principal, in which the main points raised in the students' mobility notebooks were discussed and related to the following:

- use of landmarks, clues, compass directions, kinaesthetic memory, independent familiarization and indoor and outdoor numbering systems;
- history of mobility;

- role of mobility instructor, different approaches to mobility programmes and setting up a programme in the home area(s);
- giving a talk, selection of a suitable training area;
- designing suitable mobility programmes for residential and non-residential courses;
- mobility for young children and hints for parents;
- allowing for additional handicaps and considering the effect of age, onset and degree of blindness;
- teaching congenitally and adventitiously blinded people;
- use of maps and providing after-case services;
- adapting programmes to suit the individual.

(NMC course booklet)

While these topics are, no doubt, relevant and important, they could not be described collectively as 'Mobility theory'.

At the NRAB, students had two sessions per week on theoretical aspects of mobility (a total of just under 40 hours). In this time, students had lectures, seminars, films, group discussions, further role-play practice and more sessions on mapping. They also visited practising MOs and, with the agreement of the client, observed them at work.

Anatomy and physiology of the eye

At the NMC this was allocated 15 hours. It was based on a series of lectures and seminars. The module was divided into three sections: structure and function of the healthy eye, diseases and malfunction of the eye, and low vision and its wider implications. Some practical sessions and visits were also incorporated and two guest speakers gave presentations: a low-vision client, and a lecturer in ophthalmic optics. The course outline was provided by the tutor:

Structure and function of the eye (covering anatomy of the eye and orbit):
the mechanism of vision (refraction and errors of refraction);

Diseases and malfunction of the eye:
congenital conditions and syndromes conditions affecting the external eye, also the lids and conjuctiva;
skin diseases involving the conjuctiva and the cornea;
diseases of the cornea;
diseases of the lens;
diseases of the uveal tract;
diseases of the retina;

diseases of the optic nerve;
diabetes and glaucoma;
trauma;
special precautions;
drops and drugs;
Surgical techniques;
Low vision:
what it is and how we define it;
the clinical examination and assessment;
the functional examination and assessment;
the basic goals of the assessments;
use of optical aids and training with same;
sight and visual learning;
variables affecting visual performance;
visual development in congenital and adventitious blind;
visual efficiency in the discriminating learner;
training techniques;
illumination in natural and artificial light;
colour and contrast;
low light and low vision;
other useful aids in low vision.

The tutor gave three formal lectures and students were required, on the basis of individual research, to present two seminars each: one on the anatomy and physiology of the eye, and one on eye diseases. Notes of these were photocopied and distributed to the rest of the group. A guest speaker gave a practical session on the components of the eye, including dissection of a bull's eye. The purpose was to give a three-dimensional demonstration to clarify some of the points raised in lectures. A visit to a local eye hospital allowed students to witness, at first hand, the treatment of people with eye diseases and conditions. They also observed low-vision aids being prescribed and demonstrated to patients. Finally, students visited a school for the visually impaired to gain practical experience of young people with low vision.

At the NRAB, the training on anatomy and physiology of the eye was allocated 14 hours. This included lectures and an observation visit to a local ophthalmic clinic. Students had to present seminar papers, though these were not formally assessed. Course documentation stated that at the end of the course students would be expected to:

- chart the anatomy and understand the physiology of the ear and the theories of perception;

- understand the pathology of the eye and recognize the common symptoms and demonstrate a knowledge of preventative medicine relating to the eyes;
- understand how the different diseases of the eye may effect the visual functioning of the client;
- assess the degree of useful functional vision of a client for mobility training;
- describe the range of low-vision aids and how they may be acquired.

Audiology

The NMC course included 14 hours on audiology, which involved lectures presented by the audiology tutor and a seminar presented by each of the students. The course booklet described the course as covering:

Basic properties of sound: tones, measurement and description of sound, sensitivity curve of the ear; anatomy and action of the ear, theories of pitch and loudness discrimination.

Further properties of sound: acoustics reflection, refraction, interference and masking.

Audiometry: using an audiometer, testing and interpreting audiograms; types of hearing loss; hearing aids, recent research on binaural hearing aids; spatial attributes of sound.

Auditory training: sound discrimination, using sound sources, sound shadows, sound echoes; listening to binaural audiotape recordings; developing hearing skills in mobility, catering for the blind person with a hearing loss.

The audiology tutor said that she tried to develop among students a greater understanding of the problems that can be caused by hearing loss. For this reason, students were required to wear sound excluders in some sessions in order to simulate hearing loss. Three outside speakers each gave a lecture: a physicist/audiologist on hearing aids; a representative from SENSE on multi-handicap; and a specialist in audiology. These speakers were asked to set questions on their specialist areas for the final, written examination. Students were expected to learn the deaf-blind manual, and there was a visit to a special deaf-blind unit based in a home for the handicapped. On recent courses, students had also attended a weekend course, organized by SENSE, for the parents of multi-handicapped children and young adults.

The NRAB also allocated 14 hours to audiology. This involved lectures, mostly given by guest speakers, and student seminars. Students were expected by the end of the section to be able to:

- chart the anatomy and understand the physiology of the eye and the theories of perception;
- understand the pathology of the ear and recognize the common symptoms;
- demonstrate a knowledge of preventative medicine relating to the ear;
- understand how the different diseases of the ear may effect the auditory functioning of the client;
- assess the degree of useful functional hearing of a client for mobility training and demonstrate a knowledge of how to read an audiogram;
- describe the properties of sound waves and understand how a visually handicapped person may use the patterns of sound waves to help in orientation and mobility;
- describe the range of aids to hearing and how they may be acquired.

(NRAB course documentation)

Learning and teaching

The NMC allocated nine hours for this section. The tutor with responsibility for the subject said that the aim of the course was to cover the theories of learning and develop an understanding of the processes involved when teaching a client new skills. However, she felt this was ambitious, given the time available. She also aimed to link the module with the students' learning of practical mobility. The seven sessions covered the following elements:

1. introduction
   nervous system
   human brain development
   some basic features of learning
   what is meant by learning?
2. Thorndike's experiment (instrumental conditioning)
   trial and error learning
   stimulus–responses

conditional responses
reinforcement – simple.
3.   feedback
reinforcement
shaping behaviour
extinction schedules of reinforcement.
4.   external inhibition
reciprocal inhibition
stimulus discrimination
stimulus generalisation
transfer of learning overlearning.
5.   punishment
motivation
fears and anxiety
memory – short   ıd long term
remembering and forgetting
impaired memory.
6.   skills
concepts – language – visual thinking
problem-solving
age and learning
difficult learning situations.
7.   consolidation and revision
discussion of relevance to mobility
preparation and evaluation of lessons.
(Written information provided by the tutor)
Students were given a reading list but the tutor felt there was little time for them to cover much. She said that pressure of time meant students had to be 'spoon-fed'.

On the NRAB MO course, no sessions were formally allocated to learning and teaching. Instead, tutors for the various other topics were expected to reinforce this aspect throughout their teaching, particularly in the practical mobility sessions. Despite there being no separate tuition, at the end of the course students were expected to be able to:

- describe the client's learning processes;
- assess a client's capacity to learn the skills of mobility and orientation design and plan a mobility and orientation learning programme;
- teach the skills essential to a visually handicapped person for effective orientation and mobility;
- analyse the client's skill in using the mobility techniques being taught and assess the client's progress in learning

the techniques to evaluate his own performance.
(NRAB documentation)

Adjustment to visual handicap/the psychology of blindness

At the NMC, the 'Adjustment to visual handicap' section
consisted of: (a) a formal lecture which covered loss theory,
social attitudes to handicap and stereotyping and the effects of
visual impairment on a family; (b) a group discussion of
various case studies of clients; (c) a session in which pairs of
students were each given a specific case study to discuss; and
(d) a video of a visually impaired person's progression through
the various stages of mobility training. After these sessions, the
tutor expected that the students would:

- be familiar with some of the main theories of loss;
- understand some of the effects of stigma and
  stereotyping;
- understand the effects of visual loss on an age-related
  basis;
- understand the effects of loss on significant others;
- consider the effects of rehabilitation on the visually
  impaired person and his/her family, with reference to
  practical training and social cultural and financial factors,
  etc.

(Written information provided by the tutor)
At the NRAB, the corresponding section was entitled 'The
psychology of blindness'. However, it was included in the
section on 'Social studies and administration', for which there
was usually one session timetabled per week (a total of 19
hours). At the end of the subsection, students were expected to:

- comprehend the influence that congenital blindness or
  partial sight has on human growth and development;
- apply this knowledge to particular clients in order to
  facilitate their development or adjustment while
  presenting a mobility programme;
- comprehend the emotional impact of traumatic or
  progressive loss of sight;
- apply this knowledge to particular clients to facilitate
  their adjustment;
- appreciate the effects on the family which has a blind or
  partially sighted member;

- apply this appreciation to the interaction which comes about from regular contact with the family and, where appropriate, involve the family in the mobility training programme;
- appreciate the effect on a client of multi-handicap which includes blindness or partial sight.

(NRAB documentation)

Social services/social studies and administration

On the NMC course, 'Social services' was covered in one full day during which there were lectures by tutors and guest speakers. The NMC booklet described the course as follows:
1.   history, developments and function of social services
2.   specialist services, benefits, allowances for visually handicapped and partially sighted
3.   statutory requirements
4.   working in a local authority setting.

At the NRAB, as previously mentioned, 'Social studies and administration' was allocated a weekly session (a total of approximately 19 hours, including the work on the psychology of blindness). On completion of the section, students were expected to be able to:

- recognize the effect of sensory deprivation on human interaction;
- compile and write appropriate records;
- recognize the interactions between worker, client and agency;
- recognize the boundaries of his/her own autonomy and responsibilities within and to the agency;
- demonstrate a knowledge of the basic skills needed to work in a social services agency;
- demonstrate a knowledge of the historical background to welfare services for the visually handicapped;
- evaluate this knowledge in the light of current trends;
- identify the relevant welfare services for individual visually handicapped clients;
- appreciate the changing public attitudes to handicapped people;
- demonstrate a knowledge of legislation affecting visually handicapped people.

(NRAB course documentation)

Daily living skills

At the NMC this was a relatively new topic, introduced in 1977/78. It was allocated approximately three hours. The NMC made no apology for the brevity of the module; it stressed it was in the business of teaching mobility. Each student usually had two sessions. In the first, students worked in pairs in role-play exercises with each student teaching a different skill. This session was videoed and discussed with the tutor. In the second session, the whole group watched and discussed all the videos, so that students had the chance to see skills other than the ones they had actually taught.

At the NRAB, no sessions were allocated to this subject; tutors said, and course documentation confirmed, that opportunities were taken where they arose in other subjects to reinforce the 'daily living skills and recreation' that had been covered on the TO course. However, not all of the MOs trained had a TO qualification; at least one had only a Home Teacher Certificate. At the end of the course students were expected to be able to:

- demonstrate a knowledge of the basic techniques and methods available for visually handicapped people to assist them in the skills of daily living;
- list the common available aids to daily living;
- categorize the social, recreational and leisure facilities available for visually handicapped people and advise the client on their appropriate use.

(NRAB course documentation)

Braille/communication

A requirement of the NMC course was that students learn braille, mostly on their own, and pass a braille test. The course booklet specified the requirements, as follows:

- proficiency with a Perkins braille writer;
- self-instruction to Grade II level in braille writing and reading;
- students from non-English speaking countries are required to learn English Grade I braille.

The test, which could be taken as soon as a student felt ready, involved a translation from and into braille.

On the NRAB course no time was allocated to communications. Again, it seems that the students were expected to have a knowledge of this when they started the course since, at the end of the course, they were expected to be able to:

- describe and use methods of tactile communication, read Grade I moon and have a knowledge of Grade II moon;
- demonstrate a knowledge of mechanical and technological communication aids for visually handicapped people;
- read and write Grade I braille;
- demonstrate a working knowledge of Grade II braille;
- communicate with a deaf-blind person using the manual and spartan alphabets;
- evaluate research and development in communication aids and advise clients on their implementation.

(NRAB course documentation)

Counselling

At the NMC this module was just over six hours - on the 1986 course it was all covered on one day. It was a recent addition to the course. The tutor felt that the coverage was inadequate for such an important topic, but said that there was no time to extend it. The module consisted of a lecture/discussion and four practical sessions on inter-personal skills. At the end of the five sessions the tutor expected that students should:

- be able to give a definition of counselling;
- be aware of, and have practised, the basic skills necessary in counselling;
- be aware of their present potential as counsellors and of the limits of their skills;
- begin to identify other professionals who may be appropriately involved in the counselling of a visually impaired person.

(Written information provided by the tutor)

Other elements of the SRAB course

Apart from the practical mobility training at the SRAB which has been described earlier in this section, the MO course included lectures and seminars on the following topics:

1. assessment techniques (5 hours);

2. physical and mental health and the consequences of disease and disablement, both singly and in multiple form (5 hours);
3. the particular mobility problems faced by different client groupings, such as the elderly or the mentally handicapped, and strategies for coping with these (8 hours);
4. the effects of cultural differences on attitudes to disability ($1\frac{1}{2}$ hours);
5. the history and development of mobility training (1 hour);
6. assertion techniques: achieving a desired goal without resorting to aggression (2 hours);
7. auditory training: making the optimum use of hearing as an aid to mobility and orientation and the ear (3 hours);
8. interdisciplinarity: who to contact for appropriate advice or action (1 hour);
9. specialized and commercial aids (2 hours);
10. centres undertaking research in the field (2 hours);
11. vision training (2 hours);
12. records and caseload management (1 hour).

(SRAB course documentation)

The Training Officer and the mobility tutor taught most of these subjects but outside speakers covered the following topics: sonic aids; multi-handicap; cultural differences; the work of an MO; current research; and assessment. There was also a visit to one of the Guide Dogs for the Blind Association's training centres. Students also had to prepare and present a training programme for nurses in a hospital. Three sessions were timetabled for the preparation of this and an afternoon allocated for the presentation after the placement.

Placement/teaching practice

Most of the NMC students had their fieldwork placement in a residential unit or school rather than in a social services department. Between January 1983 and January 1986, 82 students went on placement, of which only 13 were in social services departments. Three main reasons were given for this. First, such places had an easily identifiable client group in need of long cane mobility training, which made placements easier to arrange. Secondly, until recently, many local authorities had no long cane mobility service and therefore potential supervisors were few. This situation was said to have improved and the number of potential locations for placements increased accordingly. Finally, mobility officers in local authorities were often required to have a car but most students did not possess their own transport.

The NMC said that it tried to make students understand while training that they may be required as supervisors in future. However, there was said to be some difficulty in finding supervisors. The Centre said that this was because some workers found the possibility of further contact with NMC threatening, as though their work was being examined. Also, it found some authorities reluctant to allow their MOs to accept a student more than once since, rather than helping to relieve some of the workload, the placement meant more work for the MO. Some MOs had indicated a similar attitude and complained that students were not ready to carry a full caseload. The NMC pointed out that training lasted for the full six months of the course and the placement was part of the training. No training was offered to potential supervisors by the NMC, other than a set of written guidelines. Some tutors felt training was necessary, but the NMC felt unable to run any courses because of a lack of time and resources.

On the placement the students were expected to spend three-quarters of their day on normal MO duties, and a quarter on work set by the NMC, including essays and a project (see sections on Projects and Assessment, pp. 63 and 65.) Students were visited three times by their NMC tutors, and once by the Principal. These visits were to observe the students working with clients and to discuss their progress. Placement supervisors were also expected to observe students working with clients and to check their written lesson preparation and notes. The overall assessment of the placement was made jointly between the placement supervisor, the NMC tutor and the Principal, although the supervisor was asked to recommend a grade for each student. After the placement, there was a group feedback session at the NMC.

The NRAB had provided all MO placements in social services departments. Between January 1983 and January 1986 this involved 11 students. The course incorporated two periods of fieldwork placement: two weeks after the first month, and 12 weeks at the end of the course; both were at the same place.

The rationale for the first placement was that it gave students a chance to become better acquainted with the supervisor and working environment before the main placement.

Prior to the start of the placements, there was a meeting of the planning group, made up of the student, an NRAB tutor, the placement supervisor and the line manager. This group co-ordinated the placement. For the first placement, the NRAB listed a number of activities that should be covered − for example observing the MO at work, teaching one or more clients. Other activities had to be planned by the students themselves with the agreement of the supervisor. Written reports on each of these activities were required. On the main placement, the NRAB tried to ensure that there was an opportunity for students to undertake a full training programme: meet the client; assess their needs; plan a programme; and implement the training. Students were expected to work with five or six different clients overall. During the placement students had to keep a workbook, similar to the one they maintained at the training centre, in which they were expected to record their placement experiences.

Each student received at least one visit from an NRAB tutor. However, the responsibility for assessment of the student's placement rested jointly with the placement supervisor and one of the two outside assessors, appointed by the NRAB, who observed the student working with clients or, when a personal visit could not be made, watched a video recording of a teaching session with a client. Both the placement supervisor and the outside assessor sent a written report on their respective students to the NRAB. They also attended the meeting of the planning group held at the end of the placement. In the event of any disagreement regarding assessment, the outside assessors were said to have the final say. At the end of the course there was a final feedback/evaluation session, involving both students and staff.

The NRAB organized two-day courses for placement supervisors, as on its TO course. However, one of the mobility tutors felt that lack of proper supervision on the placement was a major problem and that students were often working in isolation. This tutor described other problems which sometimes arose out of the placement supervisors' own situation: poor relationships with other workers in the agency; difficulties imposed by agency structure; and getting the right sort of client referrals. The General Secretary and Training Officer disagreed with much of this, saying that the NRAB was very careful to ensure that placement supervisors were able to provide the necessary level of supervision. Also that the supervisors' relationship with other colleagues was taken into consideration before the placement went ahead.

On the first SRAB MO course the placement started in the eighth week and lasted four weeks (in subsequent courses this has been extended to six weeks). The Training Officer and mobility tutor considered a placement in a social services department preferable to one in a centre or voluntary agency, particularly if the student was relatively new to the field. On the first course, three of the four students were in a social services department and one went to a rehabilitation unit.

The SRAB said it had been keen to ensure good supervision for the placements, especially since the course was in its formative stages. The placement supervisor was expected to have a lot of involvement with the student initially, but by week three or four it was hoped that the students would be working alone with clients. The mobility tutor visited each placement once and spoke to the student and, separately, to the supervisor. She did not observe students working with clients. However, the SRAB had appointed an external adviser for its new MO course, who had visited the students on placement and observed them teaching clients. The placement supervisor was responsible for assessing the student on placement but the final decision rested with the SRAB.

Project

Projects formed part of the MO courses at the NMC and the NRAB but not at the SRAB. The NMC students had to work on their project while they were on the placement teaching practice. The topic could be theoretical or practical and was the students' own choice. Students also had to give a presentation on their projects to the rest of the group on their return to the NMC and this, together with the work itself, was assessed by tutors.

At the NRAB, as at the NMC, the project was submitted at the end of the course. Projects were assessed and graded independently by three NRAB tutors before an overall grading was agreed. The projects were then examined by an outside assessor, appointed by the NRAB, who was a retired worker. In the event of a disagreement over the mark, the outside assessor's opinion was final.

The SRAB had not included a project in its course because students had already done one on their TO course and, in any case, staff were unconvinced of the necessity of having one. Instead, students produced a detailed case study of one of the clients they worked with on the placement.

Course assessment

At the NMC, in addition to continuous assessment of the students' practical mobility skills, final written examinations were given in orientation and mobility theory, anatomy and physiology of the eye, audiology and learning and teaching; there was also a test in braille. The tests were taken individually immediately after each subject module had been completed. The pass mark was 50 per cent (70 per cent in braille) and a pass was required in each subject, although examinations could be re-taken. As well as the project, the NMC students on placement completed a case study of one of the clients they were teaching and an essay. Course tutors assessed both pieces of work.

The final MO award was graded pass, credit or distinction. According to the NMC, approximately one-sixth of students received a pass, four-sixths a credit and one-sixth a distinction. Between January 1983 and January 1986 two students (out of a total of 82) failed the course.

At the NRAB there was a system of continuous assessment which was based on the practical mobility sessions, students' workbook, three essays and the project. Students also made a case study of one of the clients (including the immediate family) with whom they worked on the placement, though this could form part of the project and was not necessarily a separate piece of work.

The SRAB also used a system of continuous assessment. To demonstrate their learning in the practical mobility sessions, students had to keep a mobility notebook of every practical lesson they received or observed. The principle was similar to that in use at the NMC and the NRAB. The mobility tutor assessed these notebooks and made written comments on them, though no grading was given.

Each SRAB student had two seminar assignments, pieces of individual research, which were assessed. If a student failed one of these two assignments, a re-submission was possible. Failure of both constituted a fail.

Course tutors

The NMC had five course tutors, two of whom were part-time, in addition to the Principal. Another tutor was employed on a temporary basis to cover staff shortages. All of these people were qualified MOs and, with the exception of the Principal, were involved in teaching practical orientation and mobility. In addition, they each had responsibilities for other elements of the course. The Principal's role was mainly an administrative one; he had no experience of working as an MO in the field, having joined the teaching staff upon qualifying as an MO.

There were seven course tutors at the NRAB, including the Training Officer. The General Secretary's role was mainly administrative. The Training Officer had responsibility for course organization and a part-time teaching role on all the courses. There were two mobility tutors who, in addition to their primary responsibility for teaching on the MO and RO courses, had some input on the TO course. There was one other full time tutor who taught communications skills to TO and RO students. Three other tutors worked part-time on the TO and RO courses.

The SRAB had three course tutors: the Training Officer, one full-time tutor and one part-time tutor. The General Secretary of the SRAB did not do any teaching on the course. The Training Officer was responsible for organizing all of the training provided by the SRAB. In addition, he taught the ophthalmology and low vision sections on the training courses. The full-time tutor did all of the mobility teaching on both the TO and MO courses. The part-time tutor's sole responsibility was the braille module on the TO course. The teaching of typing was done by the Training Officer's secretary. The remaining elements of the courses, with the exception of daily living skills, were shared between the Training Officer, the mobility tutor and guest speakers.

5 Visual Impairment Workers and Organization of Services

MOs and TOs were found to work in a number of different environments and organizational structures. The supervision they received also varied considerably. The purpose of this chapter is to identify and illustrate these differences and variations and to outline briefly the main characteristics of the workers themselves. The information is taken from the questionnaire responses of 307 workers (154 MOs, 125 TOs and 28 dual qualified) and follow-up interviews with 47 of these workers (17 MOs, 20 TOs and ten dual qualified).

Worker characteristics

Gender and age

Among visual impairment workers who responded to the questionnaire, there were almost twice as many women as men. There was a fairly even distribution of workers according to age: 21 per cent were 20–30 years; 33 per cent were 31–40 years; 29 per cent were 41–50 years; and 16 per cent were 50 or over. Twice as many TOs as MOs were to be found in the over 50 age group.

Reasons for working with visually impaired people

There was no single route to becoming a specialist worker with the visually impaired. Of those interviewed, the largest group (approximately one-third) already worked in social services departments. However, the others had come into the field for a whole variety of reasons: their own visual impairment; a wish for a complete career change; the desire to work in a 'caring profession'; involvement in voluntary work with the visually impaired (often in conjunction with looking for a job); or contact with visually impaired children through residential childcare. Examples of those looking for a career change included: an ex-policeman, someone who took early retirement from the navy, a secretary and a teacher.

Those who already worked for a social services department were often unqualified social work assistants or welfare assistants. Some said that contact with visually impaired clients or with MOs or TOs (or both) resulted in an interest in working with the visually impaired and encouraged them to find out more about the training courses. Others said that, despite having no formal qualification, they found their work already involved visually impaired people, often because they dealt mostly with the elderly. Indeed, what expertise they had was developed 'on the job'. It seems that it was common practice in many areas for responsibility for the visually impaired – in the absence of a qualified MO or TO – to be given to workers near the bottom of the social services ladder who were generally unqualified: 'Like many welfare assistants, I ended up doing the work with the visually handicapped.' Faced with this state of affairs, several of the workers interviewed said that they had pressed their superiors to be allowed to do the TO or MO course. In other cases, the original idea for specialist training was suggested by management, often because they had difficulty in filling a vacant post.

Some workers who had a visual impairment themselves said that their motivation to seek work with other such people stemmed from a belief that their own experiences could help and from their strong criticisms of the quality of service they had encountered. However, others said that they had had very positive contact with a worker and/or a rehabilitation service, and this had prompted their desire to become qualified themselves.

Other qualifications and training

Three-quarters of all questionnaire respondents indicated that they had O-levels. While there was little difference in the numbers of TOs and MOs who had O-levels, it is clear that

Table 5.1: *Other qulaifications held by MOs, TOs and dual qualified workers*

	MO		TO		Dual qualified		Total	
	N	%	N	%	N	%	N	%
O-level(s)	119	77	94	75	19	(68)	232	76
A-level(s)	68	44	35	28	8	(29)	111	36
Degree	39	25	14	11	3	(11)	56	18
Certificate of Education/PGCE	17	11	11	9	1	(4)	29	9
Home teacher	21	14	2	2	–	(–)	23	7
CQSW	11	7	10	8	4	(4)	22	7
CSS	6	4	2	2	4	(4)	9	3

Note: The figures in this table do not correspond to the total number of workers since some possessed more than one qualification; percentages are out of the total number of respondents in each category: MO 154; TO 125; and dual qualified 28 (total = 307).

many more MOs had higher academic qualifications. Another point which may be of interest is that nine per cent (29) of workers held a teaching qualification, and seven per cent (22) had a Certificate of Qualification in Social Work (CQSW) (see Table 5.1).

Number of posts held since qualifying as MO or TO

Interviews with 47 workers revealed that 30 had remained in their first job after qualifying; 14 had held only one other position, and three had had two other jobs. To put this in context, it helps to look at the length of time spent in these jobs. Nine workers had been in their current posts for less than two years, 15 had been in post for between two and five years, 18 had been in their current position between five and ten years and the remaining five had spent ten years or more in their current job.

Career plans

All but one of the 47 interviewees expressed a strong commitment to continuing in the visual impairment field. However, there was widespread dissatisfaction with the almost total absence of career development opportunities for MOs and TOs. Four of the interviewees had gone on to obtain a CQSW after becoming a visual impairment worker and two had a CSS. A further seven said that they would like to do a CQSW course. Some were concerned that if they obtained such a qualification, there would be pressure on them to do generic work, and none of them was prepared to do this. Their reason for obtaining a CQSW was to 'get on' in social services departments. They defined this in terms of promotion, getting on to a social work salary scale instead of an unqualified social worker scale (although some authorities already employed visual impairment workers on the social worker scale), and acquiring status in the eyes of social services colleagues. Some workers also felt that it would enhance the service they could offer to clients.

Eight interviewees, four MOs and four TOs, had plans to obtain the other visual impairment qualification in order to become dual qualified. The proposals for introducing a rehabilitation officer/worker course played a part in engendering such interest. Some said they had noticed the increasing number of job advertisements for dual qualified people. Four of the TOs interviewed were visually impaired. One was not interested in becoming dual qualified, but two expressed serious concern over the prospect of getting left behind in the job market because they felt that their visual impairment would prevent them from doing MO training. One commented: 'I see a very depressing future for visually handicapped TOs'. However, the fourth TO had been offered a place on the MO section of the rehabilitation worker course at the SRAB.

Where workers were employed

Nearly three-quarters (223) of visual impairment workers were employed by social services departments (see Table 5.2). The table also shows a considerable difference between MOs and TOs in this respect − a much higher proportion of the latter worked for social services.

Half (42) of those workers not employed by social services worked in education. Most of these (32) worked with children in schools run by local education authorities or voluntary organizations. The remainder - all MOs - worked in voluntary sector colleges of education or training. In total, the education

Table 5.2: Employers of MOs, TOs and dual qualified workers

Employer	MO		TO		Dual qualified		Total	
	N	%	N	%	N	%	N	%
Local authority social services	99	64	102	82	22	(79)	232	73
Other	55	36	23	18	6	(21)	84	27
Total	154	100	125	100	28	100	307	100

sector accounted for 34 MOs and six TOs, which indicated that the main role of visual impairment workers in this area was the teaching of practical mobility skills.

One worker was a freelance MO who was engaged by local authorities to teach specific clients, either because there was no MO in post or because an MO had too many clients waiting for mobility training. The remaining workers were all employed by voluntary organizations. In some areas they offered a service in addition to that of visual impairment workers in social services; in other areas they provided a service where the local authority did not employ specialists

Table 5.3: Supervisors of MOs, TOs and dual qualified workers with a visual impairment (VI) qualification

Workers' supervisor	MO		TO		Dual qualified		Total	
	N	%	N	%	N	%	N	%
VI qualified	56	36	39	31	10	(36)	105	34
Not VI qualified	87	57	84	67	16	(57)	187	61
Missing	11	7	2	2	2	(7)	15	5
Total	154	100	125	100	28	100	307	100

Supervision

Who were the supervisors?

In the questionnaire workers were asked to give the job titles of their supervisor: the result was a list of over a hundred titles! The most common were: team leader or deputy team leader, 18 per cent (54); principal social worker or senior social worker, 13 per cent (41); senior rehabilitation officer, 4 per cent (12); and headteacher, 4 per cent (13). In the latter group, all but one supervised an MO.

Table 5.4: *Number of supervisors with a visual impairment qualification in social services, compared with other employers*

	Social services		Other		Total	
	N	%	N	%	N	%
Supervisor with visual impairment qualification	54	24	52	62	106	35
Supervisor without visual impairment qualification	165	74	21	25	186	61
Missing	4	2	11	13	15	5
Total	223	100	84	100	307	101

The majority of workers – 61 per cent (187) – had supervisors who were not qualified in visual impairment (see Table 5.3). In social services, proportionally fewer workers had supervisors with a visual impairment qualification: 24 per cent (54) (see Table 5.4). Very often, the supervisors were social-work trained. Many of them were senior social workers or team leaders in charge of a team with responsibility for a specific client group – for example elderly, physically handicapped, specialist services (a multi-disciplinary team). Of the 34 per cent (105) who said they were supervised by someone with a visual impairment qualification (MO, TO or home teacher), 78 per cent (82) described themselves as working in a team of visual impairment specialists, 16 per cent (17) said that they worked alone and 6 per cent (6) said that they worked in some other team.

Advantages and disadvantages of supervision by a visualimpairment specialist

Of those interviewed who had supervisors with a visual impairment qualification, the majority clearly stated that this was an advantage because the supervisor was more able to appreciate their specific problems and could offer advice and help. As one put it, 'the supervisor knows the language'.

before her, was not au fait with many of the new developments on the NMC course, yet tried to influence how she taught mobility to clients. Another worker, who was dual qualified, said that having a supervisor with only a Home Teacher Certificate was of limited use when it came to mobility training because she 'did not know the problems involved, nor how to deal with them'.

Following the same trend as the questionnaire respondents, two-thirds of those interviewed were supervised by someone other than a visual impairment specialist. There was no dominant opinion among them about the implications of this. Some found it a problem; others felt that it was quite acceptable, while some even felt it was an advantage. The main concern of those who found it a problem was that they could not get specialist advice from their supervisor. The inability to discuss specific problems related to visual impairment was felt most keenly. Those who found their supervision adequate, despite the absence of visual impairment expertise, were commonly very experienced and confident of their ability. Because of this, they seemed to feel that the level of general supervision which they received was quite adequate. Also, when more specialist expertise was needed, several said that they contacted visual impairment workers in other areas or authorities.

Overlapping with this group to some extent were a small number of workers who found that having a supervisor who was not a visual impairment specialist had its advantages in terms of personal autonomy. Some said that it meant that they could concentrate on the elements of their work that they most enjoyed; others said that it meant that they could do as much or as little work as they liked since their supervisor was not in a position to know what could be expected from a specialist worker. However, other workers described this as a disadvantage.

A further group who also felt that having a supervisor who was not a visual impairment specialist had advantages expressed this in more positive terms. They appreciated the different approach and insight of the non-specialist supervisor and found that having to justify why they were, or were not, going to take a certain course of action made them think about what they were doing more than they would have had to do with a visual impairment specialist. They felt that these advantages helped to offset the obvious drawback of having no specialist advice to hand.

Visual impairment workers who were supervisors

The questionnaire asked workers to say whether they supervised anyone. Over a quarter indicated that they did. This figure was higher among MOs than TOs: 33 per cent, as opposed to 19 per cent. Thirty-six per cent of dual qualified workers were supervisors. Mostly, those supervised were other qualified visual impairment workers or general care assistants and voluntary workers. MOs were more likely to supervise the former and TOs the latter. The interviews reflected these same patterns.

The frequency of supervision sessions varied considerably and bore no relation to whether the worker was MO or TO trained (see Table 5.5). Almost a quarter (23 per cent) saw their supervisor at least once a week. Most met once every two to four weeks. However, over a quarter of all workers (27 per cent) met their supervisor less often than that.

Table 5.5: *Frequency with which MOs, TOs and dual qualified workers met their supervisors*

Frequency of meetings	MO		TO		Dual qualified		Total	
	N	%	N	%	N	%	N	%
More than once a week	17	*11*	11	9	5	*(18)*	33	*11*
Once a week	19	*12*	17	*14*	1	*(4)*	37	*12*
Every 2–3 weeks	27	*18*	32	26	5	*(18)*	64	*21*
Every 3–4 weeks	34	22	28	22	6	*(21)*	68	22
Less often	43	28	32	26	9	*(32)*	84	27
Missing	14	9	5	4	2	*(7)*	21	7
Total	154	*100*	125	*101*	28	*100*	307	*100*

Nature of meetings with supervisor

The majority of workers interviewed who had supervisors with a visual impairment qualification (11 out of 16) said that supervisory sessions included discussion, in varying detail, of clients with whom they were working. The rest had more general discussions about the work, except for one who felt there was no point in discussing his work at all. (This seemed to be linked to the fact that he was an MO and his supervisor's qualification was a Home Teacher Certificate.)

Most of those workers with a supervisor who did not have a visual impairment qualification generally did not discuss the individual clients with whom they were currently working. In some cases, the supervisor was said to have no idea of the work being carried out by the worker. One specialist stated, with frustration, that no one knew how many clients he was seeing – or even if he *was* seeing clients.

Those who said that they normally discussed clients with their supervisors (nine out of 30) were divided in their estimation of the usefulness of these sessions. Some said that these were necessarily general discussions because the supervisor lacked the knowledge to engage in a detailed analysis of the worker's actions in individual cases. These were all workers who felt their supervisors' lack of specialist qualification was a disadvantage. Of the rest, three said they would normally discuss only those cases which were particularly difficult. One of these workers said that these were cases which would enhance the supervisor's knowledge and appreciation of working with the visually impaired. Another said that her supervisor was mainly concerned that she kept up to date with the paperwork.

The other three workers were different in that they discussed with their supervisors the work they were doing with each client. One appreciated the supervisor's questioning of her continued involvement with clients, which meant that cases were not kept almost permanently open for the sake of it. Another described having to explain and justify the work being done with each client, as well as whether to increase or reduce his involvement or to refer the client to another social services worker. He went on to say that it all depended on the team leader. Some would simply 'rubber stamp' whatever he did; others, like the present supervisor, would ask questions in order to 'make you think about the action you've taken'. The third spoke appreciatively of the 'different perspective' the supervisor brought to each case.

Job titles

Specialist workers had a variety of job titles – the survey revealed at least 65! While some specialists were employed in schools and centres where other duties were reflected in their title, the profusion of titles does point to a general lack of uniformity of service provision. Sixty per cent of workers were covered by one of four titles: 'mobility officer' (18 per cent); 'rehabilitation officer' (18 per cent); 'technical officer' (12 per cent); and 'social worker for the visually handicapped' (9 per cent). However, these four titles were not necessarily allocated according to the workers' qualifications; for example, some specialists with only an MO or TO qualification were called rehabilitation officers, while others who were dual qualified were called TOs or MOs. Also the TOs were sometimes called 'social work assistants' or 'welfare assistants'. To add to the confusion, some of those called 'social workers' were MO or TO qualified but had no social work qualification. Clearly, many employers did not associate the attainment of a TO or MO qualification (or both) with a specific post. In some cases, however, workers' job titles reflected their employment scale – for example a rehabilitation officer would receive a higher salary than an MO or TO.

Further confusion was created by local authorities who used the titles of TO and MO to describe jobs which had nothing to do with visual impairment, such as a TO whose job involved repairs to council property and an MO who dealt with transport for the elderly or handicapped. In some authorities, the title 'rehabilitation officer' was given to occupational therapists.

Work situation

The structures in which visually impaired specialists worked varied considerably. Some local authorities employed teams of visual impairment specialists, including at least one MO and one TO, who worked as a team. In some cases, these teams were responsible for a specific area of the authority; in other cases, they covered the whole authority. This was not necessarily linked to the size of the area covered or the number of visually impaired people. Other local authorities also employed an MO and TO, but each was responsible for one part of the authority. In some of these cases, there was no overlap between them that would allow clients access to the skills teaching each worker could offer. Sometimes workers were attached to other teams such as area social work teams, or teams with responsibility for a specific client group such as the elderly or handicapped. The extent to which these workers operated as a team varied a great deal, depending on supervision, perceptions of one another's role, and so on. Some workers had such a degree of autonomy that they could not be considered to work in a team at all — they appeared to be linked only for organizational convenience.

In order to identify the types of work situations which actually existed, rather than the formal organizational structure of teams, the questionnaire asked workers to indicate which of three situations they felt best described their own position. One-third (100) said they worked alone, just over a quarter (79) said they were part of some other team and the largest group, 41 per cent (127), felt they worked in a team of visual impairment specialists (see Table 5.6). Almost twice as many TOs as MOs described themselves as working in some other team. Proportionally more MOs said that they worked in a team of visual impairment specialists. This related to the fact that a larger proportion of MOs worked outside social services alongside other MOs. Dual qualified workers generally worked alone or in a visual impairment team. The type of 'other' team to which workers most commonly belonged was a generic social work team (44 per cent).

The type of work situation described by questionnaire respondents was one of the criteria used to identify a sample of workers for interviewing. These interviews revealed that there was some confusion regarding the concept of working 'alone' and 'in a team'. Sometimes colleagues who clearly worked in the same, or a very similar, organizational structure felt very differently about the realities of their work situation. One of the key elements here was the contrast between formal structures and workers' day-to-day contact. Another aspect concerned the sorts of relationships and practices which were felt to be necessary before workers felt themselves to be part of a team. In order to illuminate some of these issues, the following section looks at some of these anomalies and also explores what the various work situations involved.

Table 5.6: *MO, TO and dual qualified workers' perceptions of whether they worked alone, in a team of visual impairment specialists or in some other team*

Perceived work situation	MO		TO		Dual qualified		Total	
	N	%	N	%	N	%	N	%
Alone	52	34	36	29	12	(43)	100	33
Team of VI workers	71	46	43	34	13	(46)	127	41
Some other team	30	20	46	37	3	(11)	79	26
Missing	1	1	–	–	–	–	1	1
Total	154	101	125	100	28	100	307	101

Workers who perceived themselves as working alone

The interview sample included 15 workers who said that they worked alone. Seven of these were officially attached to a visual impairment team, four were nominally attached to generic social work teams and two were attached to teams with a specific responsibility: occupational therapy; and elderly/handicapped. The remaining two were employed by voluntary societies and were not attached to a fieldwork team. The following three sections give details of the circumstances of these workers who described themselves as working alone.

Attached to generic teams

The four workers nominally attached to generic teams had certain features in common. Most important, they were the only visual impairment workers in their teams. They had a great deal of autonomy and organized their own work without direction from supervisors or discussion with team members. Another feature was that although they shared an office with other members of their team and attended team meetings, this did not affect their working patterns or their feelings of isolation. They were not required to carry out all the duties assigned to the social workers – for example taking a turn as a duty officer. Moreover, they were responsible for a wider geographical area than their colleagues which meant that they had as much, if not more, professional contact with members of other teams as with their own. In response to their feelings of isolation, some workers had developed informal links with visual impairment specialists in adjoining areas.

Example:

Ms A. was a TO who said she worked alone. She was attached to a 'patch' team which included social workers, occupational therapists and home helps. Her supervisor was the team leader. They were all based in the same office and had fortnightly team meetings. These afforded her the opportunity to inform the others of developments in the visual impairment field, and vice versa. Following the team meeting, the social workers had a case allocation meeting. However, all visual impairment referrals went directly to Ms A. Although she was officially attached to this team, she was responsible for five other patch teams and dealt with all their visual impairment referrals. In addition to team meetings, the authority's visual impairment specialists organized their own monthly meetings.

Attached to visual impairment teams

Two of the seven workers who said they worked alone, though they were officially part of authority-wide visual impairment teams, operated on a similar basis to those who were attached to generic social work teams, as described above. These two workers were located in different authorities, but were similar in certain respects. They were the only visual impairment specialists in their area, had a great deal of autonomy and organized their own work. However, rather than being attached to generic teams, they were officially part of visual impairment teams which covered the whole authority, with one worker based in each area. Both workers attended team meetings which brought together all the specialist workers in their authorities, but this was the only time they met.

The remaining three workers in this category were actually based with other visual impairment specialists. However, all three felt that they worked alone because of the independent manner in which they worked and the different skills they taught.

Example:

Ms B. was a TO who, along with another TO and two MOs, ;was employed by a voluntary society. The other TO was based in the society's rehabilitation centre, while the

MOs and Ms B. worked in the community. She acknowledged that her view that she worked alone would annoy her colleagues, but explained that she had no contact whatever with the Centre – she simply had a desk there. The other three workers indicated that they worked in a team. The authority employed social workers for the blind who were not MO or TO trained, but through whom many new referrals were channelled. Although quarterly meetings were organized between voluntary society MOs and TOs and these workers, Ms B. said that she had stopped attending these meetings because she felt that they were not relevant to her work.

Unattached workers

Only two workers, who said that they worked alone, were not attached to any team. Both were employed by voluntary societies. One, who was TO trained, was based in a residential home for elderly blind and partially sighted which was run by the voluntary society. Most of his referrals came via social services. He worked with some clients in a rehabilitation unit attached to the home, and others in their own homes. His manager was the warden in charge of the residential home. There was no supervision. He contrasted his experience of working alone unfavourably with his previous employment in a local authority team: 'I feel a sense of isolation very strongly'. In order to alleviate this, he had established informal contact with visual impairment specialists employed by the local social services department. This usually took the form of lunchtime discussions.

The other worker was dual qualified. He was employed by a voluntary society which was part-funded by the local authority. His immediate manager was responsible for running the society. This person was not qualified in visual impairment and did not discuss clients with the worker. No supervision ever took place. The social services department employed two social workers for the blind, one of whom was formerly a home teacher. They had limited contact with the worker through involvement on rehabilitation courses that he organized. Despite their job title, they had a generic caseload but were responsible for initial assessments of visually impaired clients.

Workers who *perceived* themselves as working in a visual impairment team

The interview sample included 18 workers who felt that they worked in a team of visual impairment specialists. Twelve of them were in teams made up entirely of workers with a visual impairment qualification. In five of these teams there was at least one worker (as opposed to a supervisor, who did not work with clients) who was also CQSW trained. Two of the 18 were in a visual impairment team which included a trained social worker who did not have a visual impairment qualification. (This team is discussed in Chapter 7.) Another worker was employed by a voluntary society but was the only person with a visual impairment qualification. A further three workers, although they described themselves as working in a visual impairment team, were based in teams which were not visual impairment teams: one was in an occupational therapist team; one in a team for the physically handicapped; and one in a sensory loss team. With the exception of one, these 18 workers shared an office/premises with all members of their team. Also, the majority had regular team meetings.

The other aspect that this group of workers had in common was the division of their work. This was most commonly done on a skills-related basis – i.e. TOs covered daily living skills and communication work and MOs gave mobility training.

> *Example:*
> Ms C., an MO, was part of a team of visual impairment; specialists which covered one county. The team was made up of three MOs, four TO/home teachers and a dual qualified supervisor. This team had a central base in a multi-purpose, social services day centre. Workers were subdivided into smaller teams with responsibility for separate parts of the county. Ms C. covered one area with a TO. Originally they tried working together very closely, visiting a different social services office together each day to collect new referrals and visit clients. However, they found this impractical, and each started to operate from their nearest social services office. This has resulted in a system in which each worker covered a certain number of social services teams, taking all their referrals. However, Ms C. did all the mobility training and the TO did all the communications work. Daily living skills were covered by them both. They spent one day per week at the day centre,

running a rehabilitation course. In addition, they ran a class on improving communication and indoor mobility skills in a local hall one morning a week. They met together with their supervisor at least once a week, and a formal supervision session, again including all three, occurred every two weeks. In addition, there was a quarterly meeting of the whole visual impairment team.

Workers who perceived themselves as working in another sort of team

The interview sample included 14 workers who said that they were attached to a team, but not a visual impairment team. Five of these were based with generic social work teams. Four were attached to teams with a special responsibility: three of these teams were for the elderly and physically handicapped; and one was for the hearing impaired. Four belonged to teams of mixed specialists: two were in a team comprising ten other fieldworkers with various responsibilities including the deaf and hard of hearing and young people with special needs; a third was a member of a sensory loss team, which included two visual impairment specialists and two hearing impairment specialists; and the fourth worked in a residential school for visually and physically handicapped children. The final worker in this group, an MO employed by a voluntary society and based in a home for the elderly visually impaired, described working with the staff of the home and the society.

Liaison with social workers and opthalmologists

Social workers

The previous section has already indicated that some workers were attached to social work teams. However, most visual impairment workers, regardless of what sort of team they were in, had some contact with social workers through the referral of clients. Social workers were a major source of referrals. Unfortunately, visual impairment workers were often critical of the referrals made. Many of them found that social workers had a tendency to refer all people with sight loss to the visual impairment worker regardless of their needs – for example, one referred a client whose immediate problem concerned burst pipes in his home; and another asked a specialist to make arrangements following the death of a visually impaired client. Other referrals were described where there was a request for skills training which an initial visit revealed was out of the question. In contrast, some visual impairment workers found that many social workers seldom, if ever, referred clients for specialist training, even where there was an obvious need. Often such clients were encountered inadvertently through some other source. MOs and TOs alike expressed these common frustrations which, in their view, were caused by social workers' ignorance of visual impairment and the specialist worker's role in relation to it.

There would seem to be some grounds for their complaints. Social workers interviewed in the course of the research were asked about the input on visual impairment in their CQSW training. The usual response was either that there had been none whatever, or that visual impairment had been covered in an afternoon. A number of MOs and TOs who had gone on to do a CQSW course said that they had been asked by course organizers to give a talk on the visually impaired to the rest of the group which was the sole input!

Apart from a perceived lack of knowledge of the function of workers with the visually impaired, there was sometimes said to be a tension in relations between the two groups. Many visual impairment workers felt that social workers did not consider them or deal with them as professional equals, ranking them instead with unqualified social work assistants or home helps. This was probably linked to the disparity in status and salary between social workers and visual impairment workers. Many of the latter were paid as unqualified social workers; some were on the bottom grade of the social work scale. In view of the differences in length and recognition of the two types of training, this is not particularly surprising, but appeared to work against good relations. One worker said that area managers in her county were very negative towards her skills, believing that there was 'nothing to it' and that visual impairment 'comes low on their list of priorities'.

The problem appeared to be exacerbated by lack of contact with social workers. Many, though not all, workers who were attached to social work teams had developed what they considered to be good working relations with their colleagues. However, where the worker was more isolated, this occurred less often. Some visual impairment specialists said that most of the other social services workers, even though they were based in the same building, did not know who they were, nor what work they did. This raises questions regarding the quality of the service visually impaired clients receive if other social services workers lack a proper understanding of a specialist resource. It also indicates a need for visual impairment workers to be able to establish themselves and their role within the overall context of social services provision. A number of workers recognized this as part of their role, and attributed the fact that many MOs and TOs failed to do so to the lack of reinforcement of this need on the training courses.

Ophthalmologists

Ophthalmologists are responsible for the clinical assessment of vision and, where necessary, registering people blind or partially sighted. Client assessment/information is recorded on the DSS form BD8. Normally, these forms were sent to social services and allocated to the relevant social work teams. In some areas they were then passed on immediately to the visual impairment worker; in others, a social worker made the initial visit to the client and then, if they thought it necessary, made a referral to the visual impairment worker. Given that many social workers had little knowledge of visual impairment, this meant that some referrals were inappropiate, while other people who could have benefited from skills teaching were not referred at all.

Usually the BD8 form accompanied the social worker's referral form, though some visual impairment workers did not receive copies of the BD8 forms. Some ophthalmologists were not prepared to release them, or, more commonly, social services would not allow anyone other than qualified social workers access to them. Also, some workers employed by voluntary societies were unable to have access to the BD8 form because they were not employed by social services and it was felt that clients' details should not be released to voluntary agencies. Sometimes, social workers paraphrased or quoted some of the information on the BD8 form and sent this instead of a copy of the whole form to the visual impairment worker.

Most workers felt that the BD8 form was important because clients often wanted to discuss their eye condition. Also, knowledge of the particular disease gave workers some idea of how the client's condition was likely to develop and skills teaching could be planned with this in mind. One MO, who received BD8 forms routinely, expressed amazement that not all workers received the form: 'How on earth can they make an assessment when they haven't previously read the BD8?' However, a number of workers felt that they did not need the information contained in the BD8 form, usually because they viewed the clinical assessment made by ophthalmologists as bearing little relation to the functional assessment that they aimed for. One TO summed this up when he said: 'I don't place a lot of importance myself on their actual sight, but on how they behave'.

There was almost no direct contact between ophthalmologists and visual impairment workers. What little contact there was involved workers talking to ophthalmologists' secretaries on certain queries regarding clients, usually by telephone. Some workers felt that the lack of communication was rooted in the division between the provision of medical and social care. Some workers also felt their status to be under question: 'Consultants don't view visual handicap workers as professionals.'

Many workers were critical of ophthalmologists' dealings with clients. Common among the complaints was that workers had to try to sort out clients' confusions and traumas about the nature of their eye condition because they had been given little or no information by the ophthalmologist. One TO said that ophthalmologists: 'Do not see the emotional, psychological and economic effects [of visual impairment because this] has not been part of their training.' A number of workers felt that clients whose problems could not be overcome through medical help were seen by the ophthalmologists as 'failures'. A further complaint on the part of many workers concerned the length of time it took for the ophthalmologists to complete the forms after seeing clients. Often this was weeks or even months, with the result that referrals came through to the worker in a large batch, rather than in a regular flow, which meant that clients were having to wait long periods for a visit. They saw this as another indication of the lack of concern for the client.

It has to be stressed that these are the *workers'* perceptions of social workers and ophthalmologists. It was not our remit, nor was it possible for us to verify how well-founded the critical comments were. They are reported here because the sentiments on which they were based were widespread and deeply held. Whether well-founded or not, they are of concern for the barrier to effective information exchange and collaborative working that such negative perceptions constitute.

Summary

Almost three-quarters of workers were employed by social services; the remainder were employed by voluntary societies or education authorities in schools, colleges or rehabilitation centres. Inquiries into the supervision of this group of workers revealed an extremely diverse situation as the extended list of job titles suggests. The majority had supervisors who were not qualified in visual impairment; usually they were senior social workers in charge of a team. Those workers who were supervised by someone with visual impairment expertise felt this was a clear advantage, and many of those who were not in this position felt that the nature of the supervision suffered as a result, usually because they did not discuss individual clients or problems specific to visual impairment. However, a few workers felt that this was not particularly a problem and that the different experiences and training of the supervisor had certain benefits. The frequency of supervision sessions varied a great deal, but the majority of workers met with their supervisors every two to four weeks. However, over a quarter had meetings less often than this.

There was great diversity in the types of team in which specialist workers were based and the amount of contact with other team members. In addition to the actual differences in organization of services from authority to authority, it was clear that workers' perceptions of their team situation varied a great deal, even within the same team. The majority described themselves as working in a visual impairment team. Just over a quarter worked in some other sort of team, usually generic social work teams or those with responsibility for a particular client group such as the elderly or handicapped. However, one-third of all workers said that they worked alone. It emerged from the interviews, though, that generally those workers who said they worked alone and those who were attached to generic or other social work teams operated in a very similar way, and that usually this involved a great degree of personal autonomy and isolation from the work of the rest of the team. Moreover, it appeared that in many cases the lack of professional contact and understanding between social workers and visual impairment workers meant that services to the visually impaired were not running as effectively as they might have been. Links with ophthalmologists, or rather the lack of them, also seemed to create problems for workers and, as a consequence, clients.

6 Visual Impairment Specialists at Work

Chapter 5 described the organization of service provision and the context in which visual impairment workers operated. This chapter moves on to focus on the work patterns and various duties of MOs and TOs. The first section deals with how they organized their work and what factors affected the amount of time spent with clients. The second section describes the nature of the client contact, how much skills teaching took place and what this involved. The information was obtained from 291 questionnaire responses (149 MOs, 116 TOs and 26 dual qualified workers) and from interviews with 47 of these respondents (17 MOs, 20 TOs and ten dual qualified workers).

Two points regarding the data in this chapter require clarification. First, the number of questionnaire respondents is lower as the pilot questionnaire respondents are not included. This is because the question on which much of this chapter is based was changed following analysis of the pilot questionnaire. Secondly, this same question presents a problem, since respondents did not complete it as expected. It required them to show how their time was divided between several activities by indicating whether the activity took up 'most', 'some', 'little' or 'none' of their time. However, many respondents did not confine themselves to indicating 'most' for only *one* activity, as might have been expected. An examination of the data indicated that 'most' has been interpreted as meaning *much* of their time and as such was often circled on two or more activities. For this reason, 'most' has been replaced by 'much' in this chapter.[1]

---

1   A full summary of responses to this question is available from the authors on request.

Organization of work

Contact time with clients

The questionnaire asked workers to indicate the number of hours spent in contact with clients each week. Most workers spent 20–30 hours per week with clients. (Table 6.1 gives a complete breakdown of responses.)

Table 6.1: *Number of hours MOs, TOs and dual qualified workers spent in contact with clients each week*

Contact time with clients	MOs		TOs		Dual qualified	
	N	%	N	%	N	%
Less than 10 hours per week	12	8	5	4	1	(4)
10–20 hours per week	38	26	41	35	12	(46)
20+–30 hours per week	59	40	48	41	7	(27)
30+–40 hours per week	37	25	22	19	6	(23)
Missing	3	2	–	–	–	–
Total	149	101	116	99	26	100

Travel

Although a number of workers had large areas to cover and felt that travel was a serious problem inasmuch as it limited the number of clients they could see, the majority seemed to feel that the distances involved were manageable. Many of them said that they kept the amount of time spent on travel to a minimum by seeing as many clients as possible from the same area on the same day. Some workers had bases in several area social services offices which they visited on certain days each week. A problem with this arrangement was that some clients were seen not in order of priority, but when they fitted into the worker's travel schedule.

It had been suggested to the project team that MOs spent more time travelling than TOs because the demand for long cane training was more thinly spread than the demand for TO skills. However, the questionnaire revealed broadly similar responses regarding the amount of time spent on travel by MOs and TOs (see Table 6.2).

Table 6.2: *Amount of time MOs, TOs and dual qualified workers spent on travel each week*

Time on travel	MOs		TOs		Dual qualified	
	N	%	N	%	N	%
Much	16	*11*	14	*12*	6	*(23)*
Some	88	*59*	56	*48*	12	*(46)*
Little	32	*21*	34	*29*	7	*(27)*
None	10	*7*	10	*9*	1	*(4)*
Missing	3	*2*	2	*2*	–	–
Total	149	*100*	116	*100*	26	*100*

Table 6.3: *Amount of time MOs, TOs and dual qualified workers spent on administration each week*

Time on administration	MOs		TOs		Dual qualified	
	N	%	N	%	N	%
Much	16	*11*	36	*31*	8	*(31)*
Some	95	*64*	69	*59*	14	*(54)*
Little	33	*22*	9	*8*	4	*(15)*
None	2	*1*	1	*1*	–	–
Missing	3	*2*	1	*1*	–	–
Total	149	*100*	116	*100*	26	*100*

Administration

The questionnaire revealed that for most workers administration took up some of their time. In general, TOs appeared to spend more time on this than MOs (see Table 6.3).

Most of those interviewed spent about $1\frac{1}{2}$ hours each day in the office, and some, much longer. A few workers were expected to take a turn on duty, and left most of their administrative work to do then. Besides organizing client visits, making telephone calls and writing letters to other parties involved with clients, there was usually a certain amount of paperwork associated with new referrals and, in some authorities, annual re-referrals. The majority of workers were required to keep client records. Some authorities had set procedures already laid down, but many workers were left to organize their own records. For some, this involved making detailed notes on each client visit, while for others, the only information they kept on file were details of the referral and a short report when the case was closed.

Caseload

Most workers interviewed had great difficulty specifying a caseload size because the majority of clients were seen only once or twice before the file was closed. With such a rapid turnover, new referrals constantly being received, and few or no clients undergoing skills training, many workers were at a loss to define a caseload; some flatly refused. Others, when pressed, quoted figures of five, 20, 50, 80, and so on. One even talked of 250–300 (he worked in a day centre and estimated this was the number of clients who visited the centre each week). It must be emphasized that these figures did not necessarily relate to the same criteria: some were describing the number of new referrals waiting to be seen, while others were referring to the number of people whose file was still open, although these would not all be seen again (some cases were merely waiting for notes to be written up before being closed). Generally speaking, rather than put a number on a caseload size, workers preferred to talk in terms of the number of new referrals outstanding, or how many registered clients there were in their area.

Receiving new referrals

Most new referrals came from ophthalmologists via social workers. In some authorities these were sent direct to the visual impairment worker, in others, social work teams received them. Where the visual impairment worker received the new referrals direct, they usually visited all of them at least once to make an initial assessment. In authorities where the referrals were sent to social work teams, social workers either passed on all the referrals to the specialist worker or, more commonly, made the initial visits to clients themselves in order to make a general assessment of their needs.

Many visual impairment workers were critical of social workers' assessments of visually impaired clients. They felt that the latter did not have sufficient specialist expertise: 'Social workers haven't the knowledge to make a proper assessment.'

This was said to result in social workers failing to recognize some clients' potential for rehabilitation training. On occasions, it led to inappropriate referrals to the visual impairment worker. Sometimes a social worker's expectations were too high and the specialist would be able to do very little with a client; in other cases a client's main problem was something other than their visual impairment, which meant that the visual impairment worker was not the most appropriate person to deal with them.

Because many workers were dependent on social workers' assessments for their referrals, the number which came through varied a great deal. Some workers, who were attached to a social work team, were given only as many as it was felt they could deal with. Others, often those who had less direct involvement with a social work team, found that the pattern of referrals was erratic and that some generic teams made more referrals than others. Visual impairment workers who received referrals direct also found that numbers varied, but an average of 15–20 per month was common. (Chapter 7, which presents case studies of individual workers, explores some of these aspects in greater detail.)

Contact with clients

Initial assessment

Visits to newly referred clients for the purpose of initial assessment was a major part of specialist workers' jobs; in particular, TOs devoted a great deal of their time to this. The questionnaire revealed that over half of them (59) spent much of their time on new referrals and assessment and a further 38 per cent (44) spent some of their time on this. Only 10 per cent (12) said that it took up little or none of their time. MOs spent only slightly less time on this: 61 per cent (91) spent some of their time, and 16 per cent much of their time. Dual qualified workers indicated a similar level of activity – well over three-quarters of them spent some or much of their time on new referrals and assessment (Table 6.4 shows a full breakdown of these figures).

The interviews with workers made it possible to examine what initial assessment involved. They revealed that for MOs and TOs the process was virtually the same. Workers were about evenly divided between those who contacted clients by

Table 6.4: *Amount of time MOs, TOs and dual qualified workers spent on new referrals and assessment*

Time on new referrals and assessment	MOs		TOs		Dual qualified	
	N	%	N	%	N	%
Much	24	*16*	59	*51*	4	*(15)*
Some	91	*61*	44	*38*	18	*(69)*
Little	18	*12*	8	*7*	2	*(8)*
None	13	9	4	*3*	2	*(8)*
Missing	3	2	1	*1*	–	–
Total	149	*100*	116	*100*	26	*100*

telephone or letter to let them know that they would be visiting them soon and those who called round without prior notice. Often clients were expecting someone from social services to visit them because they had been told by the ophthalmologists, but most had no idea what to expect from the visit.

The initial assessment commonly took the form of a general conversation with clients – about their sight loss, how they were managing, their circumstances, what the ophthalmologist or doctor had said, and so on. Workers claimed that from such discussion they were able to establish clients' needs. Relatively few of the workers who were interviewed had any kind of checklist of questions which they went through with clients. Some said they felt this would be offputting. Those who did have an initial assessment form usually completed this on their return to the office, rather than during the visit. Only one worker had a form which he filled in as he talked to the client.

The initial visit usually lasted between one and two hours. Workers felt that it was important to take their time on such visits in order to ensure that clients were put at their ease and felt able to discuss their problems. Assessment of clients' difficulties seemed to be the focal point of most discussions. Although some workers described the range of services which were available, most concentrated on the areas which clients needed help with most. In particular, they wanted to ensure that basic needs were being met. One worker stated: 'I never, ever leave a client without knowing that they are able to look after themselves or that a relative is looking after them.' Accepting the offer of a cup of tea, or even suggesting one, seemed the almost universal means of establishing clients' ability to cope. The project team had the opportunity of observing some of these initial visits; a typical example is described below. The client was a woman of approximately 70 years who had been referred by a social worker to the specialist worker. The worker was dual qualified. He had been sent a referral form which contained biographical details and notes on the client's circumstances.

> The worker visited the client without an appointment. When she answered the door, he explained that he had been contacted by her social worker and was invited in. Sitting in the lounge, the worker and client had what could be described as a pleasant conversation for about half an hour. However, the worker was finding out how the woman was coping with being visually impaired (she had a certain amount of remaining vision). Her initial response had been that she was managing very well. Apparently casually, the worker went on to ask about specific tasks – for example various elements of cooking, including what sort of meals were normally eaten. The client said that she had someone to buy her food for her, but that she cooked herself a hot meal every day. Through this level of general conversation it became clear that there were a number of things with which she was experiencing difficulty. Pouring liquids was something of a problem – she said that sometimes she missed the cup or filled it too full. She had trouble writing because although she could form the letters from memory, she discovered that she often wrote over what she had already written and had resorted to asking people to make out her shopping-lists and write letters for her. The worker said that he had some aids in the car which could help with these tasks.
> He then spent some time discussing the woman's eye condition. Since the referral had been made four months earlier she had undergone an operation to have a cataract removed from one eye. The worker asked her to tell him what the specialist had said. He then explained how her eye would have reacted to this operation, describing some of the likely symptoms. The woman agreed that she had experienced these and appeared to find it a great relief to know that what she had been going through was understood by someone. He then brought in some aids from the car: a liquid level indicator; a signature guide; and a writing-frame. He showed her how to use the

signature guide when filling out her pension book and demonstrated the use of the writing frame. The woman was very pleased with both these aids. He also checked the telephone to see if a large number gadget needed to be fitted. As it was a push-button phone, this was not necessary. Next, the worker asked if they could go into the kitchen. Through more questions, he established how she managed with the cooker controls, taking things in and out of the oven, and so on. He asked her to get out the mug or cup she normally used. He then adjusted the liquid level indicator to this and showed her how to use it. While in the kitchen, he noted the layout and the items of food. The woman said she had a home help who assisted with the cleaning.

Back in the lounge the general flow of conversation continued – how the woman felt about being alone at night, arrangements for locking the door and a discussion about how she negotiated the stairs. She counted them, which the worker said was good, but he suggested that she may find it useful to count only those which came after the handrail finished. Before leaving, the worker explained again where he was based and how to contact him, either directly or through the other social services workers, if there was anything else she needed. Afterwards he explained to us that he was satisfied that she could look after herself safely and would not make another visit unless requested to do so. The only reason he could imagine for another visit was when the results of her operation became known.

Only two workers said that they assessed clients for low-vision optical aids. One of these worked in a rehabilitation unit and had a range of such aids available for clients to try. The other worker, who was dual qualified, felt that such an assessment was vital since many clients could benefit from such aids, both for reading and leisure activities and for outdoor mobility. Regarding assessment for mobility training, some MOs said that they took only those whom they considered to be potential clients for training for a walk outdoors using sighted guide methods – i.e. not all clients were given a practical assessment for outdoor mobility. Other MOs said that they would not do this on an initial visit, concentrating first on basic needs such as daily living skills.

Some workers introduced clients to basic aids on the first visit. They said that this was often a useful ploy if the client felt that the worker could not help them or if motivation was very low. Others said that this also gave them an excuse for a second visit – to see how the client was getting on with the aid. Virtually all workers said that they saw clients at least twice before closing the case, even if the client had said that they did not want any help, or if the worker felt that the client was coping without their intervention. Many of them said that this was in order to ensure that their initial assessment had been accurate since some clients were naturally reluctant to discuss their problems with a stranger on the very first visit. One TO commented: 'If there isn't any communication on a general level, why should the client start talking about their problems?' A number of workers said that assessment took a lot longer than just one visit in any case, and felt that it was important not to withdraw too soon.

Client motivation

Virtually all workers said that lack of client motivation was a big problem. For some, this was less of a problem because the social workers in their area only referred clients who were interested in learning something. However, even these people sometimes received direct referrals from family or relatives who wanted the visually impaired person to become more independent, while the person was quite satisfied having things done for them. Among the elderly, who made up most of the client group, the latter seemed to be a common problem – they preferred to rely on family, friends or social services rather than learn how to do things for themselves. Many workers said that if the client had been used to being active and doing things for themselves before their sight loss, lack of motivation, if it arose at all, was usually a passing phase. However, if the client had become increasingly dependent on others over a period of years, it was difficult for them to see any reason why they should change. Even where clients had been used to an active life before the onset of the visual impairment, some workers found that it was important for them to have some encouragement early on, so that they did not lose heart and lapse into dependency.

Most workers said that they tried in the first or second visits to motivate clients, but that if they found the client was still not interested they did not persevere. Partly, this was because they felt that there was little point; even if they could persuade them to do some training, they would not use the skills afterwards. Partly, they felt that they could not spend time on motivating clients when there were so many to see. Indeed, one MO said that unless clients showed an interest in mobility training when she explained what this involved, she did not urge them further because she already had a waiting-list. She felt that it would be giving false hopes to persuade clients that they could achieve independent mobility, only to tell them then that they would have to wait many months for such training to begin.

However, where workers felt that all a client lacked was confidence (and this was commonly said to be the case), they made efforts to overcome this by starting with some small and relatively simple task which was easily managed, for example, coin identification or telling the time. Many workers said that the key lay in finding something which the client would value being able to do by themselves – for example going shopping or going to their local pub. Other workers, while not going this far, said that their aim was to sow the seed of an idea in clients' minds, and then leave them to think it over for a while before calling back. They found that often this did the trick and that possibly there needed to be a period of coming to terms with the loss of vision before clients were prepared to take the next step. Some workers said that this period lasted several months, or even years. Several merely left their telephone number, so that clients could get in touch if they changed their minds. Others, particularly if they could see no reason for the lack of motivation, visited the client regularly in order to build up a relationship which would encourage confidence in the worker and in their own ability to succeed in rehabilitation training.

Follow-up work

In the vast majority of cases, follow-up work with clients involved one or two visits to ensure that the client was coping before the case was closed. In almost all cases, clients received some of the most basic aids – for example liquid level indicators, signature guides and telephone dials. However, many workers were not in favour of aids and stressed that they never offered these where they felt that the client could manage without. Other workers said that they found them useful in motivating the client to try to do something for themselves, and some said that they took only a small amount of time to demonstrate aids. (Table 6.5 shows the amount of time workers spent on distributing and teaching the use of aids.)

A number of workers said that they felt that the distribution of aids, and in particular the organization of the talking book service, took up too much of their time. Some of these said that they, or the authority, were planning a resource centre in which aids for the visually impaired would be on display and could be tried and purchased by clients or loaned to them. These centres could be run by volunteers or unqualified workers, thus allowing the specialists more time for teaching.

Table 6.5: *Amount of time MOs, TOs and dual qualified workers spent on the distribution and use of aids*

Time on distributing aids	MOs		TOs		Dual qualified	
	N	%	N	%	N	%
Much	8	5	15	13	5	(19)
Some	59	40	77	66	12	(46)
Little	48	32	16	14	6	(23)
None	31	21	7	6	3	(12)
Missing	3	2	1	1	–	–
Total	149	100	116	100	26	100

Daily living skills

The questionnaire indicated that virtually all TOs spent a proportion of their time on daily living skills, though perhaps surprisingly only 10 per cent said it took up much of their time.

The majority, 55 per cent (64), said it took up some of their time, and a further 30 per cent (35) spent little of their time on it (see Table 6.6). Among the TOs interviewed, there was common agreement that clients did not need very much teaching in this area. More than three-quarters (16 out of 20) said that they had never had to teach a major daily living skills programme (i.e. cooking and/or other household tasks). Two main reasons were given for this: first, the vast majority of

Table 6.6: Amount of time MOs, TOs and dual qualified workers spent on daily living skills

Time on daily living skills	MOs		TOs		Dual qualified	
	N	%	N	%	N	%
Much	2	1	12	10	3	(12)
Some	49	33	64	55	15	(58)
Little	61	41	35	30	5	(19)
None	34	23	3	3	2	(8)
Missing	3	2	2	2	1	(4)
Total	149	100	116	100	26	101

clients were elderly and relied on home help and meals-on-wheels services, spouses or grown-up children; and secondly, clients had usually suffered a gradual deterioration in their sight, which meant that those who wanted to continue cooking and doing household tasks had adapted their methods over a period of time. Some TOs also felt that the fact that the majority of clients had some useful residual vision contributed to their coping without help from them. They saw their role as responding to requests for advice on specific activities rather than planning a rehabilitation programme.

The most common need was reported to be learning how to pour hot liquids safely, usually so that clients could make a cup of tea or coffee. TOs described their work as providing clients with 'survival' techniques: making a hot drink and a snack; using the cooker safely; and being able to use the telephone. This was said to be the most that was necessary in the vast majority of cases and took only one or two visits. Many clients did not even require this level of help.

Almost as common as making a hot drink was the tactile marking of cooker controls and other kitchen appliances, so that clients could use these safely. Two TOs mentioned that the gas and electricity boards were prepared to do this for visually impaired people and that they sometimes made use of their services; however, most workers did the job themselves. One TO said that it usually took her about an hour per household and that 90 per cent of her clients need this doing for them; once done, it was often all that was required.

Of the five TOs who said they had taught a daily living skills programme, two emphasized that this was rare. One said that usually it was with housewives, the other said that it had only occurred with two clients – a young housewife who was newly married, and an elderly man whose wife had died. However, three TOs regularly taught daily living skills programmes. One said that these usually lasted between six and eight sessions and took place on a weekly basis in the client's home. He started with the basics (pouring hot liquids and cooker control markings) and progressed to labelling, peeling and preparing food, grilling, frying (although he tried to encourage grilling in preference to frying) and using the oven. He found that often clients went beyond their original goals to do washing, ironing and other housework, once the initial programme had been completed. The other two TOs worked in a rehabilitation unit where clients attended daily for a rehabilitation programme which included daily living skills. (Their work is described in greater detail in Chapter 7.)

Dual qualified workers gave broadly similar responses regarding daily living skills teaching, both in the questionnaire and when interviewed. Of the latter, three (out of ten) found that there was no demand. Four said that demand was limited: one taught daily living skills to a group of clients as part of a rehabilitation course at a local centre; another said that she had taught daily living skills programmes to young clients – commonly those who had attended schools for the visually impaired which placed greater emphasis on academic progress than on practical skills; another had taught only one client a cooking programme since becoming dual qualified two years earlier; and a fourth said that usually the only young people who needed more than basic advice were those who could already do a great deal but wanted help with something specific. As an example, she mentioned a woman who had wanted to make Yorkshire pudding! However, three dual qualified workers said they often taught daily living skills programmes; usually these covered a range of activities involving cooking and housework. Nevertheless, they all said that if the family was happy to continue doing most things, it was very difficult to motivate the client and they had to accept this, provided that the person was safe.

Only in recent NMC MO training courses has an elementary level of daily living skills training been introduced. However, the questionnaire responses indicated that over one-third of MOs (51) spent some or much of their time on daily living skills. Those MOs who were interviewed reflected a similar amount of activity in this area – only four out of 17 said that they never taught any. The majority taught clients how to pour hot liquids safely, make snacks and use the cooker and other appliances with the tactile markings they had provided, just as TOs did. Some felt that this was part of their job; others covered these things because they were the only qualified visual impairment worker in the area. Two MOs, one of whom was a qualified home teacher, spent as much time teaching daily living skills as mobility. Moreover, they both ran in-service training sessions in daily living skills for the visually impaired for other social service workers. Of the four MOs who never covered anything in this line, two worked in a rehabilitation unit with TOs; another said he always referred clients to a TO if he felt there was a need for daily living skills training; and the other said that there was never any need.

Communication skills

According to the questionnaire responses, 51 per cent (59) of TOs spent some time on communication skills (braille, moon and typing). A further 17 per cent (20) said that it was among the things they spent much of their time on (see Table 6.7). In contrast, the TOs interviewed reported that demand for these subjects was very limited. The majority, who taught clients in their own homes, had taught braille to between two and three clients per year and moon to only two clients per year. Only one TO exceeded this; she had taught an average of five clients per year to read moon.

Other workers, who organized braille or moon teaching in groups, had between four and eight clients at a time. Some of these groups, however, were taught by visually impaired people rather than the TO. The teaching of typing was said to be slightly more common, especially with younger clients, and was also sometimes taught in rehabilitation groups rather than individually.

Table 6.7: *Amount of time MOs, TOs and dual qualified workers spent on communication skills*

Time on communication skills	MOs		TOs		Dual qualified	
	N	%	N	%	N	%
Much	3	2	20	17	–	–
Some	20	13	59	51	11	(42)
Little	48	32	29	25	10	(39)
None	75	50	6	5	5	(19)
Missing	3	2	2	2	–	–
Total	149	99	116	100	26	100

The lack of demand for communications skills was invariably attributed to the age of the client group. What little teaching occurred was described by many TOs as being taught for intellectual stimulation or recreational activity. One TO said: 'I've come to realize that 80 per cent of the clients might as well be given basketwork.' Another said that the reason for the low demand for embossed communication skills was also linked to the provision of talking books – elderly people who had often not been used to reading for leisure even before their sight deteriorated were not motivated afterwards, especially when the talking book was so much less trouble. Although workers were quite happy to teach braille or moon, mainly for recreational purposes, few of them encouraged clients who did not show any enthusiasm when first asked; indeed many TOs did not even suggest to clients that they learn any communication skills.

The decision as to whether a client learned braille or moon was usually made by the worker, and reflected their own preferences. Many TOs commented that moon was easier to learn than braille, especially for elderly people or diabetics whose sense of touch was sometimes not good. Others maintained that braille was more suitable for labelling and was more useful because people could also write in braille, using the braille typewriter. The relatively recent development of the moon writer may affect this in future.

Dual qualified workers also reported very little demand for communications skills teaching. However, the enthusiasm of the worker for these subjects seemed important. Two workers said that they always spent time trying to encourage people to try either braille or moon, with the consequence that they taught more clients.

Another said that she spent much more time explaining braille and moon teaching than typing because clients did not usually know much about embossed communication. One worker acknowledged that the reason she had taught many more clients communication skills than mobility was because she enjoyed it more. Another said that he taught far more outdoor mobility and daily living skills than communication skills because he found most clients were not interested. Typing was said to be only slightly more common than embossed communications, and some workers who had taught the latter, had not taught any typing. One said that she was trying to encourage the local technical college to teach typing to visually impaired people, so that she could concentrate on more specialist skills. In some areas, this was already happening.

As could be expected, questionnaire responses showed that MOs spent far less time than TOs or dual qualified workers on communications. Fifty per cent (75) said they spent none of their time on these subjects and a further 32 per cent (48) spent little of their time on them. Most of the MOs interviewed echoed TOs' comments that there was very little demand. However, only approximately half said that if a client was interested in learning a communication skill they made a referral to a TO. The other half said that on the rare occasions that a client had asked to learn braille, moon or typing they had taught them themselves.

Very few workers had taught the deaf-blind manual to a client. They said that usually this was unnecessary because deaf-blind clients were not so severely handicapped that they could not use either their hearing or their vision, along with speech, to communicate with other people.

Indoor mobility

Most TOs interviewed said that they found very little need to teach clients indoor mobility skills in their own homes. This was borne out by the questionnaire responses which showed that 59 per cent (68) spent little of their time on this, and 12 per cent (14) spent none of their time on it (see Table 6.8). Those TOs who were interviewed said that the reason for this was that the vast majority of clients had lost their sight gradually and, as with daily living skills, had found ways of managing without specialist help. However, there was said to be a small number of clients who had problems with indoor mobility, owing to their particular mental or eye conditions,

Table 6.8: *Amount of time MOs, TOs and dual qualified workers spent on indoor mobility*

Time on indoor mobility	MOs		TOs		Dual qualified	
	N	%	N	%	N	%
Much	19	13	2	2	–	–
Some	81	54	30	26	20	(77)
Little	31	21	68	59	6	(23)
None	15	10	14	12	–	–
Missing	3	2	2	2	–	–
Total	149	100	116	101	26	100

and needed some help with mobility in the home. Generally, the principal need for indoor mobility training was said to arise when clients moved house or, more commonly, into residential accommodation. In these circumstances, TOs gave practical help with room familiarization and with location of other rooms in the building which clients would need to visit. A few workers said that they had tried making tactile maps for clients who had moved to new surroundings, but had found that they were not usually very useful because clients who were elderly and confused could not understand how to use the maps.

A few TOs interviewed spent more time on indoor mobility in clients' homes. They described the work as covering basic safety techniques such as lower and upper body protection, negotiating stairs, basic search methods and advice on arrangement of furniture. Some TOs also felt it was important to spend some time teaching the family, as well as the client, sighted guide techniques and basic mobility skills.

Dual qualified workers described their work on indoor mobility as being very similar to that of TOs. One of them said that having done the MO course, he was much more aware of the work that could be done on mobility in the home and spent more time on this than previously.

Fifty-four per cent (81) of MO questionnaire respondents said that they taught some indoor mobility. A further 13 per cent (19) spent much of their time on it. However, 21 per cent (31) spent little time on this, and 10 per cent (15) devoted no time to it. When interviewed, some MOs described their work on indoor mobility in much the same way as had TOs. However, many of them said that they felt it was the TOs' job and that they did little, unless they were going on to teach outdoor mobility to the client. Most MOs who did some long cane training said that they started the programme indoors and then progressed to outdoor work. Generally the indoor component of the programme was similar to what they had been taught at the NMC. However, some had adapted the NMC system according to their own views. One said, 'The indoor mobility I do is different to the NMC's indoor mobility – it is geared towards individual needs and does not cover a set programme.' Two said that they omitted the indoor part of the NMC programme altogether. One of these felt that it was unnecessary because the client would have no further use for their knowledge of the indoor area, such as a school or college, once the training was over. The other said that he preferred to take clients outdoors immediately because it raised their motivation to learn if the lesson was in the pleasant surroundings of a park.

Outdoor mobility

Forty-one per cent (61) of MO questionnaire respondents said that outdoor mobility was among the elements to which they devoted much of their time. A further 38 per cent (57) said that they spent some of their time on this. However, 9 per cent (13) said they spent little time on outdoor mobility and 10 per cent (15) said that none of their time was spent on this. The latter group were mainly in senior positions which involved more administration and management (see Table 6.9).

The MOs interviewed suggested a similar range of activity in terms of time spent on outdoor mobility. Moreover, they revealed a wide variety of practice in teaching it. The main thing they were in agreement over, however, was that training had to be geared to clients' physical abilities, needs and goals. Again, because the vast majority of clients were elderly, they

Table 6.9: Amount of time MOs, TOs and dual qualified workers spent on outdoor mobility

Time on outdoor mobility	MOs		TOs		Dual qualified	
	N	%	N	%	N	%
Much	61	41	–	–	9	(35)
Some	57	38	4	3	16	(62)
Little	13	9	13	11	1	(4)
None	15	10	97	84	–	
Missing	3	2	2	2	–	–
Total	149	100	116	100	26	101

were usually unwilling or unable to walk very far, and often had someone who did their shopping for them. For these reasons, many were not sufficiently motivated to undertake *any* mobility training. MOs said that even those clients who were motivated, commonly had very limited goals such as reaching the local shops or visiting a neighbour. Occasionally, however, clients had what the MO considered to be over-ambitious goals which had to be modified.

Type of cane used for outdoor mobility. Of those clients who did some outdoor mobility training, only a small proportion used a long cane. MOs claimed that the vast majority benefited more from a symbol cane or guide cane. This was because many were elderly people who had difficulty in holding a long cane in the correct position in front of them and tended to let it drop to the side. Furthermore, some tried to lean on it, rather like a walking-stick. One MO added that elderly clients were slow and that 'slow movers don't need the long cane'. These MOs felt that it was easier and safer to have a guide cane or symbol cane rather than to use a long cane incorrectly. Some also commented that clients with good residual vision were more suited to a guide cane, or even to walking without a cane at all with the help of a low-vision aid. As a consequence, out of the 17 MOs interviewed, only one said that she always tried to get clients to use the long cane in preference to any other sort of cane and even she found that many chose to use a symbol cane after they had been trained.

Long cane training. The previous section has revealed that most clients did not use a long cane. However, all but one of the 17 MOs interviewed had done some long cane training, albeit on a very limited scale. To give some typical examples, one MO had taught four clients in two years to use a long cane, but none of these had gone beyond local travel. Another had taught two people in one year and had done some new route training with a further three clients. Another said that in a ten-year period he had taught approximately 60 clients to use a long cane, but only to reach the local shops. Many MOs therefore felt that the programme they had been taught at the NMC was not relevant to the vast majority of their clients – i.e. the full long cane training far exceeded clients' inclinations or abilities.

A few had taught some full long cane programmes which had enabled clients to be independently mobile beyond their locality and included the use of public transport. One had taught four such programmes in three years, all to young clients. Another had trained 12 people in the use of the long cane in two and a half years, though only some of these had covered the full programme. Each of the MOs who taught more extended programmes said that the time spent at certain stages varied a great deal from one client to another and that generally more time was needed than the three months suggested on the training course. Also, these workers said that they omitted parts that they did not think relevant, such as revolving doors or escalators, changed the order of some of the elements, and placed greater emphasis on some parts than others.

Dual qualified workers and outdoor mobility. Although the number of dual qualified workers is small, it is notable that all but one of them said on their questionnaire that outdoor mobility took up some or much of their time. Those interviewed, however, made similar remarks as MOs about the demand for, and extent of, outdoor mobility training – that is, that most of their clients were elderly and either were not motivated or did not have the physical ability to learn to use a long cane. One commented: 'The majority of my clients have to use a walking stick, so the long cane is out of the question.' They too found younger clients were most likely to accept training. One worker said that this was often linked to the prospect of getting a job. Another said that a cane was not always necessary for outdoor mobility, since many clients had a lot of residual vision. He gave as an example one client whom he had originally trained to use the long cane when he was an MO, but having completed the SRAB TO course, he had come to recognize that a low-vision aid was more appropriate. (He had even found it necessary to blindfold this client because the level of remaining vision had hindered the person's ability to use the long cane effectively!) The worker had since retrained this client to use a low vision telescope with great success.

Using the blindfold when teaching clients long cane mobility. MOs and dual qualified workers who were interviewed were asked about their views on using a blindfold when teaching long cane mobility. Those for and against were evenly divided. Workers who used a blindfold with clients believed in encouraging clients to use what sight they had, but felt that there were certain circumstances when it was helpful for a client to use a blindfold – for example with people who suffered from night-blindness. Others said it promoted confidence in the long cane and improved auditory skills during the early stages of training.

Of those who were against using the blindfold, some were vehemently opposed, describing it as a 'useless', 'degrading' and 'terrifying' experience. These MOs placed great emphasis on using clients' residual vision for orientation as much as possible. One worker said: 'I would rather train them with the sight they have and if they lose their sight the next day then I'll go back and do some more training.' Other MOs disliked the idea of a blindfold in principle, but found some clients asked to use it, sometimes because the MO had described the NMC training and sometimes because they found their remaining vision confusing.

One worker said that the only time he had used a blindfold had been with a client whom the ophthalmologist had said would become totally blind eventually. He later felt that this had been unwise because of the upset to the client.

TOs and outdoor mobility training. Unsurprisingly, the vast majority of TOs did little or no outdoor mobility work with clients. Eighty-four per cent (97) of TOs said that they did not teach outdoor mobility. Eleven per cent (13) said that they spent little time on this. Among TOs who were interviewed, 13 out of 20 said that they did not teach outdoor mobility; clients who needed such training were referred to an MO. In one authority, where there was no MO, the social services department employed a freelance MO when the need arose. However, a further six TOs, who also made referrals to MOs, did a small amount of outdoor work themselves. For three of them this involved sighted guide techniques and introducing the symbol cane. A further two said they sometimes taught new routes to proficient long cane users and guide dog owners, but never taught the use of the long cane. The sixth taught some clients how to use a guide cane and said that this involved practice sessions with clients to ensure that they were using it properly (this TO was himself visually impaired). Although the remaining TO knew the MO in the neighbouring area, they never cross-referred clients. Hence her clients did not have the opportunity to do any outdoor mobility. She issued the symbol cane to most clients, but found that some of them used it rather like a 'magic wand', waving it in front of them or holding it above their heads and expecting pedestrians and car drivers to avoid them! She said that certain clients refused to modify this behaviour, even when she emphasized that this was not how it was supposed to be used.

Counselling

The questionnaire responses indicated that the majority of workers were involved in counselling activities (see Table 6.10). Over half of all MOs and TOs said that some of their time was taken up with it. However, it appears that TOs devoted more time to this than MOs: 20 per cent (23) of TOs said that it was among the things that took up much of their time, while only 8 per cent (12) of MOs made a similar claim. Dual qualified workers appear to function similarly to MOs in this respect:

Table 6.10: *Amount of time MOs, TOs and dual qualified workers spent on counselling*

Time on counselling	MOs		TOs		Dual qualified	
	N	%	N	%	N	%
Much	12	8	23	20	1	(4)
Some	84	56	60	52	14	(54)
Little	31	21	25	22	8	(31)
None	19	13	7	6	3	(12)
Missing	3	2	1	1	–	–
Total	149	100	116	101	26	101

over half said that they spent some of their time on counselling, but only one devoted much time to this.

Interviews with visual impairment workers revealed a range of viewpoints on the subject of counselling. Broadly speaking, these can be divided into three groups: those who believed that it was part of their job to counsel visually impaired people, at least on problems related to their loss of sight; those who did as much as they could, but referred clients to social workers if they felt that this was necessary; and those who believed that counselling and rehabilitation teaching did not mix and who would never become involved in counselling clients.

Most workers who felt it was their place to deal with the counselling needs of visually impaired clients expressed a need for training in the relevant skills. A few said that without such training they would try not to get involved in counselling – for example 'I consider myself as unsuitable for counselling without proper training.' However, many workers said that while they felt in need of training, they had great difficulty in avoiding counselling altogether. Several said that it was very easy to get involved in this during what were supposed to be teaching sessions. Some found this acceptable, but others did not. One MO said that if this was a one-off occasion it was acceptable, but if the problem could not be resolved in this time, she referred the client to a social worker because she was not able to do both skills teaching and counselling.

Several other workers who also said that they would refer a client on to a social worker said that this would occur if they felt unable to deal with the situation. In practice, however, this did not happen often. Some believed that social workers would not be equipped to deal with the problems of the visually impaired, and several said that they had found social workers were reluctant to get involved in counselling visually impaired people. One worker commented: 'It is a difficult area. People who are professionally trained in counselling have no knowledge of visual handicap, no understanding of the grieving process involved with the loss of sight which is not necessarily the same as other grieving processes.' This person believed that social workers could help up to a point, and so could visual impairment workers, but what was needed was someone who could take on the whole problem.

One worker, who was dual qualified, had been told by his supervisor that counselling was not part of his role and that he was to concentrate solely on skills teaching. He said that he chose to disregard this instruction because, in his view, counselling and teaching could not be separated – it was all part of the working relationship.

An interesting point to emerge was that many workers were unsure whether what they were doing was counselling or not. Those who said they did none appeared, in many cases, to be operating in much the same way as those who saw it is a significant part of their role. One worker said: 'I would say I am involved in counselling, inasmuch as I listen to the problems of people who have lost their sight. At times I've felt that more in-depth counselling was necessary – I've been out of my depth.' Another worker said that he did a great deal of listening, prompting and reassuring, but that this did not amount to counselling. He described what he did as little more than being a 'good neighbour'. By contrast, a TO, who had a CQSW, felt that counselling was a very important part of her role and said: 'The trick is to get them talking about it. This is part of the healing process.' Another TO, who also spent time getting clients to talk about their feelings towards their visual impairment, described this as merely allowing clients to 'offload' their emotions on to someone else. Similarly, a dual qualified worker said that he spent a lot of time listening to elderly clients' 'moans and groans'. In his opinion, this did not amount to counselling because there were no deep-rooted problems which needed 'probing' – it was simply part of the relationship with elderly clients, many of whom lived alone and had no one else with whom they could talk. Another worker, who felt that what he did was counselling, said the main thing in counselling the visually impaired was to 'show that their life has not necessarily stopped, or even changed too much. You must make them look at what they can do, not just what they can't do.'

7 Case Studies

As the previous chapters have shown, there were various organizational structures in which workers were employed which affected their role and the type of work they did. In selecting areas for case study, six were chosen to give examples of different types of working environment. The project team was able to classify the types of organizational structure into five loosely defined categories: solo worker; worker attached to a generic team; small team of visual impairment specialists; workers based in a large visual impairment team; and workers based in a rehabilitation unit. These categories applied to both local authorities and the voluntary sector. Since the main focus of our inquiry concentrated on the former, and since the majority of specialists were employed by local authorities, it was decided to choose one local authority structure exemplifying each category and one from the voluntary sector. The voluntary society chosen included a range of working environments. Where possible, efforts were made to encompass other variables such as qualifications, recency of training, and whether urban or rural.

Solo worker

This worker qualified as a home teacher approximately 20 years earlier, and had worked in the field ever since. More recently, she trained as an MO at the NRAB. She had worked in several authorities, and was currently employed as a rehabilitation officer in a large local authority. The authority was subdivided into eight districts, each with its own TO.

It also employed two MOs who were responsible for covering the whole county. The worker had been employed there for just under two years. Originally appointed as a TO (though she had the Home Teacher Certificate), she had recently been upgraded to a rehabilitation officer owing to her recent MO qualification.

The worker was based with an occupational therapist team but described her contact with them on a professional basis as minimal. Although occasionally a 'social work problem' came up which she discussed with colleagues, she stressed that she worked alone and was entirely responsible for organizing her own work.

Supervision

The worker described the purpose of the supervision meetings, held every three weeks, as basically just to give a progress report because the supervisor was not experienced in visual impairment. The team leader described these supervision sessions as a discussion of general problems rather than individual clients. She said that generally the worker dealt with the client and left the final report with her for her to look over and initial. Although she admitted to having no knowledge of visual impairment, she did not feel that this presented any problems for her as a supervisor. She also pointed out that the supervision sessions were a necessary link between the specialist worker and senior management.

Receiving referrals

The worker dealt with all new referrals herself. Most came via the ophthalmologists from three local hospitals. Other referrals came from the local voluntary society for the blind, home-helps and social workers. Also some people referred themselves, which meant that they had not necessarily seen an ophthalmologist when she first came across them.

She complained that the flow of referrals made by the ophthalmologists was unnecessarily erratic and there were frequent delays in registering a client – sometimes this was as long as two years. Also she felt that the service could have been improved through co-operation and liaison with the ophthalmologist. In each of the authorities in which she had been employed, she said she had encountered the same problem. In particular, she was concerned about the lack of information given to the client at their hospital visit.

Caseload

The worker was responsible for an urban/rural area, which had 420 people who were registered blind and 290 partially sighted. Her active caseload was 20, which she felt was unmanageable. Because of the lack of time, only eight of her clients were undergoing any sort of training programme; the others were visited periodically. With only two MOs covering the whole authority, she realized that many clients would be waiting indefinitely unless she gave some mobility training herself, and since she had recently qualified as an MO, she was keen to make a start. In addition, there were 25 newly registered people who she had not yet visited. Also, any of the clients whom she had dealt with in the past could become active cases again at any time by re-referring themselves. The worker said that even this did not represent the extent of the workload. She had recently organized a three-day training programme for staff in a local mental handicap hospital as a means of providing indirect help for visually impaired residents.

Clients

Most clients were over 60 years of age, and the majority were women. The worker said that only about 5 per cent had no useful vision. However, she felt that most clients perceived themselves as totally blind and did not make use of their remaining vision until they received some training. Owing to their age, most clients also had other physical difficulties, often as a result of arthritis or a stroke. Of the few younger clients, most were diabetic. She had few severely physically handicapped clients.

Working week

Each day between 8.30 and 10.30 a.m. was spent in the office. The worker liked to have all her paperwork and telephone calls sorted out first. Every Tuesday afternoon she visited the local blind society. She found this useful because it enabled her to deal with certain minor problems on the spot, pick up new referrals and collect messages from other clients and workers who used the centre.

On an average day she could do four teaching lessons or deal with five new referrals. Often there would be a mix of teaching sessions and new referrals, although Thursday was usually set aside entirely for teaching lessons.

Client visits were organized around the eight clients who were undergoing a teaching programme. These appointments usually took place at set times on certain days of the week and all other visits – referrals and follow-up visits – were fitted around them. Because the district covered a wide area, the worker tried to schedule visits to certain localities on the same day to save time and keep costs down. However, she said that this was not always possible.

The following outline of one week's work was provided by the worker. (All times include travelling time between clients.)

Monday

08.30–10.45	Returned from annual leave. Sorted out messages and accumulated paperwork. Dealt with telephone calls and read through new referrals.
10.45–11.45	Home visit: elderly lady requesting registration as visually handicapped. (Referral by health visitor.) Completed referral to ophthalmologist.
11.45–12.45	Home visit: braille lesson. Partially sighted diabetic/multiple sclerosis lady of 35 years.
12.45–13.30	Lunch.
13.30–15.00	Office. Returned telephone calls, made appointments, etc.
15.00–16.30	Mobility lesson: totally blind man of 24 years doing town centre routes with long cane.
16.30–17.00	Office. Wrote reports and lesson notes.

Tuesday

08.30–10.30	Office. Did paperwork, wrote reports, etc.
10.30–11.15	Home visit: elderly deaf-blind lady discharged from hospital previous day and having difficulty identifying tablets.
11.15–12.00	Planned route for future mobility lesson. This involved walking the proposed route in town centre to find suitable auditory/tactile clues for new guide dog owner.
12.00–13.00	Lunch.

13.00–14.30	Weekly visit to local blind society. Exchanged messages and information. Interviewed three blind clients with various queries/questions.
14.30–16.15	Two home visits
	a) 92-year-old visually handicapped lady who lived alone and was having difficulties with daily living skills.
	b) Occupational therapy department, mentally handicapped hospital. Worked with a 28-year- old Down's Syndrome blind lady who was being considered for a community hostel.
16.15–17.15	Home visit: moon lesson. Totally blind diabetic lady of 57 years.

Wednesday

08.30–09.00	Did paperwork, etc.
09.00–10.30	Occupational therapists' team meeting. (Held monthly to provide exchange of information, etc.)
10.30–13.00	Collected seven clients and took them to visually impaired ladies group. (This had recently started to encourage newly blind ladies under 50 to discuss their problems and meet others with a similar handicap.)
13.00–13.30	Lunch.
13.30–14.00	Interviewed a client in office. She was a 77-year-old blind lady having problems with her Telecom account.
14.00–15.30	Mobility lesson with a guide dog owner in town centre – routes to vets and post office.
15.50–17.00	Home visit: typing lesson. 77-year-old blind man with glaucoma.

Thursday

08.30–09.45	Office. Did lesson notes and planning, reports.
09.45–10.45	Supervision session with line manager (senior community occupational therapist). Discussed referrals, problems with clients, number of clients on waiting-list etc.
10.45–11.30	Home visit to collect talking book machine and equipment from home of a deceased client.
11.30–13.00	Home visit. Client was 57 years old and newly registered as partially sighted. Advised

on benefits and services available. Referred client to DHSS and low-vision clinic.

13.00–13.15	Lunch.
13.15–14.00	Made telephone calls and did paperwork.
14.00–15.15	Home visit: new referral from client's doctor. Client was 62 years old, had glaucoma, and was requesting registration as visually impaired. Referred client to ophthalmologist for BD8 and discussed mobility problems with client. Issued equipment for daily living skills.
15.15–17.00	Home visit: braille lesson. Totally blind man, 54 years old, nearing completion of course.
Friday	
08.30–17.00	All-day course organized by county council social services training officer. Theme: 'A dual handicap'.

Initial contact with clients

The first contact usually occurred via a letter to the client which explained that the worker would visit them soon. She had produced a standard letter which referred to the source of the referral – for example the ophthalmologist or occupational therapist. She was very careful about this initial contact because often the person was unaware that the ophthalmologist had registered them. The letter described her work as dealing with services for 'people with poor sight' rather than 'blind'. It was sent well in advance in the hope that someone would have read the letter to the person by the time she visited.

Most referrals were accompanied by the BD8 form. The worker felt that it was absolutely essential to have seen this before visiting the client in order to be able to make a proper assessment. Also, she sometimes discussed the BD8 form with the client on the first visit. She found that often all the person wanted to do on this occasion was talk about their eye condition. In her view, this was because they had been told very little by the ophthalmologist.

If a client was not registered, then the worker visited them to explain the situation and sometimes even accompanied them to the ophthalmologist. Occasionally she followed this up with a limited amount of teaching, if this was felt to be necessary, even though they were not yet registered.

Generally the initial assessment involved the worker getting clients to talk about their feelings, their vision loss and what their needs were, often for as long as two hours. If a client offered a cup of tea on the first visit she always accepted because she felt that this was a useful way of discovering how they were coping. Those losing their sight very gradually were usually fairly well adjusted to the idea. Often they had been on the partially sighted register before being registered blind, and therefore were aware of all the procedures. However, there were a number of clients who had experienced a sudden loss of sight and who were in need of counselling.

On the first visit she always introduced the talking book. She explained to them that she would come back to make sure they knew how to use their talking book machine once it arrived. She found that this was a useful ploy to arrange a follow-up visit, since often on the first visit the client did not want to talk about the skills teaching she could offer. Most clients were very surprised to hear that they could receive training. The worker felt that often she left clients reeling after this initial visit, having covered so much information, including the statutory benefits.

The worker said she found initial assessment very difficult because she felt under considerable pressure to see as many new referrals as possible and close the case at the earliest opportunity. However, she was very concerned that those needing help did not slip through the net. She explained that in three months she would expect to be dealing with a completely new set of referrals.

Follow-up work with clients

Often all the client received before the case was closed was a talking book machine and some basic help with daily living skills, such as how to make a cup of tea and tuition on using a guide cane. The worker said that this was all that was needed, in many cases, and normally was covered in not more than two visits. The worker also found large lettering for labels and tactile markings on cookers extremely useful and not very time-consuming to demonstrate. The most useful and commonly distributed aids were liquid level indicators, writing or signature frames and needle threaders.

Following these first two visits, any further contact was left up to the client. The worker told them that they could request a visit from her at any future time. Many clients did get in touch again if they felt the need.

Daily living skills

The most common need was to be able to make a hot drink safely and this was usually covered in the first two visits. Far fewer clients wanted guidance in using kitchen equipment, but if this was required it involved further visits. The worker said that there was rarely any need for the other daily living skills taught at the training centres such as personal care and housework, because home helps were usually involved with the client in this capacity. Also, indoor mobility training was seldom called for unless the client was about to go into an old persons' home or had recently moved house. She found that usually clients were able to find their way around their own homes because they were losing their sight gradually. On occasions, she re-arranged furniture where she saw a need to make certain routes easier. She added that the main use of her indoor mobility skills training was in teaching clients' families sighted guide and basic mobility skills.

Communication skills

The worker believed that there was neither the time nor resources to motivate people to achieve their maximum potential. However, she felt very strongly that communication skills were especially important, particularly braille. Consequently, any clients who had requested braille were given priority, even over new referrals. However, the worker found that the majority of clients had to be encouraged by her before they felt sufficiently motivated to learn either braille or moon. She sometimes used the talking newspaper to draw attention to them.

At the time of the case study, she was taking three clients for braille. Overall, the demand for either braille or moon teaching was roughly equal, though not necessarily at any one time.

The worker had two clients who were profoundly deaf, had no speech and were losing their sight. Such clients were given the main priority, even over those waiting for braille. These were the only client group who, because of their isolation, she visited regularly, even when she was not involved in teaching them any new skills.

Mobility training

The worker used the initial assessment visit(s) to decide upon the most suitable cane, usually by simply talking with clients. Sometimes the amount of residual vision rendered a long cane unnecessary. Some clients disliked the length of the long cane, which the worker believed would probably lead to them using it incorrectly. In her opinion, these clients were better suited to a guide cane. Above all, she said that the client needed to be fit and motivated to train with a long cane. Some clients requested a guide dog, mainly, she felt, for the company and because there was less stigma attached. However, she would not recommend anyone for a guide dog if, in her opinion, they were unsuitable for long cane training since a similar level of fitness was required.

The worker described long cane outdoor mobility as a very important part of rehabilitation, but only for a small number of people. She said that ideally she would have been able to give those clients needing long cane training the same priority that she gave to braille clients – i.e. there would have been no waiting-list, but that this was simply impossible at that time.

In the training itself, the worker aimed to encourage clients to use whatever remaining sight they had, although in practice she found this difficult because they tended to think of themselves as totally blind. She believed that they needed training in using their residual vision, but that once again, time did not permit her to go into this in as much detail as she would have liked. On occasions, she had worn a blindfold herself to demonstrate her ability with the long cane in order to show her clients that it was possible to be competent without any sight at all and that their task would therefore be easier because they had some sight. However, following an incident in which one of her clients had found the blindfold experience very traumatic, the worker said that in future she would consult with the ophthalmologist to find out how the client's eye condition would develop before asking them to use the blindfold.

Counselling

The worker had some strong views about counselling. She saw it as an important part of her role, but because of lack of training all she could do for clients was to listen to their problems. Although many appeared to find this a great help, she stressed that she personally felt it was often totally inadequate. She did not believe that it should be necessarily a social worker's duty to counsel visually impaired people about their visual loss for two reasons: first, clients' emotional and social responses could not be separated from their attitudes to learning and their learning skills; and secondly, the counselling skills required were special to visual impairment. However, since she did not feel that she was equipped to deal with those in need of counselling, she said she would continue to refer serious cases to a social worker. Another factor was the constant demand on her time; she felt that she was most successful in helping those clients with whom she had built up a relationship. However, with people whom she met only twice before closing the case, she found this impossible. Recently her authority's training department had conducted a survey of further training needs of workers. They had concluded that she would find a course in counselling skills helpful!

Contact with and views of other workers

Occupational therapists

Discussions with other team members revealed quite different perceptions of the liaison that went on within the team; the occupational therapists felt that there was quite a lot of cross-reference between themselves and the visual impairment worker, whereas she felt that she worked in isolation and consulted them rarely unless they shared clients. The team manager said that the visual impairment worker made regular referrals to the occupational therapists, particularly elderly clients. In such cases, the manager said that although the occupational therapist and visual impairment worker would each be working with the client, joint visits were rarely made.

However, in the reverse situation, where an occupational therapist had a client who had a sight impairment, these workers said that a referral would only be made to the visual impairment worker if this was causing a problem to the client. Yet the occupational therapists confessed to having little or no knowledge of visual impairment. The team leader of the community and elderly team said that he always encouraged his social workers to refer clients with visual impairment in order to make service providers aware of the extent of the demand.

Social worker for the physically handicapped

This level III social worker was attached to a social work team which had responsibility for mental handicap (under 65s). She was the only member of the team who dealt with physical handicap. The visual impairment worker said that she occasionally consulted with this social worker over a problem of a social nature, which she was unsure how to deal with. Also some clients were shared.

Although the social worker came across clients with visual impairment problems, she said that she seldom made referrals to the visual impairment worker. She described her approach as assessing clients to see if they were functioning as well as they might and investigating the possibilities. Although she would have liked to know more about visual impairment, she said she 'gets by'. Also, she said that she sometimes asked the visual impairment worker for advice about her visually impaired clients.

However, she also told of a particular client who could not cope with learning braille. The social worker did not consult with the visual impairment worker over this matter, but when she went on holiday she had met a visually impaired person who taught her the rudiments of braille, so she was able to help the client upon her return. This approach to the client's problems seemed haphazard and unnecessary, particularly in the light of the visual impairment worker's strong commitment to teaching braille.

Community and elderly team

This team dealt with any referrals for people over 65 who had a problem of any kind. Often the clients were found to be visually impaired, and eligible for blind registration, even though their visual impairment had not been the presenting problem – for example, a person who had a bad fall and needed to stay in hospital. Only then did it emerge that the reason they had fallen over in the first instance was because of their sight problem.

The team leader of the elderly and community team said that although a lot of the elderly had a visual impairment, he felt that the visual impairment worker did not have much time to deal with them, and that the focus was still very much on younger clients. Overall, the community and elderly team manager felt that the problem of blindness in the elderly was not picked up early enough, but only when a person failed. Then clients got very depressed because the visual impairment worker did not have sufficient time to put in all that was needed.

Communication between the visual impairment worker and the community and elderly team was obviously not all it could have been. The team leader was completely unaware of the availability of any long cane mobility training. He did not know about the two county MOs; and on learning that one of them was supposed to spend a quarter of her time in his area, he remarked that his clients would miss out because such limited resources would be concentrated on the younger visually impaired.

Another point he raised was the need for specialist help for the visually impaired in old people's homes and day centres – a need which he felt was going totally unheeded. Like the visual impairment worker, he too felt that specialist rather than generic counselling was what was required. He said that counselling the visually impaired was not part of social work, and he would expect the specialist worker to deal with it, but he recognized that the main problem was lack of long term involvement on her part.

County MOs

There were two county MOs, each with four areas to cover. This meant that each MO was supposed to spend approximately a quarter of their time in each area. However, the demands of a programme of long cane mobility training meant that it was necessary to concentrate on one area for three months, and then move on to the next area. One MO, who had only been qualified just over a year, was finding that the demand far exceeded the work of one person, and that this, combined with the travelling demands of covering four areas, meant that she was barely scratching the surface.

Other contacts

The main help that the worker received was from a TO in a neighbouring area, whom she contacted from time to time to discuss work. She had also phoned the NRAB when a problem had arisen with a specific client which she could not resolve on her own. Also there were twice-yearly meetings of all the TOs and MOs in her local authority, but the worker was critical of these, describing them as a forum for moaning about pay and conditions but very little else.

Developments in the service to the visually impaired

Although the visual impairment worker felt that with such a large authority the only answer was dual qualified workers, she was concerned that the authority may use this as a means of saving on two salaries (i.e. by employing only eight dual qualified workers instead of eight TOs and two MOs), hence a cut in what she considered already stretched services. She was also critical, as were other visual impairment workers in the authority, of the lack of career structure and the failure to give recognition to those workers who had remained in the field a long time, i.e. experienced workers. Once becoming dual qualified, it was the end of the line.

Worker attached to a generic team

This worker had the title of TO, although he was dual qualified. He had been employed by the same local authority for over 25 years, working for the first 13 years as a clerk in the educational welfare department. He completed two-thirds of a CQSW course, but the authority refused to fund him for the final year. At that time, contact with a visually impaired colleague had prompted his interest in visual impairment. He sought secondment, this time successfully, for TO training at the NRAB. After working for three years as a TO, attached to a generic social work team, he secured secondment for MO training at the NMC. Since becoming dual qualified five years earlier, he had been seeking recognition in terms of upgrading his title to that of rehabilitation officer, with the attendant rise in salary, but without success.

The authority was divided into four divisions, each with its own visual impairment worker. The worker described himself as working alone. He was based in a neighbourhood team comprising three senior social workers, eight Level I or II social workers and three domiciliary care officers. The visual impairment worker covered the 12 teams in his division: the one in which he was based, another in the town, and ten others in smaller towns and villages scattered over a large rural area.

Supervision

The worker's supervisor was the team manager. He had a CQSW and a diploma in social work. Formal supervision sessions were extremely rare. They both agreed that, because of the supervisor's lack of knowledge of visual impairment, apart from keeping an eye on the size of the worker's caseload, he could give very little support. For this reason he was very disappointed at the authority's recent decision to cease paying its annual affiliation fee to the NRAB.

Receiving referrals

Most new referrals were sent, with the BD8 form, from the ophthalmologists to the neighbourhood or area social work teams. Referrals also came from voluntary agencies, clients or their families. It was up to the social workers to decide whether to allocate clients to the visual impairment worker or conduct the initial assessment visit themselves. In practice, the two local teams referred all newly registered blind clients to the visual impairment worker. Partially sighted registrations were allocated to a social worker or domiciliary care officer, who saw the client and decided whether it was necessary to refer the client on to the visual impairment worker. In the other area teams all new visual impairment referrals, regardless of whether they were registered blind or partially sighted, were visited first by a generic worker. This person then decided whether to refer the client to the visual impairment worker. Many said that they were conscious of how busy the worker was and would not make a referral unless rehabilitation skills, such as braille or mobility, were felt to be needed. The exception to this practice was if a client had suffered a sudden visual loss, or sometimes if the client was of working age. Any client who was felt to be in need of counselling in connection with their visual loss was seen by a social worker, not the visual impairment worker.

The visual impairment worker said that his job depended on generic workers' client assessments, but that the quality of these was generally poor. He had put on courses in order to heighten generic workers' awareness of visual impairment but felt that these had had little effect, partly because so many other in-house, in-service training programmes were being given and partly because visual impairment had low status and low priority in social services locally.

Caseload

There were approximately 1,200 registered blind or partially sighted people (one-third and two-thirds respectively) in the worker's division. He had a caseload of 50, but he thought that 15 would be a more manageable number. As it was, he found that he was not able to arrange the necessary teaching sessions for some clients. He believed that the problem could only be resolved by employing more visual impairment workers.

Clients

The majority of clients were described by the worker as elderly with age-related handicaps. Very few were severely physically or mentally handicapped. The worker estimated that only two or three per cent were totally blind. There were a number of deaf-blind clients, but he could communicate with most of these people without needing to use the deaf-blind manual. Those clients who relied on the latter as a means of communication were usually referred to a deaf-blind worker.

Working week

On average, the worker saw about four clients per day. His routine involved working in the office for about an hour and a half each morning, followed by visits to clients who were fairly local. He usually called in at the office again at lunchtime, then in the afternoon he made more distant visits. Some days, because of the size of his division, he did not go into the office at all, but spent the whole day further afield, seeing clients who lived relatively close to one another in order to keep his mileage down. However, he said that travel took up far too much of his working day and that the number of teams he had to cover was too great. He also complained of having to deal with a lot of administrative work which was not his job. The following diary of one working week was supplied by the worker.

Monday

08.45–12.30	Office. Telephone calls – for example, about talking book tapes. Received post, referrals from other areas, messages from previous Friday. Completed mileage form. Call from officer regarding mapping of Heritage Coast Discussion with domiciliary care officers about clients. Wrote up case files for other areas.
12.30–13.20	Lunch.
13.20–13.45	Made telephone calls out.
13.45–14.30	Visit to client to give braille reading lesson.
14.30–15.15	Visit to advise and assess new blind client and family regarding where to get help and advice. (Referral from social worker.)
15.15–16.00	Visit to client to take aids to daily living: clock, liquid level indicator, etc.
16.00–16.30	Visit to client to advise on choice of new dwelling, following death of parent. Involved bereavement counselling.
16.30–17.00	Office and paperwork.

Tuesday

08.45–09.00	Office. Discussion with domiciliary care officers regarding adaptations in visually handicapped client's home (new residence).
09.00–09.30	Completion of case records for another area team.
09.30–10.00	Discussion of client's needs with occupational therapist.
10.00–10.30	Team meeting (began at 9.30) including allocation of new referrals.
10.30–11.05	Discussion with senior practitioner for the deaf regarding reorganization of resources and working areas for the sensory impaired specialists.

11.05–11.15 Discussion with level III social worker. Advised him of the position with regard to social workers for the deaf within our district.

11.15–11.30 Completion of more case file notes.

11.30–11.40 Telephoned the Institute for the Blind regarding requests from clients. Discussion about clients housed near to the Institute.

11.40–12.30 Case files and paperwork.

12.30–13.20 Lunch.

13.20–13.45 Discussed another client with domiciliary care officer and social workers.

13.45–14.15 Travel to another office (via a village nearby to visit another client who had recently suffered a bereavement).

14.15–15.00 Visit to district team office regarding case files etc.

15.00–16.45 Visit to client regarding guide dogs. Discussion with client of problem with working guide dog (client also had one which was retired). Agreed to contact Guide Dogs Centre to support client regarding this problem. Gave advice on micro- wave cooker and marked the controls with 'high marks'.

16.45–17.05 Visit to local office again to record the above visit.

17.05–17.25 Return visit to home base (office). (Total journey that day 30 miles).

Wednesday

08.45–09.00 Query from deputy matron of a residential home regarding a special aid for the blind. Checked where this information could be obtained and passed details on. (Previously discussed this with hospital social worker.)

09.00–09.40 Telephone calls, case files, application for a talking book, calls regarding talking book services for the blind.

09.40–09.55 Visit to a client regarding talking book selection list. (Previous one lost in post.)

09.55–10.15 Office. Completed case files and other paper-work.

10.15–10.30 Local visit to a client regarding replacement part for talking book machine.

10.30–10.45	Office. Returned to case files work.
10.45–11.25	Discussion with deputy matron of residential home regarding a proposed course for residential care staff (RCS), organized by social services training department, in which I will be presenting two sessions.
11.25–12.15	More paperwork and planning a braille lesson.
12.15–13.10	Lunch.
13.10–14.10	Case files. Discussion with domiciliary care officers in another team in local area regarding training in visual handicap. Contacted the RNIB in London regarding leaflets for the RCS course. Prepared braille material for next day.
14.10–15.50	Meeting with managers. Discussion regarding team building (new premises) etc.
15.50–16.00	Telephone call to Institute for the Blind regarding free batteries for the blind.
16.00–16.30	Planning of talks for the RCS course.
16.30–17.05	Visit to client regarding daily living skills and talking book.
19.00–19.45	(At home) planning braille lesson for next day.
Thursday	
08.45–10.00	Travel to local village for braille lesson. Dictation on Perkins brailler.
10.00–10.30	Office. Paperwork, etc.
10.30–10.50	Interview at the office with relative of recently deceased client – returned aids to daily living. Advised administration department shortly afterwards.
10.50–11.25	Visit to client within local area. Advised on services available. Aids given. Again, recorded on the case file.
11.25–11.30	Telephone calls. Contacted services with regard to maps for the blind (they commissioned the work for maps to be provided for the local area).
11.30–11.40	Query regarding 'free travel' for the blind with the relevant department.
11.40–12.15	Telephone calls in and out and administration.

12.15–12.30	Looking again at the updating of case files and a general look at the work throughout the whole area.
12.30–13.20	Lunch.
13.20–14.30	Further research for forthcoming RCS talks.
14.30–16.00	Visit to reinstate blind client in his home following severe frost damage causing burst pipes and flooding – safety check.
16.00–17.00	Continuing research for talks.
19.00–21.00	(At home) further planning for talks.
Friday	
08.45–09.15	Post. Telephone calls to training section of social services.
09.15–09.45	Query from accounts for talking books and transfer of machines to local clients. Discussed this with Administration Officer, who said he will sort out the problem.
09.45–10.00	Case file notes.
10.00–12.00	Visit to Training Centre (33 miles away) regarding RCS talks for next week and the week after.
12.00–13.00	Lunch.
13.00–15.30	Mobility lesson – long journey.
15.30–16.30	Return to Office (closes at 4.30 p.m. on Fridays). (Total travel that day 67 miles.)

Initial contact with clients

The worker usually called to see newly referred clients without an appointment. Often he found that they were expecting someone from social services to call. The first meeting involved a general assessment of the client, some guidance in aspects of safety and, very often, counselling. The worker said that he found the authority's in-house training on counselling had been very useful in this respect. However, he felt that the hospital should have a greater role in counselling visually impaired clients at the initial registration stage.

Follow-up work with clients

Daily living skills

The worker spent a great deal of his time distributing and demonstrating the use of aids and teaching daily living skills. The latter mainly involved helping people prepare and cook safely, marking cookers, housework and using the telephone.

Clients' lack of motivation was a common problem. He was especially concerned with clients who had not done very much for themselves before losing their sight and who preferred to use the services that they had relied on before, such as meals-on-wheels and home-helps. Owing to the pressure on his time, he did not pursue this issue with the majority of such clients, but said that he was not happy with the situation – he believed that motivating clients was part of his job.

Communication skills

Communication skills teaching took up less of his time. He found that the motivation to learn braille or typing was often related to work prospects. However, a number of clients were interested for other reasons. Moon was as commonly taught as braille. He explained that this was partly because moon was easier to learn, but also because many clients who had diabetes did not have a good enough sense of touch to learn braille.

Mobility training

Since qualifying as an MO five years earlier, he had taught ten people a full long cane programme of mobility. He found that younger clients usually wanted to learn outdoor mobility because it affected their employment prospects, whereas older people commonly had more limited goals. For this reason, he had taught many more clients short programmes, geared towards reaching a specific target, such as making the journey to and from the local shops or pub. However, he did not spend as much of his time on mobility as on other skills because the authority did not recognize him as a rehabilitation officer. Had he promoted mobility training as much as he would have liked to have done, he said that he would have more clients than he could possibly deal with alone.

Contact with and views of other workers

Regular contact with the worker's own team occurred through weekly team meetings and informal contact was greatly facilitated through sharing an office with members of his own team and being in the next office to the other neighbourhood team. Both team managers described the worker as a specialist resource – 'an in-house expert'. However, domiciliary care officers and home helps had more contact than the visual impairment worker with visually impaired clients, especially the elderly or those registered partially sighted. They even had their own supply of the most common visual impairment aids. These workers said that they frequently sought the visual impairment worker's advice.

The relationship with generic workers in the other area teams was considerably more limited. Although a number of workers in other teams said that they phoned the visual impairment worker when they felt they needed advice, many said that they did not make referrals because they were extremely conscious of the number of clients he already had to deal with. Some teams, who were further afield, said that owing to the size of the division the worker covered, he would be unable to visit their clients for regular rehabilitation lessons, such as braille or mobility, and therefore they did not tell clients that such a service was available. In all the area teams, emphasis was placed on clients' 'ability to cope'. Provided that they could manage, generic workers saw no reason to inform the visual impairment worker.

Training other workers

The local authority had an active training department which coordinated numerous in-service training courses. The visual impairment worker had provided a great deal of in-house training, involving talks and demonstrations. He had also given talks to most of his area teams. However, he felt that social services workers were receiving too much in-service training generally, and they were unable to assimilate all the information being put before them in a short space of time.

Developments in the service to the visually impaired

The authority had recently set up a working party, which included the visual impairment worker, to look at ways of improving services. The main finding of the group was that there was a lack of fully trained staff and other resources. Also, the group commented on the need for quicker contact between visually impaired clients and specialist workers, and for an improvement in the awareness of area social work teams about the needs and specific problems of the visually impaired.

Some months after this case study took place, the visual impairment workers in the authority were regraded to level 4/5 (unqualified social worker grade) and were given the title 'rehabilitation officer' instead of TO or MO. Moreover, the service was reorganized. Each visual impairment worker was taken out of a social services office/team and based in a 'resource centre' (one in each of the four divisions), which were described as day centres.

Small visual impairment team

The team comprised one MO and one TO. It was responsible for providing services to the visually impaired in a metropolitan borough which covered the city and outlying rural districts. The team was based in the 'Specialist Section' of the borough's social services department, along with a team of four workers for the hearing impaired. These two teams shared an office and supervisor.

The MO qualified in 1978 and had been in post for nine years. The TO had worked for the authority for a similar period, but had been an unqualified social work assistant, employed mainly with the elderly, for the first three years. In 1982 she was seconded to the NRAB for TO training. The MO and the TO had worked together for five years.

Supervision

The team's supervisor was a qualified home teacher. Her title was 'Senior Social Worker (handicapped)'. Her work was largely administrative, although she had a small caseload of families with handicapped children. Until very recently, the supervisor had left the visual impairment team to get on with the job alone and there had not been a one-to-one session with her for three or four years. Both the supervisor and the team said that discussions took place as and when the need arose because they shared the same office. However, in the weeks prior to the research team's involvement, major changes had taken place (see p. 139–40).

Receiving referrals

About half of all new referrals came via the ophthalmologists. The other half came from domiciliary care officers, social workers, health visitors, the clients themselves, their families or neighbours. The number of new referrals received each week ranged between five and 25. In the past there had been long periods when no referrals came through, followed by a batch of about 60. The problem was greatly reduced after the team contacted the ophthalmologists and explained that this was causing long delays between registration and their initial visit. However, the number of referrals was increasing due to the expansion of the ophthalmology department of the local hospital. The team said that whereas in the past they would see a new referral within three or four weeks of receiving the information, now clients could wait up to three months before being visited.

After being registered by an ophthalmologist, clients were directed to the community health team (qualified social workers), who did an initial assessment. The visual impairment team then received the BD8 form and a letter from the social worker who had dealt with the client, saying what aids and help were needed. However, the team questioned the social workers' ability to advise clients, owing to their limited knowledge of eye conditions and their implications.

Division of work

Since working together, the MO and TO had divided their cases on a geographical basis – i.e., they each covered one half of the borough. The TO described this as working as 'a team; not as an MO and a TO'. If a client needed communication skills or mobility training, the appropriate worker taught them. However, they said that the bulk of the work involved new referrals and follow-up visits rather than skills teaching.

The team had tried various ways of prioritizing new referrals, and had finally decided to see clients in the order in which they were registered by the ophthalmologists. As for balancing these new referrals with existing clients, the TO said that she spent most of her time seeing new referrals or second visits, whereas the MO said she felt that new referrals in her area tended to get neglected in favour of re-referrals. Her rationale was that those clients who had confidence that she was there to help would miss her services more than those who had never had any contact with her. However, both workers said that sudden blindness would be given absolute priority and those who were totally blind or less independent would be also high on the list.

Caseload

There were approximately 1,300 clients who were registered either blind or partially sighted; the former slightly outnumbered the latter. Both team members found it difficult to specify the size of their caseload, since in any given period they had a great many clients (anything between 40 and 80) who were 'technically' active – i.e. requiring a first visit, due for a follow-up visit or awaiting skills training.

Clients

Eighty per cent of clients were over 70 years old and many were described as having additional difficulties owing to their age, such as hearing loss or arthritis. Less than 10 per cent were totally blind. The most common visual conditions were identified as macular degeneration, cataracts and glaucoma as a result of diabetes. The number of clients being registered partially sighted was rising, although the workers felt that many of these people still had good sight, thus creating unnecessary work for them.

Working week

Both workers spent part of every day in the office. They felt that they would be unable to cope being with clients all day: 'it's very draining'. Occasionally, a whole day was spent in the office on telephone calls and paperwork. The TO said that she usually made 15–25 client visits each week, depending on the nature of the visits involved. Most clients who were receiving skills training had teaching sessions once per week, but some one-off teaching sessions (such as showing someone how to use the iron or cooker safely) also occurred.

Travel was not felt to be too much of a problem, since each worker covered half the borough and tried to see all of the clients in a certain area on the same day. Although this saved time and mileage, the workers said that it meant that higher priority clients were not always seen first. The following diary of one week's work was provided by the TO.

Monday
08.30–13.20   Office duty: telephone inquiries and clients calling into office for advice and information.
13.20–13.45   Lunch.
13.45–15.15   Visited new client (late 50s) for partially sighted registration. Benefits and aids discussed; no further visit planned.
15.15–15.25   Travelling time.
15.25–16.00   Visited client (70s), who was partially sighted and severely physically handicapped, to sort out problems he was having with his talking book machine. Discussed other problems – promised to contact nursing staff and adaptations department on his behalf.
16.00–16.05   Travelling time.
16.05–16.45   Visited a newly registered client to deliver and demonstrate talking book machine.
16.45–16.50   Travelling time.
16.50–17.10   Visited a local residential home to see client who was having a short stay there (two weeks).

Tuesday
08.30–09.05   Travelling time (from home).

09.05–10.40   Session with client (early 20s) for daily living skills session. Included instruction with client's mother as client had slight brain damage.

10.40–11.20   Transported client to Adult Training Centre. Discussed with staff at the centre the next step for lessons with the client there.

11.20–11.45   Travelling time to office.

11.45–12.35   Dealt with messages and inquiries left in office.

12.35–13.10   Lunch.

13.10–13.25   Travelling time.

13.25–13.50   Demonstrated talking book machine to client recently transferred from partially sighted register to blind register.

13.50–14.25   Travelling time. (Difficulty in finding address in small farming hamlet. Found no one at home.)

14.25–14.35   Travelling time.

14.35–15.55   Interviewed a client who was about to be registered partially sighted. Discussed benefits and provided and demonstrated aids.

15.55–16.00   Travelling time.

16.00–17.15   Interviewed another client about to be registered partially sighted. Fewer aids required as residual vision was very good.

Wednesday

08.30–10.05   Office work: telephone calls; letters to other agencies; and messages followed up and dealt with.

10.05–10.15   Travelling time.

10.15–10.30   Visited registered blind client at the request of Adaptations Department to assess need for a handrail to back step.

10.30–11.30   Visited a geriatric hospital for reassessment of a client who was registered blind 18 months earlier. Mental ability considerably improved. Discussed with client possibility of getting a talking book machine and tactile dominoes. Discussed with staff need to transfer client to another ward or establishment.

11.30–12.15	Visited an elderly registered blind client to complete an application form for a telephone. He was becoming increasingly housebound and needed to contact people more by telephone.
12.15–12.35	Travelling time to office.
12.35–13.10	Lunch.
13.10–14.15	Collected messages, telephone calls, letters to other agencies.
14.15–14.50	Discussed with supervisor a client who needed a place in Part III accommodation.
14.50–14.55	Travelling time.
14.55–15.40	Visited client who was having problems with talking book machine.
15.40–16.10	Travel to collect work from home for braille lesson.
16.10–17.50	Braille lesson with registered blind client (21 years). Previous lesson discussed and checked. New lesson explained and exercise completed.

Thursday

08.30–10.00	Office work.
10.00–10.15	Travelling time.
10.15–11.25	Typing lesson with client (late 40s), who was registered partially sighted, but losing sight rapidly; possibly needed to be registered blind.
11.25–12.05	Visited a recently registered blind client (elderly), to demonstrate talking book machine and to check suitability of tactile markings applied to cooker controls; found to be OK.
12.05–12.55	(Travelling time included). Visited a client to deliver and demonstrate talking book machine. Client was registered partially sighted, but had good residual vision.
12.55–13.00	Travelling time to office.
13.00–13.45	Lunch.
13.45–15.20	Received information that a place was available in Part III accommodation for registered blind client (77 years). Telephoned family, residential home, administration

| | section and home-help department to arrange admission and trial period. |
| 15.20–17.00 | Received a new batch of BD8s from hospital; clerical work in connection with these. |

Friday

08.30–09.10	Collected client from her home and took her to a residential home for one day assessment.
09.10–13.20	Covered office duty for colleague: telephone calls and clients calling into office.
13.20–14.00	Lunch.
14.00–14.20	Travelling time.
14.20–14.55	Visited recently registered, partially sighted client (76 years). Demonstrated liquid level indicator and ringer timer and gave advice to help overcome other problems in the kitchen.
14.55–15.25	Visited partially sighted client to return his repaired talking book machine and demonstrate its use as it was new to him.
15.25–15.45	Travelling time.
15.45–16.30	Visited registered blind client, recently moved from another area. Delivered and demonstrated radio. Discussed problems of housing with his wife but no further involvement needed as a social worker was dealing with the problems.
16.30–16.45	Travelling time.
16.45–18.20	Visited residential home. Talked to head of home about the client who had been dropped off that morning; agreed on a six-week trial period. Transported client back home and settled her in. Discussed with her daughter procedure and arrangements for re-admission the following day.

Initial contact with clients

The initial visit assessed whether the client was safe in their home and established that the person was managing for meals, etc., especially if living alone. Most clients received a follow-up visit to demonstrate the use of aids, deliver a talking book or offer some guidance on safety. Both workers expressed great frustration at the lack of time they were able to spend on rehabilitation/skills teaching owing to the number of new referrals.

Follow-up work with clients

Very little time was taken up with skills teaching. There were two reasons for the lack of demand for specialist training: first, the majority of clients were elderly and lacked motivation, and there was not time to motivate them; and secondly, some clients had a lot of residual vision and did not need much skills teaching or, at most, only wanted help with very specific problems. The importance of respecting the wishes of the clients was emphasized by both workers; if clients did not want any sort of training, they were not pushed, although the workers would go back for a second visit if it was felt that the client was still in a state of trauma.

Daily living skills

Daily living skills took up very little of the workers' time. They found that the majority of clients had lost their sight gradually and therefore had learned to adjust. Usually the most that was needed was guidance in how to make a hot drink and use the cooker safely. The aim was to give clients a degree of safety and independence in the kitchen, not to make them totally efficient.

Communication skills

The TO said that in the five years since she qualified, she had taught approximately four clients braille, four moon and four typing. She had never had to use the deaf-blind manual with a client. The MO said that any client who wanted to learn braille or moon was referred to the TO, but that there was very little demand for such skills. She had once taught a client to type.

Mobility training

The TO said that any client requiring outdoor mobility would be passed over to her MO colleague. However, the MO said that she found elderly people were not really safe with outdoor mobility using a long cane. She had trained a number of clients only to find that they seldom used the long cane afterwards. In her opinion, this was due to the strain that it placed on them. Since such training was extremely time-consuming, she concentrated only on the specific aspects of mobility which she believed clients would use regularly. With clients who had residual vision, she almost always introduced the guide cane rather than the long cane.

Distribution and use of aids

Both workers said that a great deal of their time was taken up with the distribution and use of aids. The talking book was the most common; indeed the TO described herself as getting 'bogged down' dealing with talking books and tapes which involved not only delivering and demonstrating their use, but also handling repairs.

Counselling

As far as counselling clients was concerned, both workers said that they dealt with any problems associated with the clients' visual impairment, usually by talking to the client, allaying their fears and offering support. Anyone needing more than this was referred 'to someone more qualified' - usually a social worker. However, they both felt that they would have benefited from further training in counselling skills.

Developments in the service to the visually impaired

The supervisor's immediate superior, the Principal Social Worker (handicapped), had been asked to report on the services provided by the Specialist Section. On learning that the visual impairment team was handling its own allocations (i.e., receiving referrals from the hospital direct and prioritizing these), she decided to take an active role and introduce certain changes: (a) all visual impairment referrals had to be channelled via her office, which she then prioritized, and allocated to either the MO or TO, depending on the skills teaching likely to be needed; (b) many unskilled duties, such as delivering and collecting talking books, were stopped; the workers were directed to find a neighbour or friend who would take over such tasks; (c) the team had to concentrate solely on new referrals in order to clear the backlog and follow-up visits had to cease; (d)monthly supervision sessions were scheduled which included the visual impairment team, the team supervisor and the Principal; (e) she suggested that a qualified social worker be recruited to join the visual impairment team, as a senior member.

The TO and MO had mixed feelings about the changes. They were happy to have some of the responsibility for prioritizing referrals removed and conceded that the number of referrals had been cut down. However, they felt that follow-up visits were an important part of the service and thought that the Principal was demonstrating a lack of commitment to rehabilitation. They also felt that they needed someone to take over the unskilled duties, rather than a qualified social worker.

Large visual impairment team

This multi-disciplinary team was responsible for all visually impaired people in a London borough. It comprised eight people (see Figure 7.1). The team manager's role was almost entirely administrative. The rest of the team was subdivided into two sections: one dealt with registration and assessment, the other with rehabilitation training.

Supervision

The team manager directly supervised only the two seniors: the senior social worker, and the senior rehabilitation worker. She met with each of them separately and also held regular meetings between the three of them. Both seniors were responsible for supervising the other workers in their own section. The senior social worker held individual supervision sessions which involved a detailed discussion of cases at least once per fortnight. The senior rehabilitation officer did the same.

Figure 7.1: Large visual impairment team, showing qualifications, line management and division of work between assessment section and rehabilitation section

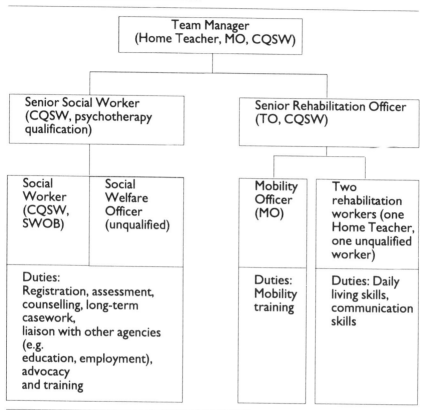

Team meetings and repercussions of the team's organization

The senior rehabilitation officer said that he spent 40 per cent of his time in meetings with other members of the team. Although he felt that the individual supervisions with rehabilitation workers were essential, he was critical of the team meetings which took up one morning a week. In these, clients were not usually discussed. Rather, the meeting was used as an opportunity to bring the workers up to date with discussions that had been going on between the three seniors in the team. The senior rehabilitation officer felt that it would have been more appropriate for the team manager to see the whole team in the first instance.

Other members of the team expressed similar reservations about the team meetings. However, these criticisms demonstrated a general dissatisfaction about the way in which the team was run, stemming partly from workers' alienation from the team manager and partly from the fact that the rehabilitation workers felt threatened by the social workers. The team manager thought this was understandable: 'Let's face it, a social worker can pick up rehabilitation work, but an RO (rehabilitation officer) can't pick up social work.' She believed that, ideally, each member of the team should have social work and visual impairment qualifications.

Receiving referrals

The vast majority of referrals came from the ophthalmologists and the district offices. These referrals were accompanied by the BD8 form. Occasionally, however, referrals came from such sources as family members, health visitors or Age Concern. If a client was referred from one of these other sources and was already known to the workers in the district offices, the visual impairment team clerk checked to see if the case was still active. If so, then there would be a joint visit with the relevant generic social worker from the district office. If the case had been closed, the party trying to make a referral direct to the specialist team was told that they had to apply to the district offices. Only if the generic social workers felt that a referral to the specialist team was necessary was a referral then made. The team manager said that this was a fairly good system because it meant that the team did not lose time on cases that were not relevant. The district offices kept the files on all clients. Hence, when the visual impairment team closed a case, all the details were sent back to the district offices.

Division of work

All the new referrals and new registrations were seen by one of the three workers in the assessment/social work side of the team. The senior social worker said he usually took the more complex cases. Because of this, he did far fewer new referral visits, most of which were done by the other social worker or the social welfare officer. The latter took mostly elderly clients. Not all clients were referred to the rehabilitation section for any skills training. Only if one of the assessment team felt there was a need for this was the case referred to the senior rehabilitation officer. He then allocated the work to the MO or one of the two sessional rehabilitation workers, according to clients' needs. Often clients doing rehabilitation saw two or more of the rehabilitation workers, usually because both daily living/communication skills and mobility training were needed.

Caseload

There were approximately 1,000 people who were registered blind or partially sighted in the borough. The team manager said that there were about another 250 people who were not registered, but with whom they were in contact. The team had 170 active cases which she considered to be far too many; further, there was a long waiting-list and new referrals were having to wait months before a worker visited. The main reasons given for this ever-increasing backlog of work was the higher number of elderly people.

Clients

Most clients were registered blind, but the vast majority of these had some residual vision. Clients were usually elderly and had physical problems associated with growing older. However, there was said to be a higher percentage of younger visually impaired people than in most areas. Those clients who had other handicaps in addition to their visual impairment were assessed by generic social workers at the district office to establish the principal handicap; work with these clients was then dealt with by the most appropriate team. The senior social worker said that peripatetic teachers tended to deal with younger, mentally handicapped people who were visually impaired, but that the visual impairment team was receiving an increasing number of referrals for such people. In his opinion, this was because the team now commanded more respect − i.e., because it had social workers.

Initial contact with clients

This took place either because a pre-registration referral had been made (for example, from a doctor, a visually impaired person or their family) or a BD8 form had come from the hospital ophthalmologists (via the central registry at the district offices). Sometimes, if a district social worker was already involved with a client, then a joint visit with a member of the visual impairment team was made. Mostly, however, one of the assessment section of the team visited the client alone. Assessment could take just one or two visits, but sometimes stretched over several weeks. Although they sometimes felt under pressure to go in, make the assessment and then pass the client on, this was felt to be potentially dangerous, and could create more problems than it solved. Both social workers said that they sought to establish, through conversation with the clients and looking at non-verbal clues, how clients were reacting to their loss of vision and whether counselling was necessary. They also described the service provided by the team and outlined the benefit entitlements. One described their role as that of 'gatekeepers of the resources' with the task of preparing clients for the next stage: 'I see my involvement ending when the clients accept their condition.' Often this initial stage took several weeks or even months.

Follow-up work with clients

This often involved a referral to the rehabilitation side of the team. Sometimes, if the social workers felt that a client might benefit from some rehabilitation training but was still in need of counselling, they made a referral, but maintained some contact with the client until they were satisfied that the person had come to terms with their visual impairment.

Daily living skills

The team had access to a rehabilitation flat which they used for teaching group rehabilitation programmes. This was a very recent development and a few, one-off daily living skills lessons were still given in clients' homes. Four staff were involved, though not all at the same time: three members of the rehabilitation team, and a social worker. Between six and eight clients were in each group. The programme ran for eight weeks, one day per week, and included practical sessions, such as reading and writing and kitchen skills, and discussion sessions.

This rehabilitation course was said to give clients the basic skills that they needed and was geared towards individual needs. However, the senior rehabilitation officer described the course as a very brief introduction to the various skills, with little or no 'real instruction'. To help overcome this, he had recently introduced a 'drop-in' afternoon once a week at the rehabilitation flat, where clients could call in if they wanted to brush up on something or needed training with something new.

Communication skills

Both moon and braille were introduced on the rehabilitation course to see if anyone was interested in learning either of these. There was very little demand for either, although moon was more popular than braille. In a one-year period, one rehabilitation worker had taught just one person braille and nine people moon. Clients who wanted to learn either of the embossed communication systems were taught at home, with one worker visiting on a regular basis to give a lesson.

Mobility training

Generally clients did not undergo mobility training and other rehabilitation work at the same time. Moreover, relatively few clients received outdoor mobility training; the MO received a referral only if it was felt that this was needed. This meant that she was dependent on the assessment made by other workers in the team. She said that usually the referrals she received were appropriate, although district social workers had occasionally asked her to take a client shopping!

The MO emphasized her belief that mobility training should not just involve teaching clients to use a long cane, or any other sort of cane, but that it started in the home. The team manager, who was also MO-trained, did not agree with this. She expected the MO to confine her work to outdoor mobility and leave indoor mobility to other members of the rehabilitation team.

The MO normally had a caseload of between four and six clients. Of this group, only one or two would be receiving an individual, 'full' long cane programme. She said that this did not reflect a limited demand for long cane training, but she felt that having more than two students during any period of time was too much for her to deal with. She would have preferred to have made the initial assessments herself rather than 'have someone else assess for me'. In her opinion, there were probably many clients who other members of the team had not recognized as needing mobility training.

The MO was required to produce a written programme of work for each client before starting teaching. She disliked this because it was too prescriptive; she said that she preferred to take her lead from clients as training progressed. However, she said that when she first visited, she required an indication of their goals and a commitment to learning. Sometimes it took several visits over a period of weeks before they were ready to accept any training; at other times, clients only needed instruction in the use of the symbol cane, and she only saw them two or three times in all.

Distribution and use of aids

Distributing and teaching the use of aids were done by one of the rehabilitation workers, as the MO was not allowed to give out any aids other than long canes. The MO felt that this was an unnatural separation of her work from other rehabilitation teaching and said that she sometimes integrated bits of rehabilitation work, such as teaching telephone dialling or using a clock, with her mobility work.

Visual Impairment Rehabilitation Unit

This unit formed part of a city council's provision of services to the visually impaired. It provided a rehabilitation service for visually impaired people throughout the city and operated in conjunction with social workers, who were deployed in area teams. The Senior Assistant, (services for the blind), who was instrumental in setting up the unit, described what its role would be:

> A rehabilitation unit which would provide a rehabilitation service for visually handicapped people throughout the city. Such a unit would provide a worker facility which the [social services] department lacked, and a professional foundation upon which other services designed to meet the needs of visually handicapped people could be developed.

There were four visual impairment workers at the unit: two MOs and two TOs. Two of them had been visual impairment workers in social services departments prior to joining the unit. The Senior Assistant (services for the blind) was also based at the unit. His post was entirely administrative; he was responsible for monitoring the services to the visually impaired, making recommendations for improving those services and liaising with social workers. Although he had overall responsibility for the unit, the senior rehabilitation officer (MO) was in charge of its day-to-day running. The other three members of the team were known as rehabilitation officers. Clients were called 'students' - a term which embodied the philosophy of the unit as a centre where people came to learn.

The building had been adapted specifically for rehabilitation purposes. It comprised two kitchens, two workrooms (typing and communication), a general workroom (also used as a dining-room), a lounge, a low-vision room, a conference room, an interview/quiet room, two bathrooms, two toilets and four staff offices, some of which doubled as workrooms when necessary.

Supervision

The senior rehabilitation officer (MO) was responsible for supervising the other three members of the team. Formal supervision sessions were not scheduled, but each of the workers said that they could arrange a meeting at any time if there was something they wished to talk over privately. Generally, however, the four rehabilitation workers raised anything they needed to discuss at the weekly team meeting. The main purpose of this meeting was to evaluate each student's progress and decide on further action. Sometimes new referrals and other issues affecting the operation of the unit were discussed.

Receiving referrals

The city was divided into four divisions which were subdivided into areas. Each of these areas had several social work teams. The social workers for the blind were usually based with the teams for the handicapped. Most of these 'specialist' social workers did not have a qualification in visual impairment; some of them had a Home Teacher Certificate. Referrals to the unit came from a variety of sources: area social workers, the social work department of the local eye hospital (the largest single source of referrals), other hospital social work departments and a number of other social services workers. In addition, requests were occasionally received from visually impaired people or their families. In these circumstances, the unit staff would involve the relevant social worker before assessing the person for rehabilitation. On average, about seven new referrals were received each month.

Caseload

There were 2,805 registered blind and 1,526 registered partially sighted people in the authority. The unit usually had five or six students following a rehabilitation programme at any one time. An average rehabilitation programme lasted about five weeks. However, some stayed for as long as 12 weeks, and others left after two. There was no set time limit; people stayed until the staff felt that their programme had been completed. In the previous year the unit had worked with 60 visually impaired people; this number was increased the following year.

Clients

The senior MO said that the majority of clients on the waiting list were over 65 years old: 'sixty is young to us'. The vast majority had some useful vision and were losing their sight gradually. Few had severe handicaps, although many had problems associated with ageing, such as deafness.

Working week

The rehabilitation team started work at 9.00 a.m. each morning; students arrived at 10.00 a.m. and left at 4.00 p.m. This created time at each end of the day for lesson preparation and reports. Students attended the unit four and a half days per week; one afternoon was set aside for the team meetings and for workers to catch up with paperwork. The working day usually had five sessions in which students were taught on a one-to-one basis. A break occurred mid-morning, at lunchtime and once during the afternoon. These were felt to be an important part of the rehabilitation process. Everyone gathered together in the lounge or dining-room and shared the duties of preparing drinks and washing up. More important, the general conversation which took place in this informal setting provided an opportunity for students to talk more easily about their visual loss with other people who were experiencing similar feelings and problems themselves. Also, those who were isolated at home usually appreciated the chance to socialize.

The senior MO spent approximately half of his time with clients, owing to his responsibility for the day-to-day running of the unit. The other three workers spent most of their time with students. The following two diaries outline one working day for one of the TOs and the full-time MO. During the period that this diary was kept the MO was responsible for supervising a student from the SRAB, who was doing the MO course and was on fieldwork placement.

MO's diary for one day

09.00–10.00	Supervision session with the SRAB student.
10.00–11.00	Low-vision training lesson with a student.
11.00–11.30	Coffee with students and staff.
11.30–12.45	Low-vision assessment and training with a visiting student (not on a rehabilitation programme).
12.45–13.15	Mobility lesson.
13.15–13.45	Lunch.
13.45–14.30	Picked up a student from home area to visit unit.
14.30–15.00	Mobility lesson.
15.00–15.15	Tea with students and staff.
15.15–16.00	Mobility lesson.
16.00–16.35	Talked to a student regarding sight loss.
16.35–18.00	Lesson notes and telephone calls.

TO's diary for one day

09.00–09.30	Administration.
09.30–11.00	(Home visit.) DLS lesson with elderly, frail blind lady.
11.15–12.00	DLS lesson: cooking lunch.
12.00–13.00	DLS lesson: general work using gas cooker.
13.00–14.00	Lunch with students.
14.00–15.00	Communication lesson: money identification; telephone dialling; discussion about equipment.
15.00–15.15	Tea with students.
15.15–16.10	Communication lesson: clocks; watches; talking calculators, etc.
16.10–17.40	Notes and lesson plans. Provided tactile markings on iron for student.
17.40–18.10	Grocery shopping for unit.

Initial contact with clients

For most students, their first meeting with rehabilitation staff occurred on the first day they attended for rehabilitation. One member of the team was assigned in advance the role of key worker with the student and was responsible for liaising with social workers and relatives about the student throughout the period of involvement with the unit. When the student first arrived, the key worker saw the student alone in the 'quiet' room for about an hour, to explain how the unit operated and to obtain basic information about the individual which was necessary in order to design a programme of rehabilitation. Although the unit already had certain basic information about the student from the referral form sent by the social worker, more detailed information about the student's needs and home background was obtained and their own objectives for the rehabilitation programme were discussed.

Follow-up work with clients

Students were transported daily to and from the unit by taxi. During the rehabilitation programme, those who were able were taught how to make the journey independently, using public transport.

Most students received some training in mobility, daily living skills communication and use of residual vision. However, each had an individual training programme mapped out which was tailored to suit their particular needs, based on the initial assessment. Lack of student motivation was seldom a problem. The workers said that most clients came wanting to achieve something. Those who were initially uncertain about the whole idea of the unit were said to derive a great deal of encouragement from meeting other visually impaired people and talking over their problems and fears with them. Competition was never a problem because students worked on a one-to-one basis with a member of the team. The only time students had group teaching was when information was being imparted, such as sessions on DHSS allowances, diseases of the eye or visual impairment aids.

Daily living skills

The TOs spent most of their time on this, with communication skills taking up just slightly less of their time. Both said that the main concern was with basic safety. All students covered at least the minimum in this respect – i.e., use of the cooker, making a hot drink, preparing food and using utensils. Beyond this, the TOs focused on aspects which people would find useful when back in their own homes.

Communication skills

The TOs said that there was not a great deal of demand for braille or moon. An introduction to both was given to students to expand their knowledge of these systems generally and to make some assessment regarding their sense of touch. With braille, more students were interested in learning Grade I, mainly for their personal use – for example, labelling purposes, recording telephone numbers. In the last two years, it was estimated that five students had completed full Grade II braille training.

Usually braille was preferred by those students requiring a system both for reading and writing, whereas for those who were interested in reading only, moon was often taught, as the full system could be learnt more quickly. All students did some work on handwriting, and touch-typing was taught when the student was interested.

Those students who wished to continue learning braille returned to the unit each week for a lesson because it took longer than the usual period of a rehabilitation programme. Also, some clients returned to brush up on their braille, or if they had a particular problem which needed sorting out. In addition to braille, moon and typing, other areas came under the heading of 'communication', such as telephone dialling and coin identification.

Mobility training

The full-time MO spent most of her time teaching mobility, although she often taught other subjects, as the need arose, except kitchen skills. She said that when she taught a long cane programme she generally followed the NMC guidelines. However, these were often modified to suit the particular needs of the student. Long cane training was felt to be unsuitable for a large proportion of students. Instead, where appropriate, they were taught to use their residual vision, possibly in conjunction with other mobility aids: symbol cane, guide cane, or solid stick. Route work and 'road sense' also formed a large part of the mobility programme.

In the two years that she had worked at the unit one MO said that many clients had learned how to use the long cane. If these clients did not complete the whole programme during the rehabilitation period at the unit, they could continue to receive training on a domiciliary basis, generally scheduled outside the unit timetable, after 4.00 p.m. or in the evenings. However, the senior rehabilitation officer said that most students required teaching at the very basic level and demand dropped off as the level of difficulty increased. Although he sometimes taught a student to travel in the city centre, very often the person had a great deal of residual vision and did not need a long cane.

Distribution and use of aids

The most common aids given out were liquid level indicators, timers, signature guides and pension book guides. Stocks were kept at the unit.

Counselling

This was not a part of the rehabilitation programme inasmuch as time was not specifically set aside. However, very often students took the initiative and talked about their problems. Workers said they were as helpful and supportive as they were able. If the problem was more than the workers felt they could cope with, they sought advice from the student's social worker. Also, at the end of rehabilitation programme, if it was felt that continued support was needed, the key worker indicated this in their final report to the social worker.

Worker in a voluntary society

This worker was a qualified MO, had a Home Teacher Certificate and a CQSW. She had been Rehabilitation/Mobility Officer at a voluntary society for the blind for six years. Until recently, she had been the only qualified worker the voluntary society employed. She was based in a rehabilitation unit which occupied the top floor of a residential home for elderly visually impaired people, run by the society. Her job involved offering rehabilitation training to visually impaired clients, both in the unit and in the community. She was also jointly responsible with the matron for the supervision of the home's care staff: six full-time and 11 part-time workers. The voluntary society had recently appointed a TO who had been seconded to the NRAB for training and had started working six months ago. He was based at the society's head office, 20 miles away, in a neighbouring county.

Relationship between the local authorities and the voluntary society

The MO and TO, employed by the voluntary society, were the only qualified visual impairment workers available to clients in an area spanning two counties. The two local authorities did not have any qualified visual impairment workers. Instead they employed workers who were designated 'social workers for the blind'. None of them had any training in visual impairment and some were unqualified in social work. The voluntary society was dependent on these workers' assessments of visually impaired people for its referrals. The local authorities' social services departments had come to an arrangement with the voluntary society, whereby they paid £65 per client per week for a residential rehabilitation programme at the unit, £1 per client per day visit to the rehabilitation unit and £3 per hour for the MO or TO to make a domiciliary visit to a client.

The social workers for the blind were based in area social work teams which had responsibility for either the elderly or the handicapped. These workers received the BD8 forms from the ophthalmologists and visited all visually impaired people, very few of whom were referred on to the visual impairment workers at the voluntary society.

One of the social workers for the blind (CQSW) was interviewed by the research team. She was based in a team of generic social workers. Her caseload comprised solely visually impaired clients (said to be approximately 250). Following receipt of the referral, she visited the client, and, regardless of whether the person was registered, issued aids and taught clients how to use them. She also often gave some basic teaching on indoor mobility and kitchen tasks which she said she had picked up since doing the job. She also informed clients about financial benefits. She seldom did any counselling. Regarding referrals to the voluntary society for rehabilitation training, she said that there was little that could be done with the elderly (most of the client group), and that unless the client was young, active and interested, she did not press them too much. Also the unit had such a wide area to cover that it took a considerable time for the MO to see someone.

In addition to clients from the two counties covered by the voluntary society, visually impaired people from other authorities were sometimes referred to the unit for training. The society charged these authorities at the same standard rate that it had arranged with its local authorities.

Supervision

The workers' supervisor was the General Secretary of the voluntary society. His position was entirely administrative and he had no qualifications in visual impairment. The worker did not have supervision sessions with her supervisor. However, meetings involving the two visual impairment workers and the General Secretary were held every three weeks, when caseloads were discussed, but not individual clients. The worker said that the main purpose of the meetings was to keep the General Secretary abreast of current rehabilitation work.

Receiving referrals

Depending on the social workers' assessments, clients were sometimes referred to the rehabilitation unit for training. Although social workers for the blind received a copy of the BD8 form, which was held by the health authority, the visual impairment workers were not allowed access to the form unless the client gave permission. Instead they received a summary of the case history and selected information from the BD8 form. Although the worker said that it would have been useful to see the BD8 form, she felt that the system was correct, and that the information should remain confidential unless the client said otherwise.

Caseload

There was a maximum of three clients attending the rehabilitation unit at any one time, often only two. The worker explained that when she had worked for a local authority, her caseload had been 40–50 clients, which meant that it had been impossible to do any rehabilitation work. When she first started working for the voluntary society, she said she had been very firm about taking only a few clients, in order to be able to train them thoroughly and then move on to the next group.

Clients

When the unit had first opened, the clients had all been residents from the home and hence were elderly. The worker said that not all of them had needed the sort of rehabilitation training that she could offer; all those who it was felt could benefit had been trained. Subsequently, the unit's clients had come from the community and were much younger; usually of working age. Often, they were gradually losing their sight and needed skills training in order to be able to hold on to their jobs. Many of these clients had diabetes or glaucoma.

Working week

The working week depended very much on whether the worker was running a rehabilitation course at the unit or making domiciliary visits. There was no set length of time for a rehabilitation programme; each was tailored to suit the client's needs. She gave an example of a period of work coming up – three weeks' intensive rehabilitation training with two young, totally blind men who were soon to go to the RNIB Torquay assessment centre. In addition to these two clients, the worker was also going to be visiting one client at home for rehabilitation work. Since this client lived locally she said that it was quite manageable; normally she would not mix rehabilitation work at the unit with domiciliary visits. After these three weeks, she was taking a week's leave, followed by three weeks' follow-up work. This involved making return visits to those clients who had received rehabilitation training over the last five or six months to check that they were putting their training into practice and to give advice on any difficulties.

Initial contact with clients

The worker always made an initial visit to clients in their own homes in order to assess their needs. Occasionally a social worker accompanied her. The visits usually lasted about an hour and involved talking to clients, and sometimes watching them do something in the kitchen to see how they managed. Since all the clients she saw had been referred because they were interested in rehabilitation training, lack of motivation was never a problem.

From the initial assessment the worker designed a programme for each client, either at home or in the rehabilitation unit. The programme specified the number of sessions that she estimated it would take the client to achieve the agreed goal. Progress was monitored through day-to-day notes and a weekly written report on each client which care staff could also have access to, if necessary.

Follow-up work with clients

Those clients undergoing a residential rehabilitation course experienced intensive training. For the first day or so, they had only a few short lessons, but these built up very quickly to six or seven hours per day with the worker. She found that clients made much more rapid progress with this kind of intensive training than with the same number of lessons, but on a weekly basis.

Clients who were taught in their own homes had less intensive training. A four week programme, for example, involved two lessons per day – one in the morning and one in the afternoon – for the first week. During the next two weeks clients had a lesson on alternate days, and in the fourth week, they were visited just once.

Daily living skills

The main component of any rehabilitation programme was daily living skills training. In the unit there was a lounge, a bedroom, a bath/shower room and a kitchen; all were furnished and gave the impression of a small residential flat. When clients first entered the unit, the worker often noted their surprise because they had expected the place to be full of special aids and gadgets for visually impaired people. She said she had deliberately avoided this because she believed rehabilitation meant working in a normal environment, resembling clients' homes as much as possible. She held this belief strongly, even though she appeared to feel that this was not the 'accepted' way.

Communication skills

The worker believed that learning braille was a great deal more useful than was popularly claimed. Although she had only taught four clients the entire braille system, most clients learned it up to Grade I. At the rehabilitation unit it was usually introduced after the first few days and from then on took place on a daily basis. Every lesson included both reading and writing in order to make it as interesting as possible. The worker preferred braille to moon, and had taught very few clients to read moon.

Mobility training

Clients were usually given some mobility training, but it was not common to give a full programme of mobility. Indoor mobility was covered in the rehabilitation unit and also in schools and colleges where the worker mapped out training areas. Her main aim was for clients to develop a good cane technique which would provide safety for the client and the public. Sometimes a guide cane was used in preference to a long cane. The worker said that elderly people, in particular, often had difficulty holding the latter correctly; the guide cane presented less of a problem in this respect.

The worker said that she always encouraged clients to use their remaining vision as much as possible. She found that often they did not seem to be aware that they could still see something and were unwilling at first to trust their sight as a guide to mobility. Often this stemmed from a fear of losing their sight altogether.

Distribution and use of aids

There were plans to set up a centre for visual impairment aids at the society's head office. In the meantime the worker kept a small number of the most common aids and gave these to clients if she felt they were necessary. She said that this was a very small part of her job.

Training other workers

The worker said that a great deal of her time was taken up with staff training. In order to avoid the necessity of channelling social services staff training through the training department, she called the sessions that she organized for social workers 'study days'. These were organized every two months. She did not do all the presentations herself, but involved some of the more recently appointed ophthalmologists who she said were happy to encourage this type of liaison. She also invited guest speakers from such bodies as the RNIB and the Partially Sighted Society. The hospital also ran training sessions for its staff and had invited the visual impairment workers to give presentations, in which they had led role-play sessions using simulation spectacles and blindfolds and demonstrated sighted guide techniques.

The worker believed that this sort of training was extremely important, mainly in altering other workers' attitudes towards the visually impaired. The main problem was finding sufficient time to organize new initiatives.

The work of the TO

The TO was based at the head office of the voluntary society, which was situated over 20 miles away from the rehabilitation unit, in the next county. Consequently, for most of the time, the two visual impairment workers operated independently. The TO made domiciliary visits to most of his clients. He was visually impaired and relied on a group of 25–30 volunteer drivers. He had a caseload of around 12 clients which he said enabled him to 'work in depth' with clients.

The TO believed that his visual impairment was a great asset in his work, mainly because it helped to develop a positive relationship with clients who felt he was more able to understand the particular problems which their loss of vision caused. Owing to the limited services to the visually impaired when the TO started work six months earlier, he found that most of his clients had been registered for several years and had not seen a qualified visual impairment worker. He found that they had come to depend on family and friends, rather than doing things for themselves, and most had not worked since being registered. Consequently, he found that they were very set in their ways and had very little motivation to start rehabilitation work.

He received 'priority' referrals for rehabilitation training from the social workers for the blind. However, he was very critical of this system and questioned the ability of social work staff to assess the needs of visually impaired clients, with respect to rehabilitation training. In particular, he felt that these workers did not regard embossed communications as important, consequently he received very few referrals for this. Also, in his view, there were many clients in his county who needed mobility training, but who were not being assessed for it because the social workers for the blind did not know enough about it. If in the course of seeing one of his clients he thought that mobility training was needed, he made a referral on to the qualified MO at the rehabilitation unit.

Developments in the service to the visually impaired

Prior to the visual impairment worker at the unit taking up post, there had been no specialist services at all – she came to a new post and for the first 18 months had spent much of her time visiting each social services area and local organizations for the visually impaired, trying to communicate the idea of the service that she could offer. She added that even with the appointment of the TO, the two of them were barely scratching the surface of the needs of the visual impairment population in so many authorities. The voluntary society was currently seconding another worker for specialist training at the NRAB on its RO course.

The TO believed that the system would be greatly enhanced if there were more co-operation and liaison between social services and the voluntary society. However, he felt that many of the social workers for the blind felt threatened because they had no specialist training and this worked against good relations. A social worker for the blind said that the situation was not ideal because they were not part of the same service. She described it as having to ask the society for assistance with a client, and being grateful when this happened.

Relations between social services and the voluntary society had become strained over the appointment of the TO.

Originally it had been suggested that the social services might employ a TO. When this was rejected, the voluntary society recruited a TO, arranged for training secondment and later approached social services with a request for assistance with funding. Following this, the Director of Social Services was said to have criticized the voluntary society for lack of consultation. Since then, the TO described the voluntary society as 'very conscious of treading on the toes of the social services'. This manifested itself in concern about visual impairment workers making initial assessments of clients and getting involved in counselling. The society did not accept that this was part of the workers' role and said that they should confine themselves strictly to skills teaching, leaving the social workers to deal with initial assessment and counselling. However, both workers felt very strongly that it was impossible to teach someone who was upset or lacking motivation without first doing some counselling.

8 Views on Training

The TO and MO training provided by the two regional associations, and the MO training offered by the NMC and the regional associations have been described in Chapter 4. The intervening chapters have outlined the working environment of visual impairment specialists and detailed the work they actually do. This chapter describes workers' views on their training; it also presents the views of students who were in training at the time of the research. The information is derived from the interviews with 47 workers and 26 students.

TO training

Working TOs trained at the NRAB

> The training gears you to thinking that clients will be enthusiastic and will be just waiting to see all that you can offer them...when you start working you fall flat on your face and you have to simply start learning how to persevere with clients. (NRAB-trained TO)

> I just felt I had the basics in everything. We were so rushed, there was no time to digest anything. (NRAB trained TO)

Daily living skills

The training given in this area was generally endorsed, but there was broad agreement that the range of topics covered was not needed with the majority of clients, who had either found ways of adapting their activities as their sight deteriorated or had people who did things for them. Some workers commented that far too much time had been spent working under blindfold, considering that most clients had some sight, and that the course should have advised them on how to adapt training in daily living skills for such people. These TOs said they had developed approaches and techniques more relevant for low-vision clients on their own initiative after qualifying, and a number of them had learned a lot from clients themselves.

Many considered the teaching to have been too rigid: its implication that there was a right and wrong way of doing things was not, in practice, a helpful orientation. Experience had shown them that clients' confidence in their own ability was all-important, and trying to teach a new way of doing something often led to a loss of that confidence. Finally, almost half the workers interviewed commented adversely on the tutor's style of teaching, which they found patronizing. Moreover, a number of them were unhappy about being taught such a practical subject by someone who lacked direct experience of working with visually impaired people.

Communications

The work on communications was a major bone of contention. This centred on the claim that students had not been trained to teach braille, moon and typing to clients; all the time had been spent on learning and practising the skills themselves. 'There should have been better tuition in the approaches to teaching communication skills' was the comment of one worker. He said that when he started work, he realized that he did not know how to set about teaching braille – whether to start with the alphabet; or whether to use jumbo or normal size work at the beginning; whether to introduce reading alone or a mixture of reading and writing, and so on. Similarly, other workers had found they were at a loss with regard to teaching typing to clients. They commented also on the mismatch between the amount of time spent on braille and typing and the low level of demand from clients for communications skills training. As one worker put it, 'Having finished the course, and lived, breathed and slept braille, it was a slap in the face to find it was hardly needed.' Finally, some workers questioned whether they should have had to do so much self-teaching: 'We were left to our own devices really to learn braille'.

The NRAB 'Deaf-blind Week' was widely felt to have been worthwhile. Workers described the week as very demanding, but felt they gained an important insight into the needs and problems of this client group.

Other subjects

Each of the NRAB-trained TOs said that more counselling work was needed. Even those who felt that counselling was not strictly part of their role found that there were times when it could not be avoided and that they felt unprepared to be of much use. One worker said: 'I feel you can't go into a client's home to teach the use of aids, to build relationships, and then turn round and call in a social worker for counselling.' Another commented: 'A lot of TOs do social work instinctively, but if they were taught their approach would be more structured.' Although some of these TOs had taken the NRAB course before counselling had been introduced, those who had trained most recently were still unhappy with the limited amount of time devoted to it.

Some workers also felt that the coverage of counselling could be improved. One said that although the marriage guidance counsellor who led some sessions had succeeded in presenting a general introduction to counselling, the emphasis needed to be more on the impact of sight loss and the specific problems the worker would need to address in this respect. Another felt that it would have been useful to discuss case studies which represented certain types of client, so that workers could identify the counselling needs of different clients.

Many workers said that the social services element of the NRAB course ought to have been more comprehensive. A number felt they had been ill-prepared for the type of environment they were going to be working in, and that a better understanding of the workings of a social services department – the people and the administrative work – would have been helpful.

General comments

Most NRAB-trained TOs interviewed said that they had not been adequately prepared to start work. Some said that although they had left the training centre feeling prepared, once they started work they realized they were not! The reasons have already been mentioned in the previous paragraphs: mismatch between content of training and clients' needs; limited coverage of counselling and teaching skills; an uncertainty as to how the training related to low vision clients; and a lack of awareness of their working environment.

Comments on the teaching focused on the balance between skill acquisition and instruction on how to teach the skills. The common view was that far too much time was given to the former and not enough to the latter. A typical comment was: 'The teaching [on] how to teach others was not very thorough, considering the time spent learning the skills.' Moreover, the role-play sessions were felt to be limited as a means of developing teaching skills because they involved teaching fellow students who already knew how to do what was being taught. This is a criticism which was made by many workers and students from all training centres. Even TOs who had been on the course when it involved a teaching practice with visually impaired people who visited the centre (a practice which the NRAB has since stopped) said that the experience was not realistic because the same people were used over and over again – a fact acknowledged by the NRAB, who said this was one of the reasons for dropping the practice. However, some NRAB trained TOs felt that the course needed to involve contact with visually impaired people before the placement.

Another general comment made by most of the NRAB-trained TOs was that too much ground had been covered in such a short course. This was felt by some to have been exacerbated by the number of assignments required and the limited library facilities. Finally, the placement was generally considered to be too short: most workers argued that a longer placement would have prepared them more adequately for their future roles.

The NRAB students

> We're given so much information at once we're not able to assimilate it. (NRAB TO student)

Daily living skills

Students felt that the daily living skills teaching on the course was useful, although they took exception to the tutor's approach. This was something which working TOs had also raised. There was a general feeling among students that they were treated as though they were still at school rather than undergoing a vocational training course for adults.

Communications

Most of the students remarked on the fact that they were left to work on communications skills themselves. One said that had it not been for a self-check braille programme on the computer he would have struggled on his own.

As with the working TOs, there was general agreement that the deaf-blind holiday had been very demanding ('traumatic', commented one student), but worthwhile. One student felt that it had given her time to think about the particular problems of this client group in a way that she would not have done had she only done the module at the NRAB. Another said that having had the experience he now felt confident to work with deaf-blind clients.

Other subjects

Again, as with working TOs interviewed, there was broad agreement that the counselling component of the course was inadequate. Students felt that the four sessions had been very good but that much more time should have been allocated. One said that, having done the placement, she realized just how much counselling came into the job. Students felt that they had learned very little about counselling, in practice, and did not feel confident about counselling clients.

Regarding social studies, in general, students again said that more time was needed to cover the content matter properly. They felt that the social services element was particularly important since it related to the professional environment in which they would be working. One student reported feeling 'totally lost' when on placement since he did not know enough about the roles of other workers and therefore who to talk to about certain problems. Another said that she had only found out what to do on initial registration visits when on placement. Two further students commented that the process of registering a client was not covered adequately. Some students felt that day visits to social services departments would have been helpful.

The teaching and learning module provoked the most criticism. Students questioned whether the teaching needed to be so theoretical, especially as it was allocated a whole morning en *bloc* which made it very difficult to absorb the information. There was a general feeling that the subject-matter would have had more relevance if it had been integrated with other parts of the course. Also, the work on task analysis was not liked and was generally felt to have been overemphasized and laboriously taught. However, one student said that having done the placement she was more able to see its relevance, and another felt that it was an important part of the course which had been approached in the wrong way – 'a lot of the theory is not relevant'.

Placement

There were two major comments from students relating to the placement. First, it needed to be longer, and secondly, the course had not prepared them for the nature of the job they were to encounter in social services. Several students remarked on their surprise that it involved more 'social work' than skills teaching. One student said that she spent a lot of time on placement watching workers counselling clients. Another found that the social work orientation of her supervisor contrasted strongly with the teaching aspect of the job emphasized at the NRAB. A third student had been told by her supervisor that it was not possible to do the job properly without a CQSW. Another student said she had been taken aback to visit a client for the first time and discover that all they had wanted to know about was welfare benefits.

Regarding the length of the placement, there was broad agreement that it needed to be longer in order to allow them to get to grips with all the new things that they were learning. Some students found that they were only just beginning to establish a relationship with a client and had no time to develop the teaching which they had begun. One student suggested that having an earlier placement, in addition to the main one, would have been helpful in this respect. Some students were satisfied that they had taught a range of skills, but others complained that they had not had dealings with enough clients, nor done very much teaching. For example, one said that he had only taught two clients and that he had been with his supervisor most of the time.

General comments

The strongest opinions regarding the course were that it was too short and that not enough time had been given to reinforcing what was supposed to be being learned: 'A lot was condensed into too little time.' Also some students felt that there needed to be more practice time; too many things were covered just once. Students also complained that they had too much work to do in the evenings and weekends and that one study afternoon per week was not enough. Moreover, some students felt that the course had portrayed an inaccurate picture of what the job would involve. One student, having had over a year's experience as an unqualified worker, said that the impression given was that clients would be able to do nothing until the worker arrived to teach them. She pointed out that this was quite wrong, and ignored the fact that most clients had developed methods of coping on their own.

Students described areas where they felt the course had been weak. One mentioned multi-handicap, which had been given only one theory session. Another said that client assessment had been given very little attention: 'I knew very little about this when I came and I still know very little about it.' A major area that all students were unhappy with was the lack of training given on how to teach the skills to clients. Comments were made to the effect that they understood they would have to pick these up on the job, which they did not feel was adequate. As one student said, 'I was surprised at how much it had been a "teach yourself" course.'

Some had found the role-play sessions useful: 'I know it's only role play, but it's helpful'; and they wanted more time to practise teaching the skills: 'We've got to learn the technique before being able to pass it on, but students only have limited teaching practice.' Others expressed strong aversion to the role-play exercises and said that they had got very little from them. There was a general feeling that the role play had not always been taken seriously and that it was impossible for students taking the part of a client to throw up the sort of problems clients would have, because students knew how to do the task, and also could not easily imitate the problems since most had little or no prior experience with the visually impaired. For these reasons, the students felt that the course should have provided more involvement with real clients, which echoed the workers' comments. For some, this lack had not been compensated for in the placement because so few clients were encountered. One student commented that it was all very well being told that they would have to adapt their teaching style for different clients, but that no instruction on this was given. Another student felt that some of the teaching on the course had been superficial – for example, having one session looking at a blank BD8 form and then, on placement, being given a completed one and being expected to be able to assess the client and act on that assessment.

Regarding the division of time between blindfold and low-vision simulation spectacles, students were unanimous that this had been heavily weighted towards working with a blindfold in the practical sessions. Some were critical of this, and thought that they should have spent more time on other eye conditions; others thought that some of the differences had been pointed out during the blindfold work. One student was surprised that there was so little information on low-vision aids. Another said that the course had been 'completely lacking' in this area and had paid only 'lip-service' to it.

Most students were happy with continuous assessment, although one thought that examinations would have been more objective. Several students commented on the lack of discussion about marks on written pieces of work. Also, one student thought that there was a need for more than one assessment in daily living skills, so that a variety of tasks and not just making a meal could be included. Several criticisms were made of the long essay requirement. One student felt that there was not enough time to do this piece of work, especially since it had to be typed and many students were new to typing. Another felt that it was wrong to require it right at the end of the course, so that an individual could pass everything else, including the placement, and then fail because of the long essay.

Working TOs trained at the SRAB

> Students are not taught the teaching skills – they are
> examined on their technical abilities. (SRAB trained TO)

Daily living skills

Many TOs trained at the SRAB were critical of the daily living skills section of the course. Much of the criticism centred on the approaches of the tutors who had been employed to teach it over the years. Some workers felt that not enough time had been spent on role play in this subject, while others felt that the lack of supervision when doing the tasks had meant that teaching points were lost: 'We were not encouraged enough as a group to sort out problems as they might arise for particular client groups – how we might apply certain techniques in particular areas.' One worker, who was a qualified MO, said that the main problem was that students were not given a clear enough idea of the type of clients who would need only certain elements of a daily living skills programme; not all clients needed a full programme, although the training implied that they would. Other workers said that more low vision work rather than blindfold work would have been helpful.

Communications

Although there was a general feeling that braille had been taught very thoroughly, most workers felt that a great deal more time ought to have been spent on how to teach braille to clients: 'Braille is learned to a very high standard, then we are supposed to be able to teach it, but there are no instructions in the teaching of the material.' Some TOs felt, in any case, that it was always possible to keep one step ahead of clients in the RNIB braille primer, and that this, together with the fact that so few clients wanted to learn braille, meant that the thoroughness with which it was taught and the amount of time devoted to it were unnecessary.

Other subjects

As with NRAB-trained TOs, a number of those trained at the SRAB who had had no previous experience of social services departments felt that there was a need for a more thorough grounding in the work of such departments, the welfare benefits for the visually impaired available and the TO's role within social services. One worker said that it was not only those lacking experience with social services, but also those who did not have experience of working with people, who needed advice on what to expect. The 'social work side' was another aspect felt by most TOs to have been inadequately addressed. As with those trained at the NRAB, SRAB-trained TOs had found that they needed counselling skills to do their job properly.

The need for the increased input on low vision and low vision aids which the SRAB course had provided in recent years was endorsed by many workers who had done the course some years before. However, many of those who had trained more recently still felt that they should have been given far more practical training with low-vision simulation spectacles, and one echoed the views of the students that the lectures on this subject were too academic.

General comments

Again, most TOs said that they had not felt prepared to start work. 'The course met only basic needs and did not equip me to begin teaching clients', said one worker. In relation to this problem, the practical role-play sessions were an aspect of the course which were frequently commented upon. Many TOs questioned the quality and the value of the role-play exercises they had participated in. However, some said that more role-play work was needed in order to develop teaching skills. Most of the criticism focused on the superficial nature of the exercises: they were simply told that they had a certain type of eye condition and had to bear this in mind when being taught by another student.

Finally, it emerged that many SRAB-trained TOs questioned the level of 'professionalism' of their course. Many expressed doubts about the suitability of the qualifications and experience of the staff who taught them. Indeed, this was alleged to be one of the reasons that so little time was devoted to teaching students how to impart the skills they learned: they felt that many of the tutors had little or no experience of teaching students or working with clients. A further comment related to the organization of the course. Workers complained of having had lectures and outside visits cancelled, and of having to miss parts of the curriculum (as published in the inter-regional course booklet) because they simply ran out of time. It was widely held that the general organization of the course needed to be addressed before significant improvements could be expected.

The SRAB Students

> Many of the ingredients of the course are excellent. The problem comes in not having enough time to do them properly. (SRAB TO student)

> A lot has been left for us to develop...we are going to have the status and responsibilities of a social worker without the training. (SRAB TO student)

Daily living skills

Students from the SRAB were very critical of the teaching which they received in this subject. They were unhappy with the way in which the tutor left students to get on with tasks themselves and expected them to find ways of dealing with problems, often without supervision. In particular, students were frustrated by the lack of follow-up discussion to these practical sessions, so that any potential benefit to be gained from them was lost. Towards the end of the course, a replacement tutor was brought in whom students commented on most favourably, although they felt that they had had insufficient time to catch up on what they had missed. Some expressed concern that, at the end of the course, they still did not know how to set about planning a daily living skills programme, although others said that they had managed to learn something of what was required from their placement.

Communications

Students were also united in their criticism of the braille teaching on the course. The general view was that this was overemphasized, in terms of the amount of time allocated to it and the high standard they were required to achieve. Some students, who already had experience in the field, said that the time allocation was excessive in view of the limited demand from clients for braille. Moreover, students criticized the lack of training in how to teach braille to clients. Although the last half-hour of the braille lessons was sometimes scheduled for teaching practice, this was said to have occurred only once or twice.

Similar difficulties were reflected in comments on the typing section. Students recognized that the problem, in this particular case, stemmed from the fact that they were taught by the Training Officer's secretary. They were dissatisfied with the fact that they were expected to spend all the time improving their own typing skills rather than learning how to teach clients. Regarding moon, students said that it was acceptable to learn this from a textbook on their own, since it was straightforward.

Low vision

Students felt that this section of the course was very important. However, there were three specific criticisms. First, the topic should have had more time allocated to it; this comment was often accompanied by references to the amount of time spent on what were considered to be less important areas. Secondly, students said that the level of teaching had been too demanding and that much of the work had been over their heads; it was described as 'too technical' and 'too academic'. Thirdly, students felt it focused too much on clinical as opposed to functional assessment. They felt more emphasis should have been placed on the practical implications of vision loss. Despite these criticisms, students said that they had benefited a great deal from this part of the course.

Other subjects

These included mobility, counselling, social services and multi-handicap. The consensus on the mobility training was that it had been excellent, especially since it had incorporated training in how to teach mobility. Also they commented favourably on the equal division of time between low-vision simulation spectacles and the blindfold. One student, who was a qualified MO, said that the SRAB's approach to mobility training had been far more realistic than the NMC programme in this respect. There was considerable concern, however, about the scant coverage of counselling. This was believed to be an important skill which would be greatly needed when working. (One student had taken counselling as the subject for her project, in order to find out more about it.) Social services coverage provoked no comment, except for one student who felt that more time should have been spent on client benefits and related procedures. Students were generally happy with the amount of time spent on the multi-handicapped, with the exception of one student who felt that the course booklet had implied that far more time would be devoted to this than the two days it actually received.

Placement

Views on the placements were mixed. Some students found the experience very rewarding and said that they had learned a great deal. However, the majority complained of having too few clients – only two or three in some cases – and too few sessions with them. One student had seen one of his two clients three times, and the other five times. There was also broad agreement that the placement needed to be longer in order to gain a wider experience of clients and working practices. All the students expressed their appreciation of the efforts taken by the SRAB to find placements which would suit them. However, these efforts were not always crowned with success – one student, who was visually impaired, had a placement with a voluntary society which could not come up with any clients for him to work with! (After four weeks the student was taken out of the placement and had to do another in a different location after the course ended.)

General comments

The most forceful impression created was that students had found the course too short, too intensive in terms of workload and extremely disorganized. In terms of the length, there was a general feeling that too much had been attempted in the time available. This was summed up by one student who said: 'I feel a jack of all trades and master of none.'

Both the amount and the standard of written work required were also widely criticized. One student remarked that the quality of work expected of them was much greater than was suggested by the O-level entry requirements for the course. Students also felt that the large amount of written work was inappropriate for a course which was supposed to be teaching them how to deliver practical skills: 'The basic requirement of our job is going into people's homes to instruct.' Several felt that it was not right that they should have to do essays on areas that the course had not covered. This was felt to be particularly inappropriate in view of the limited library facilities at the Centre.

There was broad agreement on the quality of outside speakers. With the exceptions of a speaker from SENSE and one from the Partially Sighted Society who were said to be excellent, they were described as poor – 'anecdotal' and 'ill-prepared'. Some students, who had had several years' experience of working in the field as MOs, were particularly dissatisfied at what they saw as the unprofessional and sometimes patronizing nature of these talks. Also, students felt that such talks and day visits to centres or institutions were slotted in when the training staff were busy with short courses or overstretched through staff shortages.

Another criticism related to the nature of the course assessment. Although students were in favour of continuous assessment, they were unhappy with the amount of tests they were given throughout the course. Many of them felt that this was not what continuous assessment was about. One student said: 'For me, continuous assessment is doing work in normal, class situations.' There was a feeling that so many tests generated unnecessary pressure on top of the written assignments and that they might just as well have been concentrated into one set of final examinations. The four-weekly tests in braille were a particular source of frustration, since students felt that their own performance in the subject was irrelevant and that their ability to teach it to clients was what should have been assessed.

Course organization came under perhaps the most severe criticism. Students said that they had complained to the tutors about the lack of timetabling, but were told that this was necessary in order to be flexible. This meant that they received a timetable each week for the following week: 'almost as if they are working it out as they go along', said one student. Moreover, the teaching was felt to be disjointed. 'There was a bit here, a bit there. It should have been brought together in distinct modules.'

MO training

The NMC-trained MOs

I had a terrible shock when I found out blind people could see. (NMC trained MO)

Seemed to lose touch with the fact that the object of the course was to learn to teach. (NMC trained MO)
The stereotype client we are taught to teach doesn't represent the clients in the field. (NMC trained MO)

Practical orientation and mobility

Chapter 4 revealed that the aims of the course were 'to teach students the principles of orientation and mobility training based on the long cane system of training and to encourage students to adapt that system to suit the individual mobility needs of all visually impaired people...including the training of clients whose primary travel aid is remaining vision'. The MOs interviewed fully endorsed the effectiveness of the course in accomplishing the first aim – teaching them how to use the long cane – but had serious reservations about the second aim. They all became efficient long cane travellers and could negotiate their way under blindfold in a variety of settings. Most said too that they had found the work under blindfold useful in understanding some of the problems visually impaired people encountered, although they acknowledged that the temporary wearing of a blindfold had limitations in this respect.

The second aim of the course had not been achieved, in their view, and as a consequence they had not been prepared to start work. Their main criticisms were twofold: they were not equipped to deal with low-vision clients; and they had not been taught how to teach. Workers' views on this were expressed most emphatically, particularly in the light of their experience that most clients had some useful vision: 'The course definitely fell short on the partially sighted – a point which became very clear after leaving.' This was related to another major criticism which was that the course had created an entirely inaccurate stereotype of the sort of clients they would encounter – young, fit, totally blind and motivated to learn. Their experiences had revealed to the contrary that clients were generally elderly and commonly lacked either the motivation or ability to undertake long cane training and that virtually none of them was totally blind: 'Where were all the young, blind, active clients?' One MO's observation summed up the views of the majority: although the long cane mobility practice under blindfold had been excellent, there was little or no demand for mobility training with a long cane – those who did any mobility training usually used a guide cane or symbol cane.

Following from this, many MOs commented on the inadequacy of the course in failing to provide adequate training in the use of other canes and alternative methods of teaching mobility where a low-vision aid was more suitable. Again, one worker summed up a common view when he said that the course was 'very strong on one aspect of mobility which could be used as a basis, but it wasn't; that was all of it'.

The second major criticism made by practising MOs was that the course had not trained them how to teach the skills they themselves had learned. Although reservations were expressed about the artificiality of the 'teachbacks' (where students were teaching fellow students who already knew how to perform the task being taught), workers still felt that they ought to have had more: 'They were realistic enough to want more of them.'

Other subjects

The most unanimous views on any subject, apart from mobility, were expressed in relation to counselling. Many workers said that the lack of counselling or the limited amount of time spent on counselling (depending on when they had taken the course) was a drawback when it came to dealing with clients. 'Counselling is as important as anything we do', said one worker, echoing the views of many. The relatively small number who did not feel that more counselling was needed were workers who did not see counselling as part of the MO's role. However, the majority felt that they often 'muddled through' in the absence of adequate training. It may be noted too that when workers were asked in what areas they felt they could benefit from further training, 'counselling' was the most frequent response.

Workers' views on the 'academic' subjects – anatomy and physiology of the eye, audiology and learning and teaching – varied a good deal. Most found the 'medical' information on the eye very useful when explaining to clients the details of their sight impairment. Some felt that even more work on this would have been useful and that they had not been given enough information on the effects of various eye diseases. This would have been useful not only in talking to clients, but also in planning programmes and liaising with ophthalmologists. By contrast, other MOs said that too much time had been allocated to the anatomy and physiology of the eye and that this had not been useful since they never discussed such details with clients, seeing this as outside the scope of their role. Indeed one worker said that her authority actually forbade non-medical specialists from discussing medical conditions in order to ensure that clients were not given the wrong information inadvertently. Similarly, contrasting views were given for the work on learning and teaching and audiology – some workers felt there had been too much on these subjects, while others thought that they were very worthwhile. Most workers felt that the mapmaking course had been acceptable, yet these same people questioned its value in relation to work with the majority of clients.

The other subject which workers felt ought to have been covered in more detail was social services – the single day of guest speakers was referred to as useful, but far too limited for an MO starting work in a social services department. Some workers added that they had not been equipped to operate as the only specialist in the authority.

General comments

Many MOs felt that the main reason for the limited relevance of much of the practical mobility work and the failure to prepare students for work in social services was linked to the lack of practical client experience on the part of tutors. They were particularly critical of tutors who had taken the MO course, then immediately after had become tutors. Some MOs saw this as part of the reason for their lack of preparation on the course in social services and, in particular, the almost total ignorance they encountered in social services of what mobility training was about.

Some NMC-trained MOs expressed concern over the lack of a co-ordinated approach to training. They felt that this militated against gaining the respect of other social services workers and managers of service provision, with the effect that the service to the visually impaired suffered: 'Fragmentation is preventing good training'; 'it's ridiculous that the training centres all go off in their own direction'. Some felt that the answer lay in a national college to train visual impairment workers, while others felt that external validation was what was needed: 'If I could choose just one thing, it would be external examination and accreditation.' Another common view was that the training should integrate MO and TO skills into one course since many MOs found a demand to teach the whole range.

The NMC MO students

> You are put through a set programme under blindfold and that is it. (NMC MO student)
> The course doesn't equip you to teach mobility to the partially sighted. (NMC MO student)

Practical orientation and mobility

Although students generally found the long cane training under blindfold an acceptable part of the course, there were major criticisms similar to those made by practising MOs. First, there was a general view that the use of the blindfold was overemphasized in relation to low-vision work. Students were critical of the limited amount of training given while wearing low-vision simulation spectacles, especially since their placement had made them aware that the vast majority of clients had some remaining vision. Moreover, some said that even when the spectacles were worn, the full benefit was lost because they were used to go over a route which had already been negotiated under blindfold. However, students were at pains to point out that allocating more time to wearing simulation spectacles would not be sufficient on its own to overcome the problem, especially because the spectacles were not very good at excluding all 'normal' vision. They believed that the course should incorporate the skills necessary to modify the long cane training for low-vision clients.

Secondly, students were critical that most of the practical mobility work was devoted to learning, and practising, how to travel with the long cane rather than teaching clients to do this. Most of the students said that they had not felt prepared to train clients or develop a training programme when they started their placement because of the lack of training in teaching skills. Although the 'teachbacks' were intended to facilitate this, a number of students complained that there were too few of these – most had about four – and that they appeared to be slotted in when time permitted rather than having their place in a planned programme. Thus some students had more than others – the number ranged between three and nine during the three months at the Centre.

A third criticism was that limited training was given in the use of other canes, such as the symbol cane and the guide cane, which again, having been on placement, was felt to be insufficient in view of the proportion of clients who used one of these canes rather than a long cane. This criticism related to a fourth point: that the mobility training had not prepared students for the necessity of adapting the basic programme for the needs of each individual. A commonly expressed sentiment was that the training was geared towards a certain type of client – young, fit and motivated – which was quite unrealistic. Guidance was felt to be necessary in relating mobility training to the elderly, and also to multi-handicapped people and children. Four students, whose placements had involved children, said that they had not been prepared for the adjustments to the training that would be necessary. (Minor accidents had occurred in two cases when students had been giving mobility training to a child.)

Other subjects

These included anatomy and physiology of the eye, audiology, teaching and learning and theory of mobility; they were mainly theoretical. Students' opinions of them were mixed and seemed to reflect their general comments on how difficult they had found the course. Some had enjoyed the 'academic' nature of the work in anatomy and physiology of the eye and audiology, while others seemed to have found it highly demanding. Criticisms of the module on the anatomy and physiology of the eye centred on whether so much medical information was really needed, particularly when there was such pressure on time in subjects which came up later in the course. The theory of mobility was found to be useful, although students again commented that the theoretical work on low vision would have been much more meaningful if practical work had been incorporated.

Teaching and learning was said by all the students to be too intensive. Some students also commented that the work was too demanding in terms of the level of research needed to answer some of the questions set at the end of each lesson and that the reading list was unrealistic, given the limited time available. About half of them felt that the subject needed more time in order to cover in a useful way all the elements included in the module. Others felt that some of the work could have been dropped because it did not seem to have any connection with the job of an MO; for example, one student said that she could not see the relevance of Pavlov's dogs to teaching mobility.

Some students had expected this section to equip them with information on how to teach a skill to someone else and were confused when it did not.

Placement

The major criticism MO students had of their placements was that they had not been prepared. Two dimensions of this stood out: the experience of teaching other students who already knew what the student was trying to teach had not equipped them to teach clients; and very little long cane teaching was needed. Regarding the latter, students indicated their surprise that the course concentrated so much on this, when most of their clients on placement wanted symbol or guide cane training. Often they had had experience with only one client who was learning to use the long cane. One student said that it was only on placement that she had realized that only those who were totally blind, or with very limited low vision, were suitable for training with a long cane. Another student commented on the lack of preparation in teaching the congenitally blind. She had had a placement with children and had found it necessary to spend most of her time working on pre-cane skills – posture, gait and balance – rather than the long cane.

Although they had felt ill-prepared for the placement, students seem to have found the experience extremely beneficial and would have liked it to be longer: 'I learned a lot at Birmingham, but an awful lot more [on placement].' Most said that they felt they needed to have had some involvement, and preferably teaching sessions, with visually impaired people before the start of the placement. Two said it would have helped put the NMC part of the training in context if there had been a short placement early on in the course, in addition to the one at the end.

General comments

Most NMC students said they had felt very rushed on the course and thought that it needed to be longer, although one said that with two study periods per day there was plenty of time to do the work. Favourable comments were made about the structure of the course; students liked the blocks of teaching on one subject followed by an examination before moving on to the next subject. In addition, the change of tutors for practical mobility was seen as advantageous, especially as students were of the opinion that not all the tutors taught exactly the same course components – for example, one tutor taught only one way of negotiating stairs with the long cane, but another taught two methods. Following on from this, however, some were critical of the lack of a written syllabus which tutors and students could follow and felt that the provision of a timetable sometimes as little as a week in advance was inadequate.

Over half of the students said that they felt the counselling component of the course was insufficient and that a great deal more work on the 'social work' side of the job was needed. One student, who had experience of working in a social services visual impairment team prior to starting the course, said the job involved 'so much more than just mobility work'. Also, some commented that very little guidance had been given in the organizational/administrative aspects of the work of an MO.

There was also broad agreement that having to do a project while on placement was an unnecessary burden. Although placement supervisors were requested to allow students study time, this allocation and more besides was taken up with lesson preparation, writing notes and doing a case study. One student commented that the pressures of learning how to teach clients, becoming acquainted with new colleagues and remembering how things were done in the placement location, in addition to the paperwork which involvement with clients created, were more than enough without having to worry about the NMC course-work requirements. Another student said that she felt the project was required simply to make the course 'appear a little bit more professional'.

Braille, in which students were expected to pass an examination but which was not a taught part of the course, provoked a variety of responses from students. Most seemed to feel it was quite useful to know braille, although some expressed regret that they had not learned it before starting the course, as others had done, in order to remove some of the pressure. One or two students felt strongly that it was not necessary for an MO to know braille: 'You cannot do it just for the sake of doing it; if you're not using it you're bound to forget it.'

Students were happy with the course assessment techniques. There was a feeling that the mixture of continuous assessment in the practical training in conjunction with examinations at the end of each theory block was a fair balance. Some said that the examinations provided useful feedback for them, as well as for the tutors.

The probationary period operated by the NMC appears to have had little impact on those students interviewed. They had not felt under pressure during the three-week period and many said that they had completely forgotton about it. However, one student was asked to leave the course, after failing during the probationary period and an extended period of probation.

The SRAB MO students

> You're not taught that your way is right or wrong. (SRAB MO student)
> The work is generally not about teaching [mobility] but meeting [clients'] needs. (SRAB MO student)

Practical orientation and mobility

Generally the four students had favourable comments to make about the training — they particularly approved of the fact that the training emphasized the need for flexibility and ability to adapt their skills to suit clients' needs. Their main criticism was that not enough training was given in teaching skills. Students said that more teachbacks (there were two) would have been helpful in this respect, but in particular they would have liked more opportunities to observe the mobility tutor giving mobility training to another student. They had found these sessions very useful because they enabled them to see where the 'client' was going wrong and to note the tutor's teaching points. Also two students said that although a great many references were made to the need to be flexible and adopt different teaching methods to suit different clients, they were not given sufficient examples of these alternative methods.

Students were pleased that the mobility training offered at the SRAB had moved away from the highly structured programme and the emphasis on students being good travellers characteristic of NMC training. They felt that this move reflected a more client-oriented approach which they welcomed. Students believed that having an equal amount of practice with low-vision simulation spectacles and a blindfold was a good thing, although they said that the former was more difficult and less realistic because the spectacles were not very good.

Other subjects

Students found other elements of the training satisfactory, although they commented on the degree to which they relied on the TO course for the theoretical background. Beyond this, individual students mentioned certain areas which they felt needed more time: theory of orientation; audiology and the use of sound in mobility training; and the teaching of mobility to children.

Placement

The main criticism that students raised regarding the placement was that four weeks was far too short. Two months was felt to be a more appropriate amount of time to enable them to encounter different types of client and to allow enough time to see through a substantial amount of a training programme with one client. Another point, which was made by three of the four students, was that their placement supervisors were very critical of their mobility teaching. They felt this was linked to an apparent suspicion of the new mobility training course at the SRAB, given that the supervisors had trained at the NMC. One of them described the supervisor's approach as 'bordering on nit-picking – straight down the line; do it by the book'.

General comments

Students felt that this was a new course, not only in the sense that it was the first MO course run by the SRAB, but, more important, that it diverged significantly from the traditional methods of teaching mobility – i.e., that students no longer had to achieve a high level of mobility expertise themselves in order to qualify. They commented most favourably on the training staff's 'openness and willingness to change' the training and felt that this reflected the general philosophy of MO training at the SRAB – that there was no right or wrong way to do anything and that the worker in the field must be able to respond flexibly to clients' needs: 'To get on a course where the emphasis is on people, not on the handicap, is great.'

Students thought that the course assignments (usually client profiles) were useful and spoke favourably of their relevance to the job. However, while recognizing the deliberate emphasis on practical training because the course was a supplement to their TO training, they seemed to feel that more should have been required of them in terms of written work. One student said, 'it would have been sensible to see if any of [the theory] was being retained'. Finally, students expressed dissatisfaction with the timetabling of the course, and their frustration at having elements introduced at the last minute which did not allow for sufficient forward planning; for example, students were not informed until the last week of the course that they had to give a joint presentation to a group of student nurses a few days later.

It must be emphasized that the views expressed in this chapter are those of the workers and students. It is recognized that they present a somewhat negative impression of the training, but this reflects what came across in the interviews. The comments have been reported here in some detail because they serve to highlight the key aspects of training on which attention needs to be focused.

9 The Rehabilitation Officer/Worker Courses

A 'joint' rehabilitation worker course was introduced in 1987/8, a few months before this research was due to present its findings. It was therefore agreed to extend the duration of the study to allow a brief examination of the new course and its relationship with existing courses. This chapter reports on the work of this extended phase: it includes a description of the development of the new course and the agreements reached between the three centres, course outlines, student characteristics and qualifications, and NRAB students' views on the first RO course.

Background

The training centres reported that demand from the field, both from workers and social services managers, had made it increasingly clear that in order to provide an efficient service to the visually impaired, dual qualified workers were needed. The number of authorities who were seconding their workers for a second visual impairment qualification was felt to be direct evidence of this. Negotiations between the three centres began in the 1970s with the goal of developing a new course which would incorporate all the rehabilitation skills needed for work with the visually impaired. The development of the Independent Special Option was the result (see Chapter 2). The failure of the training centres to launch this new training package was a setback in their plans to move towards rehabilitation workers in place of MOs and TOs. Further negotiations between the centres followed, but they experienced difficulties in reaching agreement over what the new course should involve. Continuing failure to agree led to the NRAB seeking the approval of its committee to run an independent RO course.

September 1985 saw the start of the first such course, which has continued each year since then.

Although the NRAB had started its own RO course, meetings to discuss a joint course continued between all three centres resulting, late in 1986, in the following statement appearing in the *British Journal of Visual Impairment*:

> Training for Specialist Workers with the Visually Impaired
> In September 1987 the National Mobility Centre, the North Regional Association for the Blind and the South Regional Association for the Blind are introducing a unified form of qualifying training for specialist workers with the visually impaired.
>
> The rehabilitation worker course has been jointly planned by the three training agencies and aims to provide a common training for all specialist workers. The course will last for one year and will integrate orientation and mobility and technical officer skills. It will also include additional theoretical and practical work on a range of topics related to the rehabilitation of the visually impaired.
>
> The rehabilitation worker course will replace the present orientation and mobility training and technical officer training courses as the basic qualifying course in specialist work. Shorter courses in either orientation and mobility training or technical officer training will be offered to candidates already posessing a recognized qualification in one or other area
> .

The course in rehabilitation work with visually impaired people started in September 1987 at the SRAB. At the NMC, because of a move to new premises, it started in January 1988. Originally the NMC believed that a January start date would be advantageous but this was not found to be the case; the NMC said that holidays were difficult to accommodate and placements were more difficult to arrange because schools were closed over the summer. (While there was a commitment to trying to secure more placements in social services, this presumably reflects the NMC practice of making placements in schools.) A joint pamphlet was produced which contained a statement of course aims; course objectives were available on request from each agency. However, the NRAB, having already run a course for two years which was called the 'rehabilitation officer course', was not prepared to change the name to 'rehabilitation worker course'. It maintained that local authorities used rehabilitation officer as a title and recognized position and, moreover, that two groups of students had already qualified with this title from the NRAB. However, the NMC and the SRAB wanted a new title to distinguish the course from what had gone before. The NRAB said that the advertisements for an RW course reflected the fact that it had been out-voted by the other agencies; it maintained that successful NRAB students would still receive certificates, issued by the NRAB, indicating their qualifying status as ROs. They would also receive RW certificates.

Development of the new courses

In developing its RO course, the NRAB said that it had consulted with a number of parties who had something to say about training needs. This included contacting organizations which represented the visually impaired and a questionnare to TOs who had been trained at the NRAB. This questionnaire asked about their views on training elements in relation to the work they did; the responses were said to have helped shape the initial RO course. The SRAB had also been engaged in consultations of its own with affiliated authorities. In Autumn 1985, as the NRAB started its first RO course, the SRAB circulated a consultative paper which outlined proposals for a 43-week course, including the numbers of hours to be allocated to each of the subjects. This was said to have evoked, in most cases, a positive response.

The discussion between the three training centres regarding the new RW course initially involved meetings between the senior personnel. Later, teaching staff from all three agencies were also involved in the meetings, but after several such meetings the attendance reverted back to include only the senior officers. The main reason for this was said to be the difficulties of getting all the staff together at one of the training centres, given their teaching commitments and the geographical constraints.

Possible variations in training approaches

The NRAB said that it was already thinking of the future beyond the current RO training. The General Secretary said that one possible development was for the training agencies to be able to take the training to the local authorities – i.e. for tutors to train social services employees in situ. This had already occurred in one authority, with NRAB tutors providing 'top-up' training, and the General Secretary said that other authorities had expressed an interest in this.

During the development of the RW course, the SRAB indicated its intention to make the training available in modular form, if it was found that there was a demand for this. The SRAB saw this as a way of appealing to employers who could not spare a worker for almost ten months, but who would be willing to release the person for shorter periods. One of the options was to offer applicants the opportunity of taking the course on a termly basis, but even shorter periods would be possible. The SRAB had not advertised these options for its first RW course; running through the whole course was more straightforward for the first time.

A unified form of training?

The negotiations resulted in agreement being reached on course length, entry requirements, course aims and the number of hours to be allocated to each subject, including the fieldwork placement. However, it was agreed that the methods adopted to achieve the agreed aims need not be the same; indeed from the outset it was understood that these would be different because the training centres would not accept certain elements of one another's training. Course assessment procedures were another aspect which none of the centres was prepared to concede; thus the NMC proposed to maintain some examinations and continuous assessment, while the regional associations intended to continue with their own systems of continuous assessment.

Despite the claims that the number of hours spent on each subject was to be the same at each of the centres, our inquiries revealed that this was not the case. At the NRAB, the number of hours spent on several subjects was different from that which had been agreed; in some cases, it was much less. At the NMC, the new Principal and other tutors said that some subjects had been allocated too much time and they had halved the time allocation in some instances — for example counselling, and learning and teaching. At the SRAB, variations were also found – for example the allocations of time to audiology, deaf-blind communications and multi-handicapped were almost halved and the time allocated to counselling was almost doubled.

Monitoring and certification of the new courses

A 'training manager's group' was created which was made up of the General Secretaries and Training Officers from the regional associations, the new Principal of the NMC and, for the NMC, a representative of RNIB. This group was concerned with broad issues including the general presentation of the course, the possibility of offering it in modular form, seeking external validation, course fees and whether visually impaired students should be accepted on the course. These topics were still under discussion in 1988.

At the time of our inquiry, another group was in the process of being established. It was intended that it should act as an interim 'validating' group until such time as the training centres could secure the recognition of an independent, nationally recognized body. It was to have responsibility for the issuing of certificates, which could be withheld if the external assessors indicated that this was appropriate (see below). It was hoped by the training centres that it would include: a chairperson (an ex social work education adviser for CCETSW), an external assessor, a representative from NAOMI/NATOB, a representative from AEWVH and observers from the DHSS, CCETSW and the British Association of Social Workers. The training agencies were also to have representatives on the board. Despite the fact that the training agencies would dominate the group, it was to be given the title of 'Independent Training Board' (ITB).

A third group had been established by the training agencies after the commencement of the NRAB and SRAB courses which was responsible for the assessment of each of the three rehabilitation courses. None of the training centres was certain of the exact composition of this group, but it appears that it was to include the following people: a representative from SENSE, a tutor from higher education who taught on courses for teachers of visually impaired children, a tutor on CQSW and CSS courses, a manager of services to the visually impaired in a local authority and a dual qualified worker who also had a CSS.

One of the training centres said that it was intended that a representative of NAOMI or NATOB should also be a member. Written documentation, provided by the NMC, spelled out the tasks of these assessors, as follows:

- to evaluate the skills and knowledge of selected students from each agency with a view to determining their ability to practise;
- to evaluate the course aims, the appropriateness of those aims and the general 'balance' of course content;
- to evaluate each agency's teaching style, placement selection and course administration – the latter concerning the methods of 'easing' the students through the necessary processes of study;
- to advise and discuss with agency staff comments on the above;
- to make recommendations to the ratifying body (ITB) regarding the certification of students;
- to give a full report to the ratifying body (ITB) every two years.

The training agencies issued guidelines for achieving the above tasks in the first year:

- agencies should identify student strengths and weaknesses – particularly the ones at the top and bottom ends of the ability scale – recognizing that these might be different for students' academic and practical work;
- placement visits to one or two students from each agency;
- examine a selection of student academic work - one or two students from each agency;
- two different assessors should each spend one day at each agency to observe teaching - particularly practical skills - and talk informally with students;
- visit two students from each agency about six months after the student has entered work to assess the relevance of the course teaching;
- assessors should receive timetables with session notes from all agencies.

Each of the training centres welcomed the idea of having external assessors. Despite the claims that a unified course had been developed, each was aware that its own course was different from the intended common pattern – and was confident that it was superior to the other two courses. The training centres said that the assessors' main task was not to assess the performance of students; this was a matter for course tutors. Rather, they were appointed to monitor the standards of the training centres themselves, including staff and syllabuses.

Course fees

The cost of the RO/RW courses varied considerably between the centres, as follows:

NRAB	Affiliated authorities	£1,200
	Non-affiliated authorities and individuals	£6,000
SRAB	Affiliated authorities	£3,000
	Non-affiliated authorities and individuals	£6,000
NMC	All applicants	£3,930

The NMC said that it could not charge any less because it did not receive a grant from central government, nor fees from affiliated local authorities. The SRAB said that it had increased its charges to come more in line with the NMC. However, the NRAB said it was determined to retain the lowest possible fee for its affiliated authorities, despite opposition from the NMC and the SRAB.

Staffing implications of the new courses

Developments in the training offered by the three centres had staff training and recruitment implications. The NRAB appointed two new members of staff. One of these was a dual qualified worker who had trained at the NRAB and whose main responsibility on the RO course was teaching practical mobility. The other new member of staff had qualifications in counselling and had worked as a counsellor in a variety of organizations. Upon recruitment, he did the MO training with other students, and after a local authority placement, he became a full time tutor with responsibility for practical mobility training, counselling and the modules on audiology and the eye and low vision. In addition, two existing members of staff, the communications tutor and the part-time daily living skills tutor, were given training in practical mobility. Neither of them had a placement to practise mobility training with visually impaired people, but they were involved in teaching practical mobility to RO students.

The NMC recruited two members of staff. One of these had trained at the NMC eight years earlier and had since worked as an MO in a social services department. Her main responsibilities on the RW course were practical mobility teaching and, temporarily until another tutor could be recruited, daily living skills. After joining the NMC as a tutor she took two one-week courses at the SRAB in daily living skills.

The other new member of staff had a social welfare officer for the blind qualification and a CQSW. At the time of joining the NMC, she took the MO training there. Previously she had worked as a social worker for the blind in social services and had spent a brief period as a tutor at the SRAB. Her main responsibilities on the RW course were the communications subjects. In addition, she had some input on the management, social studies and multi-handicap modules. In addition to these two new members of staff, the NMC had a temporary mobility tutor who was on secondment from the Guide Dogs for the Blind Association for two and a half years.

The staff changes at the SRAB involved losing the original communications tutor and recruiting two new tutors. One of these took over the communications and daily living skills module. She had MO and social worker for the blind qualifications and had worked as a social worker for the blind and as an MO, with experience of both the voluntary and state sector. The other had trained as an MO at the NMC and worked for three years in social services before taking the SRAB TO course. After qualifying, she was recruited by the SRAB as a mobility tutor. In addition, she had responsibility for counselling and social policy. She had a certificate in counselling.

The courses

Course aims

The following aims are taken from the course pamphlet:

To enable the student to develop the necessary competence in the rehabilitation of people with a visual impairment

- to enable the student to develop an understanding of the process and value of management and to work successfully within that process;
- to develop an understanding of the sociological and psychological factors which influence normal human growth and development and how the disruption of these patterns of functioning can affect both individual and family;
- to enable the student to mobilize the appropriate statutory and voluntary resources for individual clients;
- to enable the student to develop interpersonal skills, to develop an awareness of counselling as an enabling process and to appreciate the limits of his personal ability within that process;
- to enable the student to make a comprehensive assessment of individual clients as a prerequisite to programme development;
- to enable the student to develop and effect appropriate teaching programmes;
- to develop the student's understanding of the human visual system so that he can appreciate the complex nature of visual impairment and can effect appropriate programmes for making the optimum use of poor vision;
- to develop the student's understanding of sound and hearing in order to develop any client's use of sound to the maximum and to enable the student to work effectively with hearing impaired clients;
- to equip the student with knowledge of a range of communication skills and to enable the student to effect appropriate training programmes;
- to equip the student with a full understanding of the skills and processes of mobility training and to enable the student to effect appropriate training programmes;
- to provide the student with knowledge of a range of skills of daily living and to enable the student to effect appropriate training programmes;
- to develop an awareness of the problems, needs and potential of multiply handicapped visually impaired clients and equip the student to effect appropriate training programmes.

Some principal aspects of the new courses

The NRAB had decided when it ran its first RO course in 1985 that the course would be age-oriented rather than skills-oriented – i.e., based on the needs of different client age groups rather than having students learn skills in isolation. After a four-week general block of theory, the course was made up of a series of discrete blocks, starting with the elderly visually impaired and moving in turn to adults, adolescents and, finally, children and infants. Students' own skills learning was linked to the client group they were studying. The NRAB said the course was designed to enable students to look at the total needs of a client, assess these, and design an appropriate programme – for example, not just the skills to make a cup of tea but the mobility and identification skills which are also involved. In addition, there was said to be a greater emphasis than in its TO and MO courses on being able to teach skills, on counselling and on problems caused by additional handicaps.

The second NRAB course (1986–7) remained essentially the same, except that skills teaching was introduced much earlier instead of the initial block of theory. The Centre said that there was also less emphasis on the age-related blocks.

As far as the introduction of the RW course was concerned, the NRAB indicated that it had made very few amendments to its earlier RO courses. One of the main differences was that it had introduced a deaf-blind holiday – a feature of the TO training – something which the other two training centres did not have. It said that it had also tried to move further away from students learning communications skills to students learning how to teach these skills to clients. This entailed more role-play teaching sessions and use of video.

The NMC said that its RW course would have a much bigger input of practical mobility work than the MO course. Another change from the MO course was that the first term of long cane training was to involve students wearing a blindfold, and the second term using low-vision simulation spectacles. Previously the two had been mixed together, with much more emphasis on blindfold work. The new Principal said that there would still be more time spent on blindfold work, but work with low-vision simulation spectacles was easier and so students would actually cover more in less time. There were said to be more 'teachbacks' on the new course and a full day was allocated to electronic visual aids. Although the NMC maintained examinations as part of the assessment procedure, there were less of these. Also it was intended that the project should be completed prior to the beginning of the placement, unlike the MO course where students were expected to complete this on placement. Training was still organized in a series of blocks for sections on the 'eye and low vision' and 'audiology'. This was felt to be preferable because students would be unable to cope with too many topics at once. Finally, it was anticipated that more use would be made of the video; on the MO course it had been used only in daily living skills sessions.

The SRAB said that its new RW course included more emphasis on 'the management side' and counselling than its TO or MO courses had done. In addition, teaching of the section on multi-handicap was said to differ from its previous courses in that it no longer involved focusing on a series of individual handicaps, but tried to bring them all together. The mobility training offered on the MO course had changed and this was reflected in the mobility section of the RW course. There was said to be comparatively little emphasis on long cane work under blindfold and more on client assessment and the development of individual teaching programmes. Overall, the first term of the RW course had concentrated on theory and the second term on practical skills. However, it was felt that this had not proved particularly successful and was likely to be changed on subsequent courses. As at the NMC, more use was said to be made of video in recording students in practical sessions.

Course content

The courses consisted of 30 weeks' tuition at the training agencies and ten weeks' fieldwork placement. At the NRAB students spent an additional week on a residential holiday for deaf-blind people. The following list of jointly agreed sessions was supplied by the NMC.

Subject	Sessions	Equivalent no. of hours (to nearest hour)
Mobility	138	173
Communication	85	106
Daily living skills	75	94
Learning and teaching	65	81
Eye and low vision	42	53
Social studies	42	53
Deaf-blind	40	50
Counselling/interpersonal skills	27	34
Management	25	31
Multi-handicap	22	28
Audiology	20	25
Client assessment	10	13
Recreation and leisure	9	11
Study time	150	188

However, as described earlier, the number of hours allocated to the different subject areas varied, in practice, at each agency. The General Secretary of the NRAB, in a comment that reflected the opinion at the other training agencies, wrote:

> Regarding the breakdown of the number of hours spent on each subject, this is difficult as subjects are less discrete. We can provide sample timetables but feel that any breakdown into subjects would be false e.g. low vision included in mobility tutorials and daily living etc. Professional studies includes elements of social studies and skills learning etc. (Letter to project team, February 1988.)

However, the following list of sessions allocated to each subject at each centre suggests that this difficulty cannot account for all the discrepancies.

	Agreed sessions	NRAB sessions	NMC sessions	SRAB sessions
Mobility	138	70	83	90–150
Communication	85	83*	60*	60*
Daily living skills	75	53	60	50
Learning and teaching	65	60	33	
Eye and low vision	42	16*	20	
Social studies	42	26	25*	26
Deaf-blind	40	11†	13*	15–20*
Counselling	27	38	13	50
Management	25	10	17	15

	Agreed sessions	NRAB sessions	NMC sessions	SRAB sessions
Multi-handicap	22	6	22	12
Audiology	20	8*	14	11
Client assessment	10		8	7
Recreation and leisure	9	5	10	

*Plus outside visits;

†Plus deaf-blind holiday.

Note: This information has been derived from interviews with course tutors at each of the three centres and written documentation from the NRAB and the NMC. Where gaps appear, this indicates that the agencies were unable to say how many sessions there were.

The quoted objectives in the following sections were supplied by each of the training agencies and were common to all three of them.

The eye and low vision

The agreed written objectives for this section stated that, on completion of the course, students should be able to:
- explain the nature and properties of light and lighting;
- demonstrate a knowledge of elementary optics;
- name and describe the functions of the component parts of the human visual system;
- describe the symptoms and consequences of those disorders which are the most prevalent causes of visual impairment in the UK;
- demonstrate an ability to assess the nature and extent of a visual loss, and to assess and develop functional vision and visual efficiency;
- show an appreciation of the psycho-social factors which may influence the use of low vision in daily life;
- demonstrate an ability to apply the concepts of light, size and contrast to environmental and behavioural modification in daily life;
- identify, describe, supply and train clients to manage the range of equipment and services designed for people with low vision.

The three agencies had agreed to allocate 42 sessions to the eye and low vision.

At the NRAB written course documentation indicated that there were a total of 16 taught sessions, made up of lectures and seminars given by tutors or guest speakers. This compared with 11 sessions on the NRAB MO course and six sessions on 'medical studies' (including the eye and the ear) on the NRAB TO course. Visits were arranged to a resource centre and to an ophthalmologist working in a hospital outpatients' clinic.

The NMC divided the teaching of this section between three tutors and outside speakers. Tutors said that the input was to be similar to the NMC MO course but that there was more time allocated – 20 sessions, compared with 12 on the MO course. It was envisaged that this would allow more work on low vision. One day was to be spent on vision aids. It was intended that five lectures by tutors would be followed by a session from a guest speaker. Students would then each present a seminar paper. In the second term it was planned that sessions would focus on low vision.

The SRAB said that this section was given more time, particularly for low vision, than previous SRAB courses which had included approximately 26 sessions. There was also more focus on the use and amplification of light and the use of closed-circuit television

Audiology

The agreed written objectives for this section stated that, on completion of the course, students would be able to:
- explain the nature and properties of sound;
- name and describe the functions of the component parts of the human auditory system;
- describe the symptoms and consequences of those disorders which are the most prevalent causes of hearing impairment in the UK, and of those which result in a combined impairment of vision and hearing;
- demonstrate an ability to assess the nature and extent of a hearing loss and to assess and develop functional hearing capacity;
- demonstrate a knowledge of different types of hearing aid, and how these work;
- identify and describe the ways in which a visually impaired person can make use of sound in daily life.

The three agencies had agreed to allocate 20 sessions to audiology.

The NRAB course documentation indicated that there were eight taught sessions, taken by tutors and outside speakers, plus visits to an audiologist working in an outpatients' department. This was more than it allocated on the TO course (six sessions plus a visit included in the 'medical studies' section), but less than the NRAB MO course, which included 11 sessions.

The NMC audiology tutor said there were to be 14 sessions on audiology. This was more than on the NMC MO course, which involved 11 sessions for audiology. The tutor said there would be much more input on social welfare for the deaf and the causes of hearing loss than on the MO course. The format was to be similar to the MO course, with the tutor giving one or two introductory sessions and then students taking turns to give seminar papers. Outside speakers were again to be invited to give lectures, as on the MO course.

The SRAB had allocated 11 sessions to audiology. This was less than on its TO course which had approximately 14 sessions. The tutor said that the main emphases would be on hearing impairment and the implications for a client's learning programme and the use of auditory skills in mobility training.

Mobility

The agreed written objectives for this section stated that, on completion of the course, students would be able to:

- demonstrate a knowledge of the cognitive, sensory and motor skills involved in travel;
- demonstrate an ability to
  assess client's orientation and mobility needs, and design and implement appropriate training programmes
  teach the use of a range of different aids to mobility
  teach the use of low-vision and auditory skills in a variety of mobility situations
  survey routes, make and teach the use of different methods of providing geographical information;
- demonstrate an understanding of the ways in which visual and auditory clues vary in different environments, and identify strategies for coping with these variations;

- show an appreciation of the methods of independent travel which are taught by other specialized agencies.

The three agencies had agreed to allocate 138 sessions to mobility.

The NRAB's documentation stated that there were 70 mobility sessions: 60 practical and ten discussions. This was less than on the NRAB MO course which had 60 practical sessions and 32 theory sessions, including teaching practices. The NRAB said that more recently mobility work on the MO course had been reduced, so that it was now allocated the same amount of time as on the RO course. The General Secretary said that this had been achieved by reducing the blindfold work and the overlap between 'mobility' and 'teaching and learning'. There were fewer teaching practices on the RO course and students did not visit practising MOs to observe clients being taught. The original mobility tutor on the RO course said that the theoretical input was not sufficient. In practical sessions, students were taught individually, in pairs and in groups. On the MO course far more one-to-one teaching occurred, although this was said to be changing towards more pair and group work. Students changed tutors every half-term so as to experience different styles of mobility teaching. They were required to keep workbooks, as on the MO course, and a resource file (for each topic) for assessment purposes.

At the NMC, 83 practical mobility sessions were scheduled, which was to include 20 sessions using low-vision simulation spectacles rather than the blindfold. Overall, there were to be 23 more mobility sessions on the new RW course than on the MO course. It was hoped that this would allow more time for discussion of teaching points and work on other canes, in addition to the work on the long cane. Tutors said that the method of teaching would remain basically the same (i.e., one-to-one practical sessions). However, certain changes were planned. First, as well as having more work with low-vision simulation spectacles, the low-vision training was to come in a block in the second term; the first term would be spent entirely on blindfold long cane travel. Secondly, the low-vision travel would be taught using different canes, not just the long cane. This would mean more work on other canes than on the MO course. Tutors said the separation between the blindfold work and the low-vision and other cane work was being viewed as an experiment. Thirdly, there would be just one change of mobility tutor at the end of the first term, instead of the two changes on the MO course. Finally, there were to be 20 'teachbacks', ten in each term, which would be three times as many as commonly took place on the MO course. The work on mapping was going to be similar to that on the MO course and had the same amount of time (15 sessions) allocated to it. Mobility theory was going to be spread throughout the course, with an average of about one session every two weeks. This would mean a maximum of 15 sessions, compared with ten on the MO course.

Tutors at the SRAB estimated that students had between three and five mobility sessions each week; a total of between 90 and 150 sessions. This was more than on the MO course (approximately 56 sessions). There was some one-to-one teaching at the beginning, but students soon worked in twos, threes or larger groups. This included practical work, which was not always supervised by tutors. Initially, time was divided between work with the blindfold and low-vision simulation spectacles, but after the input on low vision in the 'eye and low-vision' section, students spent much more time working with low-vision simulation spectacles. (More blindfold work had recently been introduced into the mobility training in response to criticism from placement supervisors and the external assessor for the MO course that students might be unable to teach a totally blind client.) Tutors emphasized the different goals of their mobility training to that at the NMC. They were mainly concerned that students had the ability to motivate clients to try to learn some mobility skills. The tutor with principal responsibility for mobility at the SRAB said that the mobility training had moved even further away from training students themselves in the skills needed to become a long cane traveller and was geared much more to motivating clients. In her view, it mattered less that a client occasionally bumped into something than that they were actually prepared to go out and have a go. Consequently, more time was spent on the motivation and assessment of clients and the development of individually designed mobility training programmes. This took precedence over the teaching of the full long cane training programme.

Daily living skills

The agreed written objectives for this section stated that, on completion of the course, students would be able to:

- demonstrate an ability to:
    assess clients' needs with respect to home
    management, personal care and other daily living
    skills, and design and implement appropriate
    teaching programmes
    teach food preparation, cooking, serving and eating
    skills
    teach personal care, hygiene and grooming skills with
    sensitivity
    teach home care and home management skills;
- describe how a range of household electrical appliances
  work, and teach the safe use of electricity in the home;
- identify ways in which current advances in technology
  could either benefit or disadvantage visually impaired
  people;
- identify, describe, supply and train clients to manage the
  range of aids and equipment which are associated with
  daily living, both specially designed and commercially
  available.

The three agencies had agreed to allocate 75 sessions to daily
living skills.

At the NRAB the daily living skills tutor said that RO and TO
students had almost identical teaching; often they were brought
together for lectures because the two courses were so similar.
However, documentation showed that more than twice as much
time was allocated to daily living skills on the TO course than
on the RO course: 120 sessions and 53 sessions respectively. As
with the TO course, assessment took the form of a workbook
kept by students which contained all written coursework, a
teaching practice, a task analysis, a 'dinner essay' (see Chapter
4) and a resource file.

The NMC provided written documentation which stated that
there were to be a total of 60 sessions; 30 formal lectures and
30 sessions made up of practical sessions and teachbacks. At the
SRAB, the daily living skills tutor said there were approximately
50 sessions on this subject on the new RW course; on the TO
course 62 sessions were allocated. Lectures and seminars were
used as well as practical sessions which involved either role-play
teaching practice sessions with students working in pairs, or all
students wearing blindfolds or low vision simulation spectacles.
The latter were said to be used far more frequently because the
majority of clients had some residual vision. The groupwork
involved students being given a particular task and having to

work out what the potential problems could be for certain client groups. The tutor had dropped the assessment formerly used on the TO course which involved students preparing a three-course meal while wearing a blindfold or low-vision simulation spectacles (i.e. the NRAB's 'dinner essay'). She felt that this was too elaborate for the needs of most visually impaired clients.

Communications

The agreed written objectives for this section stated that, on completion of the course, students would be able to:
- give an account of the evolution of embossed type for visually impaired people;
- demonstrate an ability to:
  assess the communication needs of clients, and design and implement appropriate teaching programmes
  read and write Grade II braille and moon fluently and efficiently
  teach braille and moon fluently and efficiently
  teach braille (Grade II) and moon
  touch-type and teach typewriting skills
  teach handwriting skills
  teach effective verbal communication skills
  teach tape recording skills
- identify, describe, supply and train clients to manage the range of equipment and services associated with communication.

The three agencies had agreed to allocate 85 sessions to communications.

At the NRAB, course documentation indicated that there were approximately 83 sessions on communications. This was far less time than on the TO course at the NRAB, which included 192 sessions. The assessment in each of the communications subjects was similar to that on the TO course. For typing, the tutor taught RO and TO students together (see Chapter 4).

At the NMC, the communications tutor said there were to be approximately 60 sessions on communications: 24 braille; 24 typing; and 12 moon. Some sessions were also timetabled for non-verbal communication and the new work based around computer programmes; and ten visits were planned. Outside speakers would give lectures on adult literacy, children and the multi-handicapped. When planning this module, the tutor had visited the other agencies to try to ensure a similarity between the courses.

At the SRAB, students worked on moon, tape-recording and handwriting in the first term. In the second term they had approximately two sessions on braille and two sessions on typing each week – a total of 60 sessions. These subjects were also allocated approximately 60 sessions on the TO course, but the teaching input on the RW course was virtually absent; students spent most of the time in self-instruction, with the tutor monitoring their progress. Despite this, the new tutor maintained that there was more emphasis on students' ability to teach these skills than on previous SRAB TO courses.

Deaf-blind

The agreed written objectives for this section stated that, on completion of the course, students would be able to:
- demonstrate an ability to communicate effectively, using a range of appropriate methods, with people having a combined impairment of vision and hearing;
- demonstrate an understanding of the problems experienced by visually impaired people who also have a loss of hearing;
- show an appreciation of the implications of the onset of visual impairment before a hearing impairment and vice versa, and demonstrate an ability to deal adequately with these;
- demonstrate an ability to assess the needs of clients having a combined impairment of vision and hearing, and design and implement appropriate training programmes;
- identify, describe, supply and train clients to manage the range of equipment and services designed for people having a combined impairment of vision and hearing.

The three agencies had agreed to allocate 40 sessions to deaf-blind work.

At the NRAB, in preparation for the 'Deaf-blind Week', a total of 11 sessions were timetabled on deaf-blind communication, which included visits to deaf-blind residential units; RO students went on the one-week deaf-blind holiday with the TO students. Assessment procedures were similar for both groups. As well as deaf-blind communication, RO students were expected to practise their mobility and daily living skills on the holiday. The third RO course included a 'Deaf-blind Week' for the first time. The NRAB felt that it served an important function, namely, the establishing of a team spirit which was felt to be conducive to their learning.

The NMC had allocated 13 sessions on the deaf-blind, in which students were to learn the deaf-blind manual and hear various guest speakers. On the MO course the work on the deaf-blind had been included in the audiology section. There were to be a number of role play teaching sessions in which students, taking the part of clients, would wear sight and sound excluders. In addition, each student would be expected to attend a local deaf-blind club for one session and visit deaf-blind centres where they would communicate with the clients. To compensate for what was described as the lack of time scheduled for this module, the tutor intended to show videos on aspects of the course during the lunchbreaks, for which attendance was optional. There was to be no 'Deaf-blind Week'; though the tutor saw the advantages in such a week, the NMC felt it could not spare the time. Students were scheduled to attend a weekend organized by SENSE during which they would run a crèche for multi-handicapped children and young people in the mornings and attend workshops and discussion groups in the afternoons. On the NMC MO course, work on the deaf-blind had been more limited, forming a small part of the audiology section.

At the SRAB there were between 15 and 20 sessions timetabled, in which students learnt but mostly practised their deaf-blind communication skills. There were also a number of role-play teaching practice sessions. A representative from SENSE gave a talk about the deaf-blind. The SRAB had not reinstated the 'Deaf-blind Week' as it still considered this unnecessary (see discussion of the SRAB TO course, Chapter 4). Students were to attend the same SENSE weekend as the NMC students.

Social studies

The agreed written objectives for this section stated that, on completion of the course, students would be able to:
- define 'group dynamics' and explain the roles of group members and patterns of communication within groups;

- demonstrate an ability to implement a rehabilitation group for visually impaired people and to introduce a client into a group for rehabilitation purposes;
- identify and describe reactions to loss and the process of recovery;
- state how attitudes are acquired and identify personal and social attitudes towards visual impairment;
- identify and describe different types of family structure and function and the problems which may arise when one or more members are visually impaired;
- identify the major historical factors which have led to the present system of assistance for visually impaired people;
- demonstrate an understanding of current legislation as it affects visually impaired people;
- discuss the rationale of registration as blind/partially sighted and interpret the information given on a BD8 form;
- identify the benefits and concessions available to visually impaired people, both obligatory and permissive, and how these can be obtained;
- identify, describe and evaluate different types of educational provision for visually impaired people;
- identify and describe training and employment provisions for visually impaired people.

The three agencies had agreed to allocate 42 sessions to social studies.

The NRAB's written course material indicated that 26 sessions had been timetabled, which included some input from outside speakers.

There were lectures, practical exercises, role-play exercises, videos and, most commonly, seminars and group discussions. Sometimes students from all three courses had a social studies session together. On the TO course social studies was allocated 50–70 sessions, although other topics were also included which did not fit in elsewhere.

The NMC said that the time allocated for this section included some overlap with other sections. Course documentation indicated that there were to be 25 teaching sessions, ten sessions allocated to visits and seven sessions of students' study time (total = 42). The section was intended to remain basically the same as on the MO course, with considerably more time spent on each topic; the MO course had allocated three sessions to 'adjustment to visual handicap'.

At the SRAB there was a section described as 'social policy' which seemed to cover both 'social studies' and 'management'. The tutor said that about 26 sessions were scheduled and topics covered included: attitudes to visual impairment; legislation; and relationships between management and worker. More use was made of formal lectures than on other parts of the course, but students were also required to prepare seminar papers. This was a new section at the SRAB, compared with the small number of one-off lectures on the TO course.

Multi-handicap

The agreed written objectives for this section stated that, on completion of the course, students would be able to:
- identify and describe a range of theories of disability;
- show an appreciation of the network of problems created by multi-handicap;
- demonstrate a knowledge of various disabilities and the effect these have on individuals;
- demonstrate an ability to assess the needs of multi-handicapped clients and design and implement appropriate training programmes;
- identify, mobilize and co-ordinate appropriate help from other professionals and agencies.

The three agencies had agreed to allocate 22 sessions to multi-handicap.

The NRAB's course documentation indicated that six sessions were timetabled, most of which were given by outside speakers.

The NMC said that they planned at least 22 sessions, which were all timetabled for term two. Teaching would involve lectures from the tutor and guest speakers; there was also a visit to a multi-handicap club.

A tutor at the SRAB estimated that students would have a total of 12 sessions on this subject. Students would spend much of the time undertaking individual research into different disabilities and would present the results to the rest of the group. Two outside speakers were to give talks on working with the multi-handicapped: one from the point of view of an MO, and the other from the TO side. The main emphasis was to be on the ways of working with these clients, and the other professionals and agencies to be involved. The approach to this subject was said to have changed on the new course. Whereas students on other SRAB courses had been introduced to individual handicaps one after another, there was now much more integration. Client profiles were to be used to present a range of disabilities in relation to one client.

Learning and teaching

The agreed written objectives for this section stated that, on completion of the course, students would be able to:
- identify and evaluate a range of major theories of learning
- demonstrate an ability to:
    interpret and apply this knowledge to a range of learning and teaching styles and methods;
    formulate and implement strategies designed to motivate clients to acquire new skills and to transfer old knowledge into new situations;
    structure and implement sequentially planned teaching programmes, adopting a flexible approach in responding sensitively to client need;
    monitor the learning progress of clients;
    critically analyse his/her own effectiveness in promoting learning;
    recognize the symptoms of, and take steps to alleviate stress or anxiety in a client under instruction.

The three agencies had agreed to allocate 65 sessions to learning and teaching.

The NRAB described this section as 'professional studies' and had timetabled 60 sessions; there were 48 on the TO course. This was an increase over the first RO course. Occasionally the tutor gave a joint session for TOs and ROs, but generally she said that more was expected of RO students. Role-play teaching exercises sometimes involved a TO and an RO. More recently, attempts had been made to link the work with practical skills teaching. This included occasions when the professional studies tutor would be involved in a skills-teaching session. She also said that more emphasis had been placed recently on helping students with 'return to learning' skills.

At the NMC approximately 33 sessions were to be allocated to learning and teaching. This was much more than on the MO course, which had included seven sessions. In addition, some input was planned in practical skills-teaching sessions – for example mobility and daily living skills. The course content on the RW course, it was said, would be similar but would place more emphasis on the practical implications for teaching.

The SRAB was unable to say exactly how many sessions were timetabled for this subject. The Training Officer said that it concentrated on the management of learning and models of learning. He said that he did some work on how to adapt teaching styles to different types of client. The section was divided between lectures on the theory and role-play teaching sessions. The tutor believed that students would only fully appreciate this section when they began the teaching placement, that is when they were expected to teach a variety of real clients.

Client assessment

The agreed written objectives for this section stated that, on completion of the course, students would be able to:
- define 'assessment' and explain its importance and limitations;
- demonstrate a knowledge of different methods of assessment;
- demonstrate an ability to:
    apply appropriate assessment techniques;
    assess the potential of clients to acquire and develop new skills;
    select programmes of instruction appropriate to the needs of individual clients;
- identify other professionals and agencies which may be appropriately involved in the assessment process.

The three agencies had agreed to allocate ten sessions to client assessment.

The NRAB emphasized the need for students to be able to assess all of a client's needs and to develop a teaching programme geared to them. The teaching sought to cover the differing needs of clients of different ages, abilities and possible additional handicaps. Client assessment was also said to be part of the practical skills sessions.

At the NMC this module was a new development; eight sessions were allocated. The tutor said that she planned to give introductory and concluding lectures, between which outside speakers would give five sessions, each on the assessment of different client groups. A final session would be held on students' return from placement. The tutor pointed out that aspects of client assessment could also be covered in other topics – for example the assessment of a client for typing would be covered by the communications tutor.

At the SRAB, this section was referred to as 'assessment and rehabilitation'. It was said to include models of disability and perceptions of disability and to pose the question: 'What is rehabilitation?' There was more input, estimated at about seven sessions, on this section than on previous SRAB courses. In addition to these separate sessions, there was said to be some overlap with other subjects.

Management

The agreed written objectives for this section stated that, on completion of the course, students would be able to:
- demonstrate an understanding of:
    the role and function of management in voluntary and statutory agencies;
    supervision and the ways in which it can be effectively utilized;
    the effects of change in organizations and the individuals within them;
    caseload and time management, and the principles involved in decision-making and setting priorities;
    budgeting, negotiation and resource management and skills necessary for public speaking;
- describe the role of committees in the functioning of voluntary and statutory agencies;
- identify and describe the functions of the separate officers and members of a committee;
- demonstrate an ability to:
    organize a meeting and record proceedings;
    write coherent reports and keep efficient records;
    design and implement training courses for different groups of workers;
- demonstrate a knowledge of staff training resources;
- describe ways in which volunteer help can be utilized and supervised.

The three agencies had agreed to allocate 25 sessions to management.

At the NRAB, course documentation indicated that there were ten timetabled sessions given by tutors and outside speakers on management. Previously it had not been presented as an identifiably separate section. There was said to be some overlap between this section and the one on social studies. Topics covered included: use of volunteers; the role of voluntary societies; interviewing techniques; caseload management; record-keeping; public speaking; and the role and functioning of committees.

The NMC said that this section was effectively an extension of the 'social services day' on the MO course. Course documentation stated that there would be 17 sessions made up of lectures and seminars given by tutors and guest speakers. The topics to be covered were: development of public speaking skills; purpose and organization of meetings; structure and function of social services departments; managing a specialist team; voluntary agencies and the visually impaired; role, function and procedures of committees; organizational change; working with volunteers; decision-making and priority-setting; record-keeping and report-writing; supervision and accountability; and the training of non-specialist personnel.

The SRAB scheduled weekly sessions on this topic during the first term. A particular emphasis was on the relationship between management and rehabilitation theories. Other topics included: supervision; the management of time; and negotiations. Again, there was more input than on previous SRAB courses.

Recreation and leisure

The agreed written objectives for the section stated that, on completion of the course, students would be able to:
- identify and describe a range of recreational activities suitable for a variety of clients;
- identify a range of organizations which provide resources for recreation and leisure;
- demonstrate an ability to assess the suitability of specific leisure activities for individual clients, and to facilitate access to these activities.

The three agencies had agreed to allocate nine sessions to recreation and leisure.

The NRAB had not previously had a section on recreation and leisure although one-off lectures were given by guest speakers. Course documentation indicated that there were five sessions on the RO course, given by tutors and outside speakers.

The NMC had ten sessions timetabled. The tutor with responsibility for this subject felt that it was an important area which tended to be the first to be cut on the MO course if time was short. The section was similar to that introduced on the MO course: there were two lectures, the rest of the time was taken up with practical sessions. Activities, during which students wore blindfolds or low-vision simulation spectacles, ranged from keep-fit to outdoor activities such as archery and golf. There were also weekend fieldtrips during which students experienced canoeing, climbing and camping wearing blindfolds; the purpose was to demonstrate to students that visually impaired people can lead active lives.

Counselling/interpersonal skills

The agreed written objectives for this section stated that, on completion of the course, students would be able to:
- demonstrate an ability to practise effective counselling skills, in both group and individual circumstances;
- identify agencies which undertake counselling, and show an appreciation of realistic timing and means of client referral to these agencies in appropriate cases;
- identify factors which can influence an interview and demonstrate an ability to undertake an interview in both formal and informal settings;
- identify various forms of non-verbal communication and describe the ways in which these are used;
- describe common difficulties experienced in non-verbal communication by both sighted and visually impaired people.

The three agencies had agreed to allocate 27 sessions to counselling.

The NRAB tutor with responsibility for counselling was unable to say exactly how many counselling sessions there were, but estimated that it would amount to about seven and a half days (equivalent to 37-8 sessions). The tutor explained that students did not have weekly sessions but instead,would have a half-day every few weeks. There were four sessions on counselling on the NRAB TO course, mainly conducted by outside tutors. Teaching was now the responsibility of a new NRAB tutor who had counselling qualifications and experience.

The NMC planned to schedule 13 sessions, compared with five sessions on the MO course. The new Principal said this was adequate and explained that it was not the intention to make the students into good counsellors, but to make them aware of certain basic issues. A part-time counsellor, who was partially sighted, had been invited to give ten sessions on the course; an NMC tutor was to give introductory and concluding sessions. The latter was to take place after the placement.

The SRAB said that this section began in week five, from which point students had two sessions per week, giving a total of 50 sessions and representing a huge increase on previous SRAB courses. A new tutor, who had taken a short course in counselling, was responsible for the module. She described it as the link between the various sections of the course; the course philosophy revolved around building relationships with others. Emphasis was placed on: making students aware of how a good worker–client relationship helps the skills teaching; interpersonal skills; and the student/worker's limitations as a counsellor. A number of role-play teaching exercises took place.

Placement

The training agencies had agreed a ten week placement. The NRAB followed the procedures established for its TO and MO courses, with a two-day course for supervisors, pre-placement meetings between the relevant parties, an agreed placement programme and the fieldwork placement guide. Since the RO course began most students had been placed with dual qualified workers in social services departments. The NRAB was keen that students gained some appreciation of the range of activities and responsibilities of social services departments. It was also considered important that students had direct experience of the initial contact between a visually impaired person and the social services, specifically the registration process. Because of this, only a limited number of placements in voluntary societies were considered potentially suitable. However, the NRAB on the 1987–8 course experienced more problems than usual in finding enough placements which were acceptable. This seemed to be linked to the increased number of students on the course (16).

The NMC planned to use the same supervisors for the RW course as previously, wherever possible. In cases where a worker was only MO-trained, the NMC said it would look for a TO working in the same team or area to contribute to the supervision. Placements would be in a range of environments –

social services, institutions and schools. The problem of social services requiring students to be car drivers remained. The placement for the new RW course was two weeks shorter than that on the MO course. For the past two years placement supervisors had been invited to the NMC for the day to talk to students and tutors. The new Principal gave a short session on the nature of supervision. It was hoped that this input for supervisors could be extended. Guidelines issued to supervisors were similar to those for MO placements.

The SRAB said that the main difference in the RW placement was that they were looking for supervisors who were dual trained or for a working environment in which both a TO and MO were employed, preferably in social services departments. There was no training of supervisors, but this was something that was under consideration. The Training Officer felt that the key was to find the right formula for such training sessions. There was said to have been no difficulty arranging placements, which would usually be in social services departments. There was no problem concerning students' ownership of transport, but the SRAB did make the point that efforts would be made to arrange placements for visually impaired students in urban areas.

Project

The NRAB required RO students on placement to produce a case study of a client they had worked with or a project. Examples of the latter, which the NRAB outlined in their original RO assessment booklet, were:
- setting up a volunteer group;
- organizing a specific activity for a group of visually handicapped clients;
- integrating a particular client into a sighted group (this should not be just a description of the activity, but show an understanding of the theory used).

The NMC required students to submit a project, as on the MO course, but this now had to be completed before students went on placement.

The SRAB RW students also had to do a project although reservations about the usefulness of the exercise (see Chapter 4) remained. It was emphasized that tutors had to ensure that students covered areas which would be useful in their future work – for example a teaching pack. Students were encouraged to complete as much of the project work as possible during their time at the SRAB so as not to have too much to do on the placement.

Assessment

Each of the training agencies produced their own written assessment schedule.[1] At the NRAB, RO students were required to keep resource files (containing all relevant material gathered during the course) for each subject. Also a new procedure was introduced for assessing student attitudes. This was based on tutors' perceptions of the students, following certain criteria. Otherwise assessment remained similar to that introduced for the original RO course.

At the NMC there was to be a move away from examinations on the RW course. Three subjects were to retain examinations: mobility; eye and low-vision; and audiology. The new Principal said that in mobility 50 per cent of the marks were on the written examination, 25 per cent on the teachbacks and 25 per cent on the notebooks. In the eye and low vision and audiology, 25 per cent of the marks would be based on the preparation and presentation of a seminar; 75 per cent on the written examination. Examinations were scheduled at the end of the course rather than immediately after each subject block. This represented a return to the system the NMC had operated formerly. Instead of an examination in learning and teaching, students would be required to present an essay. The NMC said that, in agreement with the regional associations, there would also be an assessed essay for the social studies section. The tutor said that the list of possible titles included topics from the management section. For practical mobility, in addition to a solo city centre journey under blindfold (as on the MO course), students were to undertake an outside exercise wearing low-vision simulation spectacles – for example a shopping trip to a supermarket.

The SRAB said that in the assessment of students there was much more emphasis on a student's ability to teach certain skills on the RW course. There was also more written work required: five assignments plus a project. The assignments were intended to draw the different elements of the course together.

---

1 Copies of these schedules are available on request from the authors.

RO/RW student characteristics and recruitment

Student numbers

Each of the three centres was asked to supply basic information on the students on the 1987/8 RO/RW courses (for the NRAB this was the third group of RO students). The student numbers at the start were: eight at the NMC; nine at the SRAB; and 16 at the NRAB. However, each centre had lost some students early in the course: the NMC had two students who left (one of whom was said to be unable to cope with the long cane training under blindfold); the NRAB had lost three (one was said to have found the academic work too demanding); and the SRAB had lost two (one on maternity leave, and an overseas student who had insufficient funds to complete the course – both were expected to return to complete the course in the future). Thus the eventual numbers were: NMC, six; SRAB, seven; and NRAB, 13.

Numbers at the NMC were said to be lower than on MO courses because of their move to new premises. In future it was hoped to accept more students, up to a maximum of ten which its commitment to one-to-one practical mobility teaching imposed. The NRAB said that 16 was the maximum number that it could accept on a course. The SRAB felt that a group of nine students was large enough for the first course because of the inevitable teething problems that would arise. However, in addition to the students taking the full RW course, others, who already possessed a TO or MO qualification, had been accepted to do part of the RW course (depending on what qualification they already had) in order to qualify for RW status. This obviously raises questions about the integrated nature of the skills training since these students were not staying for the full academic year.

Entry requirements

The course pamphlet stated that:
- candidates should normally have completed the training between the ages 21–45 years;
- candidates must demonstrate an ability to study at A-level standard;

- candidates must meet the appropriate temperamental, physical, sensory and medical requirements in order to complete the training course and carry out the subsequent work;
- candidates should be aware that training and practice can be exhausting, both physically and emotionally; training may have to be given outdoors in all weather conditions.

These requirements were almost identical to the criteria established for the original NRAB RO course, the main difference being that candidates should normally be under 45 rather than 50. The requirement regarding A-level standard was new to both the NMC and the SRAB.

Information available to applicants

A course pamphlet had been prepared. This was very brief, containing an outline of the role of a rehabilitation worker, a statement of the agreed course aims, a brief outline of the methods of assessment and details of the application procedure. Course objectives were not included; these were available on request from each of the training agencies.

Interviewing

Each centre had its own interview procedures and saw only those students who applied to it. The NRAB maintained the system they used on the other courses (see Chapter 3). At the NMC, since the appointment of the new Principal, two members of staff – usually the new Principal and deputy – conducted the formal interviews. Applicants still were blindfolded and given some basic orientation exercises but they were now also required to do a written piece of work, which was used to assess their command of written English and general academic ability. At the SRAB the formal interview remained the same, as did the requirement of a written piece of work. However, the informal session which preceded the panel interview had changed considerably. It involved a series of group exercises, said to be similar to the management games industrial organizations and others use as part of their selection procedures. In these, tutors observed and assessed applicants on their contribution to the sessions, their interactions with the group and the general attitudes they exhibited.

Visually impaired applicants

Both the NMC and the NRAB said that they would not accept visually impaired applicants on their courses. In both cases, the reason given was that they felt they lacked the necessary expertise and were therefore unable to offer the mobility component to such students. The NRAB suggested that the three training agencies needed to find a way of allowing visually impaired people to obtain an RO Certificate which did not involve taking the mobility component and yet was not, as a consequence, regarded as a second-class qualification. The SRAB took a different view and explicitly rejected the notion that the training agencies lacked the necessary expertise to teach visually impaired students to be mobility instructors. It was suggested that what was lacking was not the expertise but the willingness to tackle the subject. The SRAB said it would accept students with a visual impairment who had a reasonable chance of passing the mobility component and, indeed, had two visually impaired students on the first RW course. Also a qualified TO, who had a visual impairment, had been accepted to do the MO component of the first RW course. It was envisaged that the teaching of a visually impaired student would involve different strategies (for example with the tutor staying nearer to the student) but that this would not be an insurmountable problem. Having said that, visually impaired applicants were said to need a certain amount of residual vision to be accepted on the course. The three training agencies had agreed that, in the immediate future, no totally blind person would be accepted for the RO/RW or MO courses.

Student characteristics

Over two-thirds of the students were female (19 female and seven male students). Thirteen students were aged between 20 and 30, 11 between 31 and 40, one between 41 and 50 and one student (at the NMC) was over 51 years of age.

Work experience

Four of the NMC students had some previous experience of working with the visually impaired; in two cases, this was with people with additional handicaps, and the other two, including one in a voluntary capacity, had worked in rehabilitation centres for the visually impaired. The two remaining students had social/welfare service experience, one as a general social work assistant and the other working with the elderly and handicapped.

At the NRAB, there were four students who had worked with visually impaired people. Of these, two had been home visitors (one for the deaf-blind) and two had worked for local voluntary societies for the blind (one as a projects officer and one as a voluntary worker/receptionist). Five students had some social/welfare service experience: a child care officer; a social work visitor; a welfare assistant; an instructor at a social education centre; and one who had spent time prior to joining the course as a trainee rehabilitation worker in her sponsoring authority. Four students had no relevant work experience.

At the SRAB, two students had worked previously with visually impaired people. Both were employed by voluntary societies and one had also worked as an ophthalmic nurse. Two students had some social/welfare service experience: one with young people and one assisting occupational therapists. Three students had no relevant work experience.

Education and other training

At the NMC, two students had degrees and one had A- level qualifications. Of the remaining three, one had a CSS, one was a registered general nurse and one had O-levels.

At the NRAB, eight students were qualified at A-level standard or above. Two of these held an additional social/welfare service qualification (counselling; deaf-blind communication) and one held a vocational qualification (dental nurse). Of the remaining students, two had social/welfare service qualifications (both CSS) and one had a vocational qualification (police). Two students were qualified to O-level standard.

At the SRAB, four students had higher education qualifications. Of these, three had additional social/welfare service qualifications (diploma in social administration; certificate in social work; occupational therapist's helper course) and one had a vocational qualification (lawyer). Of the other students, one had vocational qualifications (state-enrolled nurse and ophthalmic nurse), one student had O-levels and one had no formal qualifications.

NRAB RO students' views on the course

Students on the first NRAB RO course were interviewed by the project team. The following is a brief summary of their comments on the training.

Generally the students were concerned that the course was too short. They found that they had not had sufficient time to assimilate fully what was being taught before moving on to a new topic. The private study sessions and written handouts which tutors often issued to accompany lectures were welcomed but were not sufficient to overcome this problem. Students also criticized the lack of planning on the course. Apparently, students and staff received a timetable for a three-week period only; and towards the end of this period, a timetable for the following three weeks was issued. Students also said they received little feedback from staff regarding their progress, which they found disconcerting.

On the practical skills teaching, students expressed most satisfaction with the mobility section. Most work was done using a blindfold and some students would have liked more work with low-vision simulation spectacles. In daily living skills students could choose to use a blindfold or low-vision simulation spectacles for practical work – most chose a blindfold because they found it easier. Students still complained of there being more emphasis on learning the skills themselves than on learning how to teach those skills to others, particularly in relation to communications. The video was used to record students' performances in practical sessions, and this was generally felt to be very helpful. Students said they had experienced problems in role-play teaching practice sessions trying to act the part of clients. They commented that these sessions were unrealistic and had not given them enough experience of teaching the skills they had learnt. They would have liked some experience of teaching people who were visually impaired.

10 Analysis and Recommendations

This report has described in detail the MO and TO courses provided by the NMC and the regional associations for the blind; it has also presented the views of students and workers on the training they received and described at length the work and working environment of visual impairment specialists. This suggests three perspectives within which to examine the training: the objectives of the courses; the implications of workers' and students' views; and the demands of the workplace. The bulk of this chapter is concerned with these three strands as they relate to each of the training courses. Some of the points that emerge relate to one particular course or training centre; others, particularly those pertaining to the demands of the job, apply to two or all three training centres. The inevitable overlap serves to highlight some of the general issues which are returned to in a final section on recommendations.

TO training

Daily living skills

Judged by its own objectives, namely that students should have a knowledge of aids, resources and techniques to enable clients to live an independent life, the daily living skills module at the NRAB appears to have been successful. Workers trained at the NRAB were generally satisfied that the course had been effective in preparing them to teach a daily living skills programme, although a number felt that the training had been a little rigid in its suggestion that there was only one way of performing each task. Both workers and students commented unfavourably on the tutor's teaching style, and expressed dissatisfaction that she had not had experience of working with visually impaired people.

The objectives of this module at the SRAB were not set out. However, the training appears to have been less satisfactory than that on the NRAB course. Students' criticisms reflected comments made by workers who had been trained at the SRAB over the years, and therefore cannot be easily dismissed. The main problem was said to be the lack of actual teaching. It was felt by some that there may well have been certain advantages in students attempting tasks themselves while wearing blindfolds or low-vision simulation spectacles – for example showing that there could be many acceptable ways of performing a task or making them understand that clients could, and in many cases would, have managed to accomplish certain tasks without assistance. However, many workers and students felt that the potential benefits of such a discovery-learning approach to daily living skills were lost through lack of follow-up discussion between students and tutor. They felt the importance of sharing experiences had not been capitalized on and that important practical and teaching points had been missed. Some workers also felt that more role-play of client/worker interaction would have been useful.

Looking at the daily living skills training in the light of the work of a TO, it seems that both agencies devoted too much time to advanced skills which were rarely, if ever, called upon – for example the 'dinner essay' assessment which involved students preparing a three-course meal while wearing a blindfold or simulation spectacles. Three-quarters of TOs interviewed had not taught a daily living skills programme; the great majority of clients required only tactile marking of cookers and advice on making a hot drink.

There were two main reasons for this situation. First, clients were generally elderly and most had other arrangements for dealing with daily living skills tasks, i.e., home-helps, meals-on-wheels services and help from family and friends. Because of this, workers found that many were not motivated to tackle these things for themselves. Secondly, workers found that because a great many people had some residual vision and, moreover, had been losing their sight gradually over a period of time, they had learned to adapt. Also, it was believed that clients' confidence in themselves were more important than trying to teach them a new method at a later stage.

These experiences would suggest that cooking, cleaning, ironing, personal care and so on were overemphasized in the training, particularly on the NRAB course. Although the tutor at the NRAB recognized the need for basic 'survival' techniques and the importance of focusing on the needs of individual clients, this had not come across in the training. In addition, too much emphasis was placed on total blindness as opposed to low vision; more advice on the modifications which would be necessary for working with clients with low vision should have been given. As it was, many workers said that they had developed their knowledge in this area after qualifying – often by watching how clients themselves managed. Although the training at the NRAB and the SRAB had included more low-vision work in recent courses, more is still needed. Finally, there would seem to be little point in students becoming proficient in carrying out daily living tasks without sight; rather the emphasis should be on the development of the relevant teaching skills. This criticism applies to much of the training and is discussed in the relevant sections elsewhere in this chapter.

Communications

The specified objectives of the NRAB communications module were generally achieved; by the end of the course it appeared that students had a knowledge of the range of aids and resources for reading and writing, the ability to read and write braille and moon up to Grade II standard, a knowledge of basic touch-typing and the ability to use a range of communication methods with deaf-blind people.

However, workers were critical of the lack of teaching in how to set about teaching braille, moon and typing to clients; again, they said that far too much emphasis had been placed on learning the skills and not enough on how to teach these to clients. Also workers were critical of the lack of formal teaching in the subjects. Students complained of having been left to get on with learning the communications skills on their own.

At the SRAB, although the objectives of the communications module were not sct down, the assessment tasks were all concerned with ensuring students' proficiency in braille, moon and typing. This was indeed achieved; both students and workers commented on the high standards that were required of them but, as with their NRAB colleagues, there was strong criticism from them that there was too much emphasis on learning the skills and too little on the teaching approaches that would be required when working with clients. Students said that although teaching skills were sometimes scheduled for the last half hour of the braille sessions, these were omitted if time was pressing. Similarly in typing, the tutor concentrated on developing students' own typing skills rather than on teaching skills. In the absence of such training, TOs who did any work on these subjects said that they improvised as the need arose. Also a number of TOs said that without practice it was not possible to maintain the standard that they had achieved on the course, but that in any case this did not matter, as it was always possible to keep one lesson ahead in the RNIB *Braille Primer* when teaching a client who progressed beyond the elementary stages.

From the perspective of the workplace, there was virtually no demand for these skills from clients. TOs from both the NRAB and the SRAB expressed strong criticisms regarding the mismatch between the amount of time spent on communications subjects in their training and the minimal work required on this in their job. They reported that clients, most of whom were elderly, were not interested in learning either braille or moon, other than perhaps for the tactile markings in the home. Most said that their clients found it easier and more enjoyable to listen to a talking book. Typing was similarly in limited demand; commonly only younger visually impaired people had any use for this, often in connection with employment, but young clients were far less common.

In the light of this situation, the SRAB Training Officer's decision to cut down the amount of course time devoted to braille seems reasonable. While there will always be a certain number of clients who will require instruction in communication skills, their predominance in the training (especially at the NRAB where just under half of the formal teaching was taken up with communications) needs to be reconsidered. Finally, it perhaps needs to be said that many TOs found that moon was more suitable for elderly people owing to their often impaired sense of touch, yet little time was spent on this at either training centre. Although moon is reported to be very simple for students to learn, there is scope for including some sessions on the teaching of moon to clients.

The objectives of the deaf-blind training at both the NRAB and the SRAB were linked to the development of appropriate communication skills. However, the objectives of the 'Deaf-blind Week' organized by the NRAB were only partly linked to the development of deaf-blind communications skills; tutors saw it as a means of experiencing one-to-one contact with clients and developing a sense of group identity among students. The SRAB could see no rationale for having a 'Deaf-blind Week' and had dropped it from the course. Both workers and students trained at the NRAB spoke of the week very favourably, indicating that they found it extremely challenging but they had gained invaluable experience of the particular problems of this client group.

From the perspective of the workplace, TOs said they had few deaf-blind clients, and that most of those were not so severly handicapped that they needed to use deaf-blind communications methods. On this basis, the week the NRAB allocated in addition to time on the course is difficult to justify. If, however, the advantages of the week lie in the nature of the experience – being thrown in at the deep end with clients and required to demonstrate interpersonal, communication and organizational skills – it would be useful for the training centres to explore the possibility of arranging a period (or periods) of extended contact with people who reflect more accurately the client group workers will encounter in their job.

Social and other studies

At the NRAB, given the time allocation of only two sessions per week, the objectives of the social and other studies component were extremely ambitious. A wide range of areas were addressed: psycho-social aspects of visual impairment; non-verbal communication; group dynamics; self-management skills required to fulfil a professional role; interviewing; counselling; case-recording; the legislation, organization, personnel and role of the personal social services, and it is not surprising that the objectives were not fully realized. In particular, workers and students were critical that two key elements of this module, social services and counselling, had not been covered adequately. (These two subjects are dealt with separately for the purposes of this analysis.)

Regarding social services, NRAB TOs said that they had very little idea before they started work of what to expect. Many felt that the course had given them very little preparation for the environment in which they would be working and had had to find out once they started about such aspects as the organization, personnel and administration in social services departments. Students had similar comments to make on these aspects and some felt that they had not gained the maximum benefit from their placements because they did not know enough beforehand about the general organization and procedures in social services. Also, the initial registration process of visually impaired people was felt by students to have been covered inadequately. They were critical of the limited time spent on client assessment – for example one session spent looking at a blank BD8 form was all the training they were given on how to make a practical assessment based on it.

At the SRAB, the objectives were again not set out, but what teaching was given on social services appeared to be inadequate; the SRAB TOs had similar comments to make to those who had trained at the NRAB. They maintained that they had not been given a sufficient grounding in what social services departments involved – i.e. what their role ought to be within them, the relationships with other workers, administrative procedures, client benefits, and so on.

It hardly needs to be said that such preparation is essential. Taken from the perspective of the workplace, two main points arise. First, many TOs found upon starting work that there were no existing arrangements regarding how their job was to be organized, either practically or administratively. Even where systems were already in operation, the infrequent and non-specialist nature of the supervision, in many cases, meant that workers had a great deal of personal autonomy. Thus areas such as caseload management, prioritizing work, initial registration visits and record-keeping were commonly the sole responsibility of the worker. In view of this, it seems that they need to be covered more fully in both the NRAB and SRAB courses. While recognizing that time is limited, the amount of work on these elements does not reflect their importance on the job. Secondly, it seems that workers were not functioning as fully integrated members of social services departments. Although the majority were formally based in some sort of team structure, in practice few were operating as part of a team. Again, the social studies section did not seem to have prepared workers for this reality, nor did it emphasize that they would need to take an active part in establishing good working relationships with social services colleagues and informing other workers of their role.

Counselling

The objective of the NRAB counselling component was for students 'to have an ability to undertake interviewing and counselling'. The four sessions were intended to develop an awareness of: what was meant by counselling; the skills involved; the worker's limitations; and when to refer a client on for more expert help. However, it appears that even these limited goals were not achieved. There was evident confusion among workers over what counselling was and the delineation between their role and that of social workers regarding the counselling of visually impaired people. The majority of NRAB-trained TOs said that they did not feel equipped to counsel clients, a view echoed by students completing their training. Some workers were also concerned that the sessions provided by the marriage guidance counsellor had been too general, and that they should have focused more on the specific counselling needs of visually impaired people.

On the SRAB TO course a counselling section had been introduced recently. However, with no one to teach the module it was reduced from the planned 18 hours to just one lecture and a video. Clearly, this was not enough to meet the objectives of introducing the section on counselling. SRAB-trained TOs were critical of the fact that they had received no training in the subject. Similarly, students expressed great concern that they had completed the course yet had barely had an introduction to what counselling involved.

As far as the work itself is concerned, there is a clear need for counselling skills. The vast majority of TOs said that they took on a counselling role, despite feeling that they had not been trained to do this. Some felt that counselling their clients, at least in connection with their visual impairment, was part of their job and did the best they could; others found that they could not avoid becoming involved because clients drew them into the situation. Others reluctantly took on some sort of counselling role because there was no one else willing to do it – many felt that social workers saw all work with the visually impaired, including counselling, as part of the specialist's role. Few workers were of the opinion that counselling and rehabilitation did not mix, and even here it was not clear that, in practice, they were avoiding counselling altogether. Moreover, although these people said that where counselling was needed they would refer the client to a social worker, few of the workers interviewed reported doing this in practice.

There can be no doubt that some training in counselling skills is needed. Until recently, the training centres have been reluctant to develop this side of the training. This may stem partly from their lack of professional expertise in the subject, but it also reflects a long-standing belief that they are in the business of skills training and that counselling is the job of social workers. This is a debate which goes beyond the scope of this inquiry. Nevertheless, the current situation, in which workers become involved in counselling clients even though they have had little or no training, must be remedied.

Client motivation is related to this area of the job. Workers reported that lack of motivation in clients was one of the main factors affecting the limited demand for skills teaching. Yet little or no training was given in even the most basic inter-personal skills. Many workers said they attempted to motivate clients by introducing low-vision aids or trying to restore confidence through achieving success in a small task. They found that often this led on to more advanced training. Other workers did little or nothing to motivate clients. Indeed it seems likely that some clients were put off by being approached at the wrong time.

Clearly, the courses need to develop students' awareness of what is involved: the lack of motivation they will encounter; the possible causes; and the strategies which can be used sometimes to overcome the problem. Moreover, students need training in order to be able to recognize the appropriate time to introduce the idea of a programme of learning to a client.

Mobility

At the NRAB, the limited aims of the mobility component were generally achieved. The nine practical sessions covered sighted guide and guide cane techniques. Students worked on a one-to-one basis with the tutor, receiving a practical demonstration after which they had to practice the same wearing a blindfold or low-vision simulation spectacles. Seminars and lectures covered the importance of hearing, the use of other senses, the environment and low vision. One session on the long cane was also given. Workers and students seemed to have found this work acceptable.

The SRAB work on mobility also seems to have achieved its objectives. Students felt that the training had been thorough, and welcomed the fact that it had involved learning how to teach the client. Also they commented favourably on the fact that the time spent practising with low-vision simulation spectacles was equal to that spent wearing a blindfold.

Most TOs found very little need for teaching indoor mobility in the home because clients had generally adapted over a period of time to their loss of sight. However, the skills learned were useful when a client had moved house or into residential accommodation. Some TOs found that they used their indoor mobility and sighted guide training to teach clients' families. It would seem therefore that the limited amount of work on indoor mobility at each centre was pitched at the right level.

Learning and teaching

At the NRAB a separate module had recently been introduced on learning and teaching. However, it seems unlikely that it achieved its objectives, since students appeared to have failed to make the connection between the work in this module, which was mainly theoretical, and the practical job which they would be doing. This theoretical approach, combined with the introduction of an extensive amount of information in each session and the scheduling of the two sessions consecutively, seems to have offset much of the potential benefit. The work on task analysis was felt by students to have been overemphasized and laboriously taught and only one student eventually saw its significance to the job. Generally students felt that the work should have been integrated with the practical skills teaching on the course.

The NRAB course also incorporated role-play teaching exercises which were intended to develop students' teaching skills. However, workers and students did not find these particularly useful. One of the criticisms they made was that they were totally unrealistic because the students they were teaching already knew how to do the task. Moreover, the fact that most students had little or no experience of visually impaired people made it all the more difficult for them to imitate the problems that a real client was likely to present. Yet despite their criticisms, some students felt that more teaching exercises would have been useful in the absence of anything more relevant.

In subsequent TO courses the NRAB has modified the original teaching format. The tutor, recognizing the problems that students encountered owing to the way in which the theory was presented in isolation, has sought to integrate elements of the theory with some of the practical skills teaching. This has involved co-operative working with other members of staff. Also the tutor has sought to make the task analysis work more relevant by linking this each time with the learning of a particular skill. Although we are not in a position to comment on the success of these changes, they would appear to represent a significant improvement on the original structure of the learning and teaching section.

At the SRAB the lectures on learning and teaching formed part of the 'other studies' section. In addition, the practical skills training incorporated a limited number of role-play teaching exercises. Workers and students held very similar views to those who had trained at the NRAB on this work. They said that the course had failed to give adequate training in teaching skills and questioned the value of the role play which they felt was too superficial. Yet they too felt that more work along these lines was needed.

Obviously the work of a TO requires teaching skills and the training centres expressed their awareness of this. However, it seems that different sorts of experiences need to be introduced into the training before students feel that they are prepared as teachers/instructors. Clearly, the way most of them learn the teaching skills at the moment is by picking them up as they go along through their contact with clients. It would therefore be useful if this type of experience could be incorporated into the training. Although this is in part the purpose of the placement, there seems to be a need for more structured experiences of this kind to be introduced earlier in the course, possibly through observation visits or a short placement before the main placement (see later comments on NRAB MO training).

Low vision and medical studies

On the NRAB course, TOs did not have a separate section on low vision. What work was done on this was included in 'medical studies' which was allocated just six sessions, mainly given by outside speakers. In these six sessions it was intended that students would: gain a knowledge of medical disorders accompanying visual impairment; learn to assess vision both clinically and functionally; understand the visual system, visual disorders and their consequences; be able to make the best use of poor vision using light, size, contrast and vision training; understand the structure and function of the hearing system, hearing disorders and their consequences; be able to operate strategies to make the best use of poor hearing; and gain a knowledge of appropriate resources for making the best use of vision and hearing and how to obtain these. This set of objectives was totally unrealistic for six teaching sessions and was not achieved.

This module was a good example of workers' and students' criticism that the course had tried to cover too much in too little time. Also, students said that the objective relating to making the best use of poor vision had barely been touched on.

At the SRAB, far more emphasis was placed on these subjects. Two separate modules existed, one dealing with medical aspects and audiology and the other with low vision. The development of the low-vision work from the original short module on ophthalmology was a recent initiative. It sought to give students training in low-vision assessment and the selection of appropriate low-vision aids to suit the needs of individual clients. It appears that the module had gone a long way towards achieving these objectives. The students indicated an awareness of the importance of client assessment and the differences involved in training clients who had residual vision. They also felt that this part of the course had been very important and that they had learned a great deal. However, most expressed concern that the module had been pitched at too high an academic level and that too much of the work had been on clinical rather than functional assessment of vision. In addition, they felt that more time was needed to cover adequately what they saw as one of the most important elements of the course.

Viewed from the demands of the workplace, it was evident that understanding low vision was essential to the job. Workers reported that the vast majority of their clients not only had remaining vision, but often to a degree which rendered the skills they had learned under blindfold of little use. They described feeling prepared for the job until starting work, at which time they realized that they lacked many of the necessary skills. These included making a functional assessment of clients' remaining vision, selecting low-vision aids and planning appropriate training. Most TOs said that they had had to pick up what was involved along the way, often from clients themselves, rather than being trained to do this on the TO course.

It was evident from workers' comments that they found it difficult to adapt the blindfold work they had done on the course to suit the training needs of clients with low vision. Therefore, the NRAB and SRAB courses need to respond to this situation. First, the blindfold work could be reduced and low-vision simulation spectacles used more in the practical training to give students more idea of their clients' problems. More important however, the training needs to include much more on low-vision assessment, for without a proper assessment the ensuing work with clients is unlikely to be as effective as it otherwise might be. Finally, advice and training are needed in the ways of making the best use of remaining vision. The SRAB course has made considerable progress in these aspects. The NRAB had introduced some work on low vision in recent courses, but needs to do much more.

Placement

The NRAB specified two major objectives of the placement: 'to meet the individual student's needs and to offer varied and relevant work experiences'. The NRAB took certain steps to try to ensure that these objectives were achieved, arranging a meeting in advance of the placement between a tutor, the student and the placement supervisor in which a placement programme was agreed. However, the NRAB itself acknowledged that, once on the placement, students were dependent on having a good supervisor. While most of the students felt that they had learned a lot from the placement, the general view was that it needed to be longer in order to develop the teaching which they started with clients. Several of them were unhappy about the limited number of clients they saw and the lack of teaching experience they had. Others expressed feelings of surprise and confusion about social services departments, in general, and about the nature of the work which took place with clients, i.e. the amount of 'social work', as opposed to skills teaching.

SRAB students had very similar comments to make to those at the NRAB. Although the placement on the SRAB course was a week longer, students said that they would have benefited from a longer placement to provide a wider experience of clients and working practices. They felt that experience with just two or three clients was inadequate and that they should have had more contact time with them.

It would seem that part of the problem with the placements lies in the training centres' almost total absence of involvement in, or monitoring of, the placements while they are in progress. Most students received only one visit from a tutor during their placement and even this did not usually involve observation of the student working with a client. Since both training centres place such great emphasis on developing students' teaching skills, it seems that they are neglecting a valuable opportunity of assessing these skills in a practical situation. After all, the placement supervisor is not in a position to compare the student's performance on the course with their placement work, nor to establish whether what has been taught on the course has been absorbed and is being put into practice. Also, informal discussions have revealed that supervisors find it extremely difficult to assess students and are reluctant to tell the training centre when they feel a student is failing. As for the number of clients seen by students and the level of supervision they receive, these are decisions which the training centre should at least be involved in – they therefore need to monitor the placement much more closely while it is in progress.

Finally, although approximately two-thirds of placements from each of the centres were in social services departments, such placements should be the norm, certainly for those students who will be working for social services after qualifying. Given the confusion which existed among students regarding the structure and functioning of these departments, the opportunity to gain first hand experience of them during the training period is very important.

MO training

Orientation and mobility

At the NMC, the daily practical training in long cane mobility under blindfold was only partially successful in achieving its objectives. Qualified MOs felt that the course had not equipped them to adapt the system to suit individual clients' mobility needs. They described the course as giving them excellent training in using the long cane themselves, but were very critical that it had not prepared them to begin teaching this to clients. Most felt that there should have been more 'teachback' sessions incorporated into the practical training, although some felt that these practices were not sufficiently realistic because they involved teaching other students who already knew how to do the task being taught. The second major criticism workers made of the practical training was that it failed to address the mobility training needs of people with low vision. Workers also felt that more training should have been given in the use of other canes and low-vision mobility aids.

Students' views echoed those of the workers. First, they were unhappy that most of the training had involved the use of the blindfold rather than low-vision simulation spectacles, especially as the latter were usually used to go over a route which had already been covered with a blindfold. However, they emphasized that simply incorporating more work with low-vision simulation spectacles would not be sufficient; what was needed was practical training in, and advice on, mobility aids and techniques appropriate to the needs of low-vision clients. Secondly, students also felt that the practical training had concentrated too much on learning the skills, as opposed to learning how to teach clients these skills. They too felt that more teachbacks would have helped. Thirdly, there was broad agreement that the practical work should have incorporated much more work using other canes.

At the NRAB, the mobility training sought to develop in students the ability to assess clients' needs and provide individualized mobility training. Emphasis was said to be less on students being good long cane travellers and more on the development of teaching skills. Also it was intended that students should become knowledgeable about other mobility aids and techniques in addition to the long cane system.

With so few MOs qualified from the NRAB so far, it is not possible to draw firm conclusions on the NRAB's success in achieving its goals. However, certain observations may be made. It is fair to say that the course incorporated elements which were likely to promote practical teaching skills. First, the role-play teaching sessions attempted to simulate different ages, visual and other physical impairments. Secondly, a video was used in some of these sessions to allow students to examine their teaching techniques and discuss these with the tutor. Thirdly, the course incorporated one session per week in which one student observed the tutor teaching another student mobility. There was discussion of the teaching points arising from these observation lessons in the weekly mobility theory sessions. Fourthly, the course involved student visits to practising MOs to observe them teaching clients.

The fact that the NRAB MO students were all experienced visual impairment workers is likely to have enhanced these experiences. Their previous contact with clients should have helped them to perform and make better use of the role-play teaching practices. Also students would have had prior experience of teaching clients, hence the course had the advantage of being able to build on existing skills in this respect. Furthermore, the students were likely to be more aware of the modifications which would be necessary for individualized client programmes.

The NRAB student we interviewed said that virtually all the practical mobility work was done under blindfold; only occasionally were low-vision simulation spectacles used. The tutor in charge of mobility teaching believed that more work with low-vision simulation spectacles was incorporated than on the NMC course, but this seemed more likely to be the result of his having trained some years earlier at the NMC, rather than a reflection of the current situation. Moreover, it seems that, as on the NMC course, little work was done with other canes or low-vision aids. Thus the stated goals of providing a knowledge of other systems of mobility and mobility aids were unlikely to have been achieved.

At the SRAB it was intended that the practical mobility work would equip students with a range of approaches to teaching mobility, involving not just the long cane, but other mobility aids. The Centre also emphasized a concern that students were prepared to meet the mobility needs of clients with low vision. There was no intention of making students proficient long cane travellers under blindfold. Since the course was new, caution needs to be exercised in judging the extent to which the SRAB was successful in achieving these objectives. Informal discussions with a variety of informed people revealed a conviction that students were indeed less proficient long cane travellers than traditionally trained students, but little else could be ascertained about the extent to which students were more knowledgeable about other approaches to mobility teaching and low vision.

SRAB students themselves (who were also qualified TOs) felt that the course had succeeded in developing an awareness of the need to develop mobility training programmes according to the needs of individual clients. They welcomed the flexible approach to practical mobility teaching on the course which they felt reflected a more client-oriented approach than the traditional system of training. Also, they commented favourably on the fact that an equal amount of time was spent practising with low-vision simulation spectacles and a blindfold. However, students said that not enough training was given in teaching skills. They found watching the tutor teaching another student very useful in this respect, and felt that more opportunities for this should have been incorporated. Finally, they would have liked more role-play teaching practices.

Since the first course, the SRAB had reduced the amount of one-to-one teaching significantly. Commonly, students worked in pairs or groups: the tutor demonstrated an activity to the group, which they then practised in pairs, taking turns to take the part of client and worker. At other times the tutor worked with one pair at a time, teaching one of the students while the other observed, after which they practised together. This was in response to feedback from the students on the first course and an increased confidence that this was a more appropriate way of preparing students for their mobility teaching role.

The demands of the workplace were revealed by practising MOs, virtually all of whom had trained at the NMC. What they quickly discovered once they started work was that the stereotype of a client which their NMC training had led them to expect did not represent the clients they encountered. Instead of being young, fit, motivated and totally blind, most were elderly with the physical limitations that often accompany the ageing process and had little or no motivation to attempt an outdoor training programme, preferring to rely on home helps and families. Moreover, the overwhelming majority were not totally blind, but had some remaining vision – often a good deal. Faced with this situation, MOs found that much of their training had very little relevance for their clients. Even those who required some mobility training tended to have very limited mobility goals and to need a symbol or guide cane rather than a long cane. Others did not need a cane at all; they had sufficient remaining vision to manage with some low-vision training, possibly in conjunction with a low-vision magnifying aid.

Inevitably, the limitations of the NMC training in terms of teaching skills, low-vision work and the use of other mobility aids meant that workers had to develop their own strategies for teaching mobility and dealing with low-vision clients, once working. This was difficult enough in cases where the worker was employed with other MOs who could pass on their experiences and knowledge. However, in a great many cases MOs did not have this peer support and were left to reconcile the demands of their job with the training they had received. Needless to say, some appeared to have been more successful than others and it is hardly surprising that some MOs did very little mobility training with clients.

The demand from the field for the incorporation of teaching skills into the training is by now evident. The practical orientation and mobility training at the NMC seemed to contain the implicit assumption that by mastering the long cane technique students would be equipped to teach the system; clearly, this was not the case. Although students had noted some differences in the teaching approaches of the different mobility tutors, these observations could not possibly provide adequate preparation for students' future role as instructors. In any case, with the concentration students needed during the blindfold mobility sessions, it was unlikely that they would be thinking about the teaching skills of the tutor. It seems that far more role-play teaching exercises need to be programmed into the practical mobility sessions at the NMC. In addition, efforts need to be made to make the teachback sessions more realistic – for example using client profiles. Finally, it seems that more practical guidance in how to develop teaching programmes for clients is needed and, ideally, more observation of teaching situations in the field.

It seems that only the SRAB, in its second and subsequent courses, had made any significant progress in responding to the need for teaching skills, involving as it did either role play or observation of teaching in virtually all practical mobility sessions. The SRAB's move away from one-to-one practical mobility teaching was a source of great concern to many advocates of the 'long cane system', centring on the belief that students who were not themselves proficient long cane travellers would not be able to teach the long cane system to clients. There is, as yet, no evidence either to support or refute this claim. However, we are inclined to the view that the worker needs to be knowledgeable about the full long cane system, but that proficiency is essential only in the fundamental principles – i.e. cane technique and safety. There is a further argument put forward by many in the field to justify students learning the full long cane programme – namely that it is the only way to inculcate a belief in the long cane system. This has also to be put to the test; it remains to be seen whether the SRAB-trained MOs will have less of a conviction that the long cane system is an effective means of independent travel than their colleagues trained at the NMC or the NRAB.

The NMC had introduced much more work using low-vision simulation spectacles in recent years, but this was still very limited. Even students on the 1986 course said that they had done little work with simulation spectacles. Similarly, the NRAB had introduced more work on low vision but yet more is needed. Given the visual impairment population with which most MOs work, the NMC and the NRAB need to focus much more on the needs of low-vision clients and correspondingly less on the totally blind. Moreover, the use of existing vision and how this relates to mobility training with any type of cane, or with other low-vision aids must become an integral part of the training, rather than tacked on to the original blindfold work with the long cane, as was the case at the NMC and the NRAB. The NMC maintained that the long cane system was applicable to work with other canes. This view was not supported by comments from MOs. There appears to be no reason, if the long cane system can be used with other canes, why the daily practical mobility sessions at the NMC and the NRAB did not incorporate work with these.

The SRAB's decision to give students equal experience of low-vision conditions and total blindness in the practical mobility work was another source of concern in some quarters. This had to do with the fear that the MOs who took this course would not have the level of knowledge and expertise to train a client who was totally blind. This too must remain an area of speculation. In any case, it is based on the assumption that every worker should be able to deal with every client. It may be that there are circumstances which would allow for the development of specialisms. It is possible that the SRAB course has moved too far in the opposite direction; that the emphasis on blindfold work has swung to the other extreme. But it is also possible that, having adopted one system, it is difficult for proponents of this system to accept that, after almost 20 years, significant changes may be necessary.

The remainder of this section on mobility training deals mainly with the NMC modules and, where teaching occurred, the NRAB work. The SRAB course, which was intended as a 'top-up' course to its TO training, included little formal teaching in other subjects.

Anatomy and physiology of the eye

At the NMC, given the time allocation of only 15 hours, it was not possible to achieve the objectives for this module. The section on low vision alone – i.e. what it is, clinical examination and assessment, functional examination and assessment, use of optical aids and training with these, sight and visual learning, variables affecting visual performance, visual development in congenitally and adventitiously blind, visual efficiency in the discriminating learner, training techniques, illumination in natural and artificial light, colour and contrast, lighting and other useful aids in low vision – could have taken up all of the allotted 15 hours and more quite usefully, yet it was only one of the three sections.

NMC-trained MOs were dissatisfied with the amount of training in low vision. These comments related to the practical training, as mentioned above, but also to the theoretical side of the course. In particular, they felt that the course fell short when it came to low-vision conditions, their assessment and the modifications to training which were needed when working with low-vision clients. In addition, more work was felt to be needed in the use of low-vision aids – assessing for these and training clients to use them. Workers were divided over the medical information contained in this module. Some felt that it had been extremely useful and would have liked to know more about the effects of various eye diseases. Others felt that too much time had been given to the anatomy and physiology of the eye.

NMC students' views on the module were mixed and seemed to relate to how difficult they had found the information to comprehend. Several questioned the need for the medical information, particularly when time on the course was pressurized.

At the NRAB, as at the NMC, the objectives of the work on anatomy and physiology of the eye were far too ambitious to be achieved in the time allocation of just 14 hours.

When considered in the context of the work, there would seem to be a case for extending the time allocation at the NMC and the NRAB to enable a more thorough grounding in anatomy and physiology of the eye, including low vision and low-vision aids. First, many MOs found that in the initial visits to clients they were often called upon to discuss clients' eye conditions with them. Since workers seem to be placed in this position of 'expert', they need to be knowledgeable in such matters. Secondly, much of the MO's job was taken up with initial assessment of clients, despite the fact they felt they lacked training in low-vision assessment. While most clients had remaining vision, only two workers said they assessed clients for low-vision aids. It seems that the training needs to spend more time on low-vision conditions and functional assessment in order to equip MOs with the skills needed to offer individualized mobility programmes to the full range of clients.

Thirdly, liaison with other professionals who also came into contact with the visually impaired was negligible. Workers felt that they were not seen as equals with other professionals in social services, and that this had an adverse effect on their work. This situation might improve if the courses provided a firmer knowledge base in terms of medical conditions and assessment, so that workers could converse as the visual impairment *specialists* they are so often called upon to be .

On a more general level, the practice at the NMC and the NRAB of requiring students to cover most of the work through individual seminar papers, presented and photocopied to the rest of the group, seems a misuse of the limited time allocated to this subject. Formal teaching from a tutor would have enabled more information to be imparted and ensured that all the relevant points were covered.

Audiology

The NMC's audiology module also had an unrealistic set of objectives, given that only 14 hours were allocated to it, and it is unlikely that these were achieved. Some of the objectives, though possibly appropriate for a more advanced or extended training course, seemed out of place in such a short module – for example testing and interpreting audiograms (not something which any MO interviewed described as part of their work). Arguably, with time so limited, the work should have been confined to the section on 'auditory training', since this information has most direct relevance to the teaching of mobility. Again, with so much information to impart, the use of lectures rather than student seminars would probably have been a more effective way of transmitting the information.

Again at the NRAB, the long list of objectives were not realistic and were unlikely to have been achieved in the 14 hours allocated. Even if students already possessed a TO Certificate, they would have had only a few hours' teaching in audiology. Moreover, there is no suggestion in the objectives for the MO course that the training was intended to develop existing knowledge in these areas. Given that a total of only 11 hours per week was taken up with any teaching on the MO course, there seems to be no reason why more formal input could not have been made by tutors. Also the use of student seminar papers again seems to fail to make the best use of the limited time allocation.

Learning and teaching

At the NMC the module on learning and teaching clearly attempted to cover too much in just nine hours. Workers criticized the work in this section for being too theoretical and too intensive. Students had similar comments to make and added that they found it difficult to see the connection between the theoretical concepts and the practical mobility training on the course.

There was no separate section on the NRAB MO course on learning and teaching. Tutors were supposed to reinforce the principles involved in other sections of the MO course. Most of the specified objectives seemed appropriate to the work of an MO, but we are not in a position to say whether these were achieved (see section on orientation and mobility, above).

In terms of the demands of the job, it has already been clearly stated that the job of an MO requires teaching skills and an ability to develop a teaching programme; the NMC course did not seem to address these needs. Rather than present a formal programme covering a range of learning theories, the section needed to focus much more on the application of certain elements of learning theory. In particular, it ought to have concentrated much more on linking the practical mobility sessions and students' own experiences of learning practical mobility to discussion of teaching techniques. As it was, the 'discussion of relevance to mobility' and 'preparation and evaluation of lessons' formed only one part of one of the six sessions. Similarly, 'age and learning', which was included with five other areas in a single session, should have been given far more prominence in view of the elderly client population and the problems this posed for MOs who were expecting to be teaching young, active, motivated clients.

Counselling

At the NMC, the counselling section consisted of a one-day module comprising a lecture and four practical sessions on inter-personal skills. At the end of the day, the tutor intended that students would: understand what counselling was; have practised some of the basic skills; be aware of their potential and limitations as counsellors; and know where to turn for more specialist help. Given the limited scope of these objectives, it seems likely that they were achieved. However, the associated module on 'adjustment to visual handicap' seems unlikely to have achieved its objectives which, though appropriate, were unrealistic for the four hours the section was allocated. For example, it would have been possible to spend the whole four hours developing students' understanding of 'the effects of rehabilitation on the visually impaired person and his/her family with reference to practical training and social, cultural and financial factors etc'. Most workers felt very strongly that the course had neglected the importance of counselling, and that much more work on this area was needed. Indeed they demonstrated a confusion over what counselling was and whether what they did constituted counselling or not.

At the NRAB the work on 'psychology of blindness' was included with the 'social studies and adminstration' section. Together they were allocated a total of 19 hours. In the light of such limited time, it is unlikely that the objectives were fully realized (see comments on similar section in TO course, page 221).

From the perspective of the workplace, it emerged that many MOs, like TOs, became involved in counselling clients. Moreover, some felt that forming this type of relationship was an important part of the confidence-building which had to take place before teaching could begin. Some felt that the skills involved were a matter of common sense, but many felt that what they did was inadequate and that proper training should have been given. Some felt that counselling clients was not part of their role, but found it difficult at times to extricate themselves from situations in which counselling skills were called for. Others said that they did what they could for clients in the absence of someone else to fulfil the role; they found social workers unwilling to get involved with visually impaired clients. However, in situations where social workers worked more co-operatively with visual impairment workers or, indeed, formed part of the same team, it seems that the situation was improved and referrals for counselling by a qualified person were made.

In view of the demands made upon most MOs, and the importance many workers attached to being in a position to be able to counsel their own clients, it is evident that the training at each of the centres needs to pay much more attention to counselling skills; one day is not sufficient time to cover such an important and complex subject.

Social services

The objectives of the NMC 'Social Services Day' were not achieved. Workers and students said that there should have been much more work on this. Although the talks given by guest speakers from social services were said to have been interesting, there was a general feeling that this was not enough, in itself, to prepare them for the working environment of social services. Some students expressed concern that so little guidance had been given on the organizational/administrative part of their future work.

At the NRAB the objectives of the social studies section focused on the essential points. However, the extent to which these objectives were met must depend to a large extent on the previous experience of the students. The course did not specify that students had to have a visual impairment qualification. For those without work experience in social services, it is unlikely that the objectives could be met in the time allocated. Again, the lack of formal teaching on the course does not seem justified, given the amount of study time MO students had. In practice, all of the NRAB MO students had work experience as TOs or home teachers. It is thus reasonable to conclude that the course objectives were achieved in these instances because it was possible to build on existing knowledge. However, the course objectives say nothing about this.

From the perspective of the workplace, it was clear that more training was needed on social services departments and the MO's role within them. MOs complained of finding themselves the only specialist in the authority and being expected to get on with the job with little or no help from supervisors or colleagues. The fact that they had been given so little preparation on the workings of social services departments, setting up case files and record-keeping, making referrals, prioritizing clients and organizing their own workload left them feeling very vulnerable during the early stages of taking up post. Clearly the lack of team and supervisory support is a problem beyond the scope of the training centres. Nevertheless, workers need more initial preparation in self-management skills and social services organization.

In relation to the NMC course, it is regrettable that the majority of the placements did not provide experience of social services departments. Until such a situation can be remedied, it is even more important that this part of the taught course is developed.

Placement

At the NMC, although no written objectives for the placement existed, tutors comments suggested that there were two main goals: to practise teaching the long cane, and to gain experience of the future working environment. The first of these was generally achieved, but the second was only rarely fulfilled since over 80 per cent of placements were in schools and colleges rather than social services departments.

NMC students had found their placements a useful experience, but said that the course had failed to prepare them properly. Their main criticism centred on the fact that little long cane teaching was required. Most taught only one client the long cane; the other clients used symbol or guide canes. A second criticism voiced by students, most of whom had had placements with children, was that they were ill-prepared for the different approaches which would be needed. Two of them described situations in which children they were teaching had minor accidents. These students felt that this was the result of their not being alerted to the need to modify the teaching approach when working with children. Another student said that she had been taught nothing of the pre-cane skills which were required when working with congenitally blind children.

At the NRAB, the objectives in mind for the two-week placement early in the course (in addition to the main 12-week placement at the end) seem to have been achieved. It enabled the students to become familiar with the environment in which the main placement would take place and to get to know other workers in the placement setting. It probably also helped to put the training which followed into context. This was something which a number of students on other courses at the NRAB and elsewhere felt was lacking. With only one student's experiences to call upon, it is not possible to make a definitive statement about the objectives for the second placement.

At the SRAB, the placement was too short to achieve its objectives. Students were dissatisfied with this situation and felt that two months would have been a more appropriate period. As it was, they felt that they saw too few clients and did not have enough time to develop a teaching programme with any of them.

As far as meeting the requirements of the workplace is concerned, the NRAB provided placements for all its MO students in social services and the SRAB did the same for three of its four students. The NMC recognized that it was failing to provide the most suitable experiences for students since most would be working for social services, once they qualified. However, it appeared to be making little headway in changing the situation. This meant that many students did not have the opportunity to experience what it was like working in a social services department – the role of the MO, the type of clients, organization of the workload, the relationships with other workers and the administrative responsibilities – before starting work. In addition, the placements in schools meant that many students did not even have the opportunity to practise teaching adults before taking up post.

It is difficult to understand why so much written work was set by the NMC for students to complete while on placement. The requirement that students completed a case study of a client seems reasonable, but the further requirements of a project and an essay seemed unnecessary and likely to detract from the main point of the placement. The appropriate time for this type of academic endeavour was while students were based at the training centre, where books were available and two study periods per day were allocated.

On a more general level, the NMC discharged its responsibilities well in relation to the monitoring of students while on placement. Its students received three visits from their NMC tutor, as well as one from the Principal. Moreover, NMC staff observed students working with clients, conducted their own assessment of this and held individual discussions with the students and supervisors. Joint responsibility for assessment of the placement lay with the tutor, the placement supervisor and the Principal. This system seems to have worked well. By contrast, the NRAB and the SRAB maintained their policy of effectively relinquishing their responsibility for assessing students on placement to the local supervisors. They continued the practice of visiting students only once on placement. In our view, this does not seem satisfactory and is not conducive to getting the best value out of the considerable period of time spent on the placement (see comments on their TO courses).

Finally, the SRAB recognized that the placement on the first course had been too short and extended the placement on subsequent courses to six weeks. However, even this is possibly too brief a period in which to establish relationships with clients and develop a mobility training programme to any extent. Moreover, as with the TO training, the SRAB made no attempt to observe the students working with a client. The same comment must therefore be made: the training centre relied too much for its assessment of students' practical teaching abilities on placement supervisors.

General comments on NRAB and SRAB courses

On the NRAB MO course, mobility took up seven and a half hours per week. The remainder of the teaching took up an average of just over three hours per week. The course was not advertised as a top-up course, although so far only people who already had a visual impairment qualification had been accepted. However, even for these people, the limited amount of tuition – $10\frac{1}{2}$ hours per week – cannot be justified. Furthermore, in some cases the NRAB MO students had taken their first qualification several years earlier, before many of the new elements in the training had been incorporated, and one had only a Home Teacher Certificate. The NRAB said that students were expected to undertake private study and prepare assignments. However, the low academic entry requirements and the principal aim of preparing students to teach practical skills raise questions about the value of this approach.

At the SRAB, the MO course was available only to those with a TO qualification. Moreover, only TOs who had trained recently or those who had done preliminary sessions to bring them up to the 'required standard' were considered. Even this stipulation did not overcome all the problems, however. There were certain elements which were not covered adequately, even in the most recent SRAB TO courses which the MO course did not seek to address – for example counselling and social services. Furthermore, there are some subjects which may have been given sufficient emphasis for the needs of TOs, but in which MOs are likely to need more extensive training – for example audiology.

RO/RW training

The introduction of the new RO/RW training so near to the end of this project allowed for only a brief examination. However, certain points arise in relation to it.

Written objectives for each subject area were agreed between the three training centres. This represented an advance in itself, particularly for the SRAB and the NMC which had little or no written details of this kind on their other courses. Moreover, on paper, these objectives indicated a significant improvement on earlier objectives for MO and TO training. In each subject area students were required not only to learn a specified body of knowledge, but also to be able to *apply* that knowledge by making an individual assessment of needs, planning a teaching programme, drawing together the necessary resources and implementing the programme. Setting out these objectives seems to demonstrate an increased awareness of the demands of the work of visual impairment specialists. Moreover, there appears to be a greater emphasis in certain subjects on developing an awareness of the psycho-social factors which may affect rehabilitation.

However, our inquiries revealed that the training centres were not sticking to the agreed time allocations for the various subjects. Considerable differences emerged in the actual time allocations between the three centres. For example, it had been agreed that mobility would be allocated 138 sessions, but the NRAB had allocated 70 sessions and the NMC 83 sessions; the SRAB found it difficult to be definite, but said that it would be between 90 and 150 sessions. Similarly, it had been agreed that 27 sessions would be allocated to counselling. The NRAB allocated 38 sessions, the NMC allocated 13 sessions and the SRAB allocated 50 sessions. Such divergence so early in the joint venture is somewhat surprising, to say the least.

In course content and teaching methods the differences which had existed in the training between the three agencies remained. In many subject areas the new courses appeared to be seen as an opportunity to cover the same ground but at a more reasonable pace. Moreover, there were indications that former 'specialisms' were still to the fore – for example the NRAB's emphasis on communications and re-introduction of the 'Deaf-blind Week', the emphasis on mobility training at the NMC, and the eye and low-vision work at the SRAB.

Teaching methods were another aspect in which the different philosophies of each centre had changed very little. For example, the NMC continued to have much more work with the blindfold rather than low-vision simulation spectacles and to maintain the daily one-to-one practical mobility teaching. However, it planned to have many more 'teachbacks' and to incorporate the use of other canes as well as the long cane in the low-vision simulation work. The SRAB had re-introduced slightly more blindfold work in response to pressure from its MO course assessor and other quarters. However, there remained a huge gap between its approach to mobility teaching and that at the NMC and, to a lesser extent, the NRAB. Very little one-to-one teaching was involved and low-vision simulation spectacles were used much more than at the other two centres.

Student assessment methods, despite some modifications, also continued to differ. The NMC had increased the amount of assessed coursework, but retained some examinations. The NRAB continued with its existing assessment procedures; the only difference was the introduction of an attitude assessment procedure which it had planned for some time. The SRAB also introduced this procedure, but not the NMC. The SRAB had also introduced a project, in line with the other two centres.

While recognizing the historical divide between the three training agencies, it is difficult to accept that even in the new training these differences are continuing. Overall, very little evidence of a joint approach to training was found. There were considerable discrepancies in time allocation, course content, teaching methods and assessment. It is reasonable to assume therefore that despite agreed objectives, the outcome of each of the courses will not be the same. This will be for the 'independent training board' to decide. However, it may experience some difficulty in this, owing to the way in which it has been set up. With each pair of assessors having responsibility for only one centre, they will not be in the best position to make comparisons.

The great discrepancies between the fees charged for the new training (£2,730 between the highest and lowest figure) and even the failure to agree a title militates against even the impression of a unified approach to training. The training centres themselves acknowledged the differences we have highlighted, and claimed that one of the main reasons for launching the 'joint' course was to present a united front which would enhance the likelihood of their securing external validation.

Summary of Recommendations

In this final section we want to highlight recommendations which cut across individual courses and course components.

1. There was an overwhelming emphasis on students learning the skills themselves, as opposed to learning how to transmit the skills to clients. In the training, the balance needs to be switched so that the development of teaching skills and strategies is the main focus of the practical skills sessions.

2. Much of the training seemed to assume that clients would be waiting to learn new skills or modify existing ones, whereas in practice there was very little call for skills teaching. This is due in part to a lack of client motivation; students need to be made aware of this and receive training in the inter-personal skills necessary. Also, many clients have developed their own strategies for managing without the help of a specialist worker. Students need to understand this and be prepared to take on the role of adviser rather than instructor. Furthermore, a large proportion of visually impaired clients, owing to their advanced years and like many other elderly people, have limited aspirations in terms of travelling, cooking, and so forth. Again, students need to understand this and be conscious of the modifications that will be necessary to training programmes.

3. The training was geared towards total blindness rather than low vision, even though totally blind clients make up only a small percentage of the client group. There was an assumption that workers would be able to adapt the training for work with clients with residual vision but in practice this was extremely difficult.

Although the training centres would claim that they have made progress in introducing training in low vision with simulation spectacles, much more work is still needed. Indeed the balance between these two needs to be switched around.

However, the practical simulation of low-vision conditions is, in itself, not enough. There has been for many years now a separate body of knowledge on low-vision which needs to form a major part of the training – in particular, as it relates to assessment, aids and making the best use of remaining vision.

4. Working relations between specialist workers and other professionals within the social and health services need to be improved. Workers were often isolated from colleagues and suffered from a perceived lack of prestige. Much of the problem stems from organizational factors beyond the control of the training centres. However, the situation could be improved somewhat if students were alerted to these issues during the training. More should be included on inter-professional ways of working and the need to act as an advocate for visually impaired clients and services in their area. In connection with this, students need a much greater understanding of the workings of social services departments and their role and responsibilities within them.

5. Most workers felt that in order to do their job properly, they needed to be able to offer counselling. With little or no training, they did what they could with varying degrees of effectiveness and confidence. Although the training centres have been reluctant to offer training in counselling skills, some sessions have been included in recent courses. However, this needs to be expanded considerably. Students need to know what counselling involves and when to refer clients for more specialist help, but also they should be given the opportunity to develop some of the basic skills themselves.

This analysis has highlighted areas where elements of the training do not match the requirements of the work of visual impairment specialists. Recommendations have been made which would improve the situation within the existing structures for training. However, training issues present only one set of problems. Others arise from the organization and deployment of specialist workers in social services departments.

Despite formal team structures, workers commonly experienced a great deal of isolation and an unjustifiable degree of personal autonomy stemming from infrequent and non-specialist supervision. This problem was also identified by a DHSS inquiry and the subsequent report discussed these issues in some detail (DHSS, Social Services Inspectorate, 1988). We feel we must endorse the view that this is an intolerable situation; steps need to be taken to establish the employment of visual impairment workers in social services departments on a proper footing.

References

ABEL, R. (1987). Identification of the blind, 1834–1968: a study of the blind register and the registration process. PhD thesis, University of London.

ASH, E. (1985). *Training for Workers with Visually Handicapped People (England)*. London: CCETSW.

BARCLAY REPORT. (1982). *Social Workers: Their Role and Tasks*. London: Bedford Square Press.

BARON, J. (1987). 'Amalgamation of professional organisations in the social services field', *Association for the Education and Welfare of the Visually Handicapped Bulletin*, Autumn, 15–16.

BIGGS, G. (1982). 'Blind mobility training services in English local authorities', *New Beacon*, LXVI, 785, September, 225–229.

BLEDSOE, C.W. (1980). 'Originators of orientation and mobility training.' In: WELSH and BLASCH, B. (Eds) *Foundations of Orientation and Mobility*. New York: American Foundation for the Blind, pp. 581–624.

CASTLE, F. (1979). *Proposal in Principle for Independent Special Option of Certificate in Social Service on Visual Handicap*, North Regional Association for the Blind.

CENTRAL COUNCIL FOR EDUCATION AND TRAINING IN SOCIAL WORK (CCETSW) (1972). *Social Work: People with Handicaps Need Better Trained Workers*, Paper 5. London: CCETSW.

CENTRAL COUNCIL FOR EDUCATION AND TRAINING IN SOCIAL WORK (CCETSW) (1983). *Training for Work with Visually Handicapped People*. Report of a Workshop held at the Beeches College, Birmingham. London: CCETSW.

CENTRAL COUNCIL FOR EDUCATION AND TRAINING IN SOCIAL WORK (CCETSW) (1987). 'Minutes of Meeting, 14.2.87, between CCETSW, RNIB, NMC, NRAB, SRAB and NFER'. London: CCETSW.

CROUSE, R. (1969). 'The long cane in Great Britain', *New Outlook for the Blind*, 63, 20–22.

DEPARTMENT OF HEALTH AND SOCIAL SECURITY, SOCIAL SERVICES INSPECTORATE (SSI) (1988). *A Wider Vision: The Management and Organisation of Services for People who Are Blind or Visually Handicapped*. London: DHSS.

DODDS, A. (1987). 'NAOMI mobility officer survey', *New Beacon*, LXXI, 839, March, 71–73.

HALL, T. (1987). 'Training social workers for tomorrow', SRAB Annual Lecture, reprinted in *British Journal of Visual Impairment*, Autumn, 83–84.

JAMES, P. (1986). 'Some thoughts on mobility training: past, present and future', *British Journal of Visual Impairment*, IV, 3, Autumn, 91–93.

JOINT STATEMENT ON TRAINING FOR WORK WITH VISUALLY HANDICAPPED PEOPLE, RNIB, NMC, SWRAB, NRAB and CCETSW (June, 1984). Appendix, in: ASH, E. *Training for Workers with Visually Handicapped People (England)*. London: CCETSW.

NATIONAL ASSOCIATION OF ORIENTATION AND MOBILITY INSTRUCTORS (NAOMI) (1985). Recruitment leaflet, NAOMI.

NATIONAL MOBILITY CENTRE (NMC) (1980). *Proceedings of the Twelfth Annual Course*, NMC.

NEW BEACON. (1973). 'Home news', *New Beacon*, LVII, 669, January, 8–12.

NEW BEACON. (1986). Advertisement, *New Beacon*, LXX, 831, July, 223.

NEWTON, T. (1984). 'The community – living with visual impairment', *British Journal of Visual Impairment*, II, 3, 76.

NORTH REGIONAL ASSOCIATION FOR THE BLIND (NRAB) (1985). *Seventy-ninth Annual Report, 1st April 1984–31st March 1985*, NRAB.

NORTH REGIONAL ASSOCIATION FOR THE BLIND (NRAB) (1986). *Eightieth Annual Report, 1st April 1985–31st March 1986*, NRAB.

NORTH REGIONAL ASSOCIATION FOR THE BLIND (NRAB) (1987). *Eighty-first Annual Report, 1st April 1986–31st March 1987*, NRAB.

OLIVER, M. (1983). *Social Work with Disabled People*. London: MacMillan.

PHELAN, P. (1984). 'Are we producing the goods?', *British Journal of Visual Impairment*, II, 3, Autumn, 70–73.

SEEBOHM REPORT (1968). *Report of the Committee on Local Authority and Personal Social Services*, Cmnd 3703. London: HMSO.

SOUTHERN REGIONAL ASSOCIATION FOR THE BLIND (SRAB) (1968). 'Report of a Conference on the Mobility of Blind Persons, with Special Emphasis on the Long Cane Technique', *Conference Report 57*, July.

SOUTHERN AND WESTERN REGIONAL ASSOCIATION FOR THE BLIND (SWRAB) (1978). 'The special needs of the visually handicapped', *Southern and Western Regional Association for the Blind, Regional Review*, Supplement 2, SWRAB.

SOUTHERN AND WESTERN REGIONAL ASSOCIATION FOR THE BLIND (SWRAB) (1979). 'Report on 1978 conference – the challenge of blindness: planning, training and the provision of services for the visually disabled', *Regional Review*, Supplement 1, SWARB.

SOUTH REGIONAL ASSOCIATION FOR THE BLIND (SRAB) (1985a). *Letter to Directors of Social Services Outlining Proposed Training Strategy*, September 1985, SRAB.

SOUTH REGIONAL ASSOCIATION FOR THE BLIND (SRAB) (1985b). *Annual Report 1984–85*, SRAB.

THORNTON, W. (1968). In: SOUTHERN REGIONAL ASSOCIATION FOR THE BLIND (SRAB) 'Report of a Conference on the Mobility of Blind Persons, with Special Report Emphasis on the Long Cane Technique', *Conference Report*, 57, July, p. 13.

WELSH, R. and BLASCH, B. (Eds) (1980). *Foundations of Orientation and Mobility*. New York: American Foundation for the Blind.

YOUNGHUSBAND REPORT (1959). *Report of the Working Party on Social Workers in the Local Authority Health and Welfare Services*. London: HMSO.

Legislation

1946 National Health Service Act
1948 National Assistance Act
1948 Children Act
1970 Local Authority Social Services Act
1970 Chronically Sick and Disabled Persons Act
1972 Local Government Act

THE NFER RESEARCH LIBRARY

Titles available in the NFER Research Library

TITLE	HARDBACK ISBN	SOFTBACK ISBN
Joining Forces: a study of links between special and ordinary schools (Jowett, Hegarty, Moses)	0 7005 1179 2	0 7005 1162 8
Supporting Ordinary Schools: LEA initiatives (Moses, Hegarty, Jowett)	0 7005 1177 6	0 7005 1163 6
Developing Expertise: INSET for special educational needs (Moses and Hegarty (Eds))	0 7005 1178 4	0 7005 1164 4
Graduated Tests in Mathematics: a study of lower attaining pupils in secondary schools (Foxman, Ruddock, Thorpe)	0 7005 0867 8	0 7005 0868 6
Mathematics Coordination: a study of practice in primary and middle schools (Stow with Foxman)	0 7005 0873 2	0 7005 0874 0
A Sound Start: the schools' instrumental music service (Cleave and Dust)	0 7005 0871 6	0 7005 0872 4
Course Teams–the Way Forward in FE? (Tansley)	0 7005 0869 4	0 7005 0870 8
The LEA Adviser – a Changing Role (Stillman, Grant)	0 7005 0875 9	0 7005 0876 7
Languages for a Change: diversifying foreign language provision in schools (Rees)	0 7005 1202 0	0 7005 1203 9
The Time to Manage? department and faculty heads at work (Earley and Fletcher-Campbell)	0 7005 1233 0	0 7005 1234 9

	HARDBACK	SOFTBACK
GCSE in Practice: Managing assessment innovation (Grant)	0 7005 1239 X	0 7005 1240 3
Moving into the Mainstream: LEA provision for bilingual pupils (Bourne)	0 7005 1235 7	0 7005 1236 5

For further information contact the Customer Support Department, NFER-NELSON, Darville House, 2 Oxford Road East, Windsor, Berks SL4 1DF, England. Tel: (0753) 858961   Telex 937400 ONECOM G Ref. 24966001

PRACTICAL INTEGRATION IN EDUCATION

A new series of books focusing on the practical aspects of integrating children with special needs into mainstream schools.
Each book focuses on a particular handicap and will provide you with:

- Relevant factual information about the handicap

- Suggestions for overcoming problems

- Methods of helping these children to integrate

- Practical tips on aids, equipment, classroom design and career advice

Following the 1981 Education Act pupils who would formerly have attended special schools were integrated into ordinary schools. The Practical Integration in Education series investigates the problems of integration experienced by pupils and their teachers. The series puts forward a number of suggestions of ways in which successful integration may be facilitated making it an invaluable addition to any teachers bookshelf.

Partially Sighted Children is the first in the series and brings together a wide range of knowledge and experience about the educational needs of children with partial sight to enable mainstream teachers and nursery teachers to cater for the needs of visually impaired children in their classroom. It draws on information gained through experience and research on aspects such as special equipment needs, classroom design, mobility problems and their solution – including a chapter devoted to sport and leisure activities – and the future career prospects open to partially sighted students.

The authors, Gianetta Corley, Steve Lockett and Donald Robinson, are all experts in the field of visual impairment and the book benefits from their breadth of experience and different perspectives. Donald Robinson who has retired as Head of a school for the visually impaired, spent his career teaching blind and partially sighted children; Steve Lockett works as a Mobility Teacher and Gianetta Corley is an Educational Psychologist for visually impaired children.

ISBN 07005 1198 0 Code 8311 021 – Price £6.95

Coming soon:
The Motor Impaired Child
Myra Tingle

For further information, please contact our Customer Support Department on (0753) 858961, or write to the following address:

NFER-NELSON, Darville House,
2 Oxford Road East, Windsor,
Berkshire SL4 1DF

NFER-NELSON JOURNALS

TOPIC — PRACTICAL APPLICATIONS FOR RESEARCH IN EDUCATION

Keep up to date with the latest research information as it affects you. *TOPIC* is a new, looseleaf forma journal from the NFER, designed to draw out the *practical implications* of a range of research projects. I short leaflets and reports, which may be photocopied, will be particularly useful to teachers, lecturer advisers and students, highlighting the implications of research findings for their daily work. Published i the Spring and Autumn of each year and edited by David Upton of the NFER. **This is our newest journa submissions are particularly welcome.** Preferred article length: 1000 to 4000 words.

EUROPEAN JOURNAL OF SPECIAL NEEDS EDUCATION

Published in response to the need for a journal that moves beyond the confines of conventional articles wi a narrow research base, the *European Journal of Special Needs Education* presents studies, reports a information of international significance. Abstracts are translated into French, German and Spanish. Ea issue includes contributions from a variety of different countries. Launched in 1986, the journal continu to grow and develop and will appeal to teachers, advisers and students as well as researchers. Published March, June and October and edited by Dr Seamus Hegarty of the NFER. Preferred article length: 4000 7000 words.

RESEARCH PAPERS IN EDUCATION

A unique forum for high-quality research papers in all fields of eduation, *Research Papers in Educati* specializes in the publication of longer, in-depth research reports, providing readers with more detail tha usually provided in conventional article format. The journal draws from theses, interim and final reports major research programmes, planning papers for major projects and spin-off results from major resea findings. Published in March, June and October and edited by Professor Ted Wragg of the University Exeter. Preferred article length: 10,000 to 16,000 words.

THE JOURNAL OF MORAL EDUCATION

An international journal published for the Social Morality Council. The *Journal of Moral Education* is only international journal in the field of moral education. Its contributors and readers include education at all levels and from a wide variety of disciplines including philosophy and psychology. Articles range fr theoretical analyses and discussions to reports of empirical research, case studies, and description classroom practice. The *Journal of Moral Education* has regular special issues on relevant topics. Publis in January, May and October and edited by Monica Taylor on behalf of the Social Morality Cou Preferred article length: 3000 to 6000 words.

EDUCATIONAL RESEARCH

For information on the latest research from Britain's leading educational research institute, the Natie Foundation for Educational Research (NFER), subscribe to the termly journal *Educational Resea* Drawing on projects being undertaken at universities, colleges of education and other insititution Britain, including the NFER itself, the journal aims to disseminate research findings at all levels of educa — from policy making to classroom teaching. Articles include a wide variety of research studies and rev of research, summaries of research findings in more specialized fields and comprehensive reviews of books. In addition, the latest projects being carried out by the NFER are summarized. Published in Sp Summer and Winter and edited by Dr Clare Burstall, Dr Seamus Hegarty and David Upton of the N Preferred article length: 5000 words.